W9-BKZ-713

SEASON OF THE

SEASON OF THE

76ers

---

*The Story of Wilt Chamberlain
and the 1967 NBA Champion
Philadelphia 76ers*

WAYNE LYNCH

Foreword by Billy Cunningham

Thomas Dunne Books / St. Martin's Press 🐾 New York

THOMAS DUNNE BOOKS.
An imprint of St. Martin's Press.

Extract on pp. 144–146 reprinted by permission from the April 13,
1967, edition of *The New York Times* © copyright 1967 by The New
York Times Company.

All photos courtesy of Urban Archives, Temple University,
Philadelphia, Pennsylvania, unless otherwise noted.

Book design by Michael Collica

Library of Congress Catologing-in-Publication Data

Lynch, Wayne.
    Season of the 76ers : the story of Wilt Chamberlain and the 1967
NBA champion Philadelphia 76ers / Wayne Lynch ; foreword by
Billy Cunningham.—1st ed.
        p. cm.
    ISBN 0-312-28277-X
    1. Philadelphia 76ers (Basketball team) 2. Chamberlain, Wilt,
1936–1999 I. Title

GV885.52.P45 L96 2002
796.323'64'0974811—dc21

                                                        2001052502

First Edition: February 2002

10 9 8 7 6 5 4 3 2 1

CONTENTS

AUTHOR'S NOTE

This book is a compilation of many historical facts, stories, and quotes appearing initially in a variety of newspaper accounts, magazines, books, sports publications, and other materials in the public domain, primarily from the mid-1960s. I have supplemented this research with new information garnered from personal interviews completed over the past three years with many members of the 1966–67 Philadelphia 76ers and others who were extremely close to the team.

ACKNOWLEDGMENTS

This book could not have been written without the help and encouragement of several people. First, I want to thank my brother, Kevin, for finding and buying the old 1967–68 Philadelphia 76ers yearbook at a sports collectors' show in our hometown of Pittsburgh. He gave it to me as a birthday gift in early 1999, and it started me thinking that I could write a book about my longtime favorite team. Second, I want to thank my mother, Rita, for giving her 16-year-old son the money to buy a season ticket to the six games played by the 76ers in Pittsburgh's Civic Arena back in 1966–67. Seeing the team in person forged my fanaticism forever.

Thanks go also to Paul Paolicelli, fellow broadcast journalist and author, for helping me connect with my great agent, Tony Seidl. And to Tony for helping me connect with my editor at St. Martin's Press, Pete Wolverton. And to Pete and his associate editor, Carolyn Dunkley, for all of their tireless work bringing this book to completion.

I am especially appreciative of all the help given me by Ted Kosloff, son of the 76ers' co-owner in the championship era. Ted

ACKNOWLEDGMENTS

opened his personal scrapbook to me, and it was vital to my research. My research was also made so much easier thanks to the great, hardworking people at Temple University's Urban Archives Library in Philadelphia.

I also appreciate the work of Bruce Sanford and Bruce Brown at the Washington, D.C., law firm of Baker & Hostetler in reviewing the manuscript.

My thanks to the 76ers, especially Dave Coskey and Amy Cohen, for granting permission to excerpt that 1967–68 yearbook and other material here. I am also grateful to Erik Levin of NBA Properties, who granted me permission to excerpt material from NBA.com through NBA Media Ventures, LLC.

Along the way, many others helped me with this work, but there are too many names to mention here. I say thanks to all of you. You know who you are.

And, finally, this book is dedicated to my son, Matt, and to my wonderful wife, Karen, the person who has supported and encouraged me most through it all.

FOREWORD

This book, *Season of the 76ers*, brings back fond memories of when I played as the sixth man on the 1966–67 76ers world championship basketball team; the days when basketball wasn't synonymous with money and fame, but with a love of the game and team unity.

After coaching the 76ers to another title 16 years later, I now have a greater respect for the sacrifices and achievements of that first team.

With only 10 teams in the league then, competition was fierce. The previous season we had the best regular season record, but the Boston Celtics demolished us in the playoffs. Not only were we disappointed in ourselves that we didn't go all the way, we were determined to make amends.

The next season, the memory of that previous year's loss lit a fire, as did our new coach, Alex Hannum. He brought a certain respect and discipline to the team. He reminded us that we were there to win a championship, and he made the game as enjoyable as it could be.

Alex also had a great group of guys to work with. We played smart and had a wonderful chemistry. Everyone understood each other's strengths and weaknesses and knew how each other would respond to different situations on the court.

Another of our strengths was that we had talent in all the key positions, and a very physical lineup. We had Wilt Chamberlain, whom we all respected because he was so far ahead of his time, so outspoken. But he was a soft touch, a pussycat, extremely bright, caring, doing so many wonderful things for others and seeking no recognition.

Even with Wilt's presence, I believe that Luke Jackson was the key player, because he sacrificed his individual statistics for the benefit of the team's success.

We also had Chet Walker, the bachelor, who always had a smile on his face. All he needed was the ball and a little space.

Hal Greer was the pure jump shooter. He always knew where he was most effective, 15 to 18 feet out.

Wally Jones brought energy to the team. He would harass his man up and down the court.

And I can't forget Larry Costello, who started the first 42 games, during which we were 38–4, before an injury all but ended his career.

But we didn't have to rely only on our starters. We had other great pros like Dave Gambee, always ready to contribute whenever called upon. We also had two rookies, Matty Goukas and Bill Melchionni. Matty gave a great contribution in game six of the championship series and then went on to a long playing and coaching career. And Billy, my travel roommate, could always be counted on to give us a spark with his great shooting.

By the time we got to the playoffs, we realized we weren't going to win one championship, but two. First, we had to dethrone the Celtics, who were as dominant a franchise as any. They had won 8 straight championships, and 9 of the last 10. Beating them in the semifinals was a championship in itself.

Then we had to play for the world championship against the Warriors, who were led by basketball legends Rick Barry and Nate Thurmond.

We were drained after what should have been the clincher at home on a Sunday. We had to pack and, once again, fly to San Francisco for game six the next day. That final game, we came from behind to beat the Warriors by three points.

When I coached the 76ers to the NBA title in 1983, about two million people turned out for the parade down Broad Street.

In 1967, I remember no parade, just a bunch of guys celebrating for a long time in the locker room.

We were like a family, and the bond that we created is everlasting. Yes, we have lost Wilt and with time we have all gone our separate ways, to different parts of the country. But I know that if I ever need anything, I have my old teammates to count on.

Wilt's death was a great loss to all of us. He is someone I will always think about, and this book wouldn't be written now if it weren't for what he did for us back then.

Our team was ranked the best in the first 35 years of the NBA.

Do I agree?

I would have to say that, at the least, we were as good a team as has ever been assembled, and I strongly believe that we would have gone on to win a few more championships had we not been broken up a year later with trades.

The story of this team has never been fully told, until now.

Season of the 76ers is a long-overdue scrapbook of our memories, and your chance to see us for the team that we were.

—BILLY CUNNINGHAM

INTRODUCTION

I know exactly why and when I became a fanatic for the Philadelphia 76ers. It was an early spring night in 1965. I was just 15 at the time, gangly, nerdy, complete with the requisite black, horned-rim glasses, and very much into my own little world. I was into music and sports—not playing, but listening.

I was hooked on clear-channel, 50,000-watt AM radio stations. The big rock 'n' roll music stations like WKYC in Cleveland, CKLW in Windsor, Ontario, and WLS in Chicago nightly lured me and countless other teenagers to sample the hot deejays and soak up the sounds of rock, roll, and soul.

But there were also the stations that carried sports. I would pump up the volume on the professional play-by-play of all the games I could find. That meant plenty of major league baseball and buckets full of basketball—especially NBA basketball! It didn't matter if the words wafted from Don Criqui at WHN in New York, Vince Lloyd on WGN in Chicago, Ed Kennedy on WCKY in Cincinnati, Jerry Gross ("Grab a bottle of Busch, we're goin' into overtime!") on KMOX in St. Louis, or, as on this night, the gravel-throated Johnny Most on WHDH in Boston. Tapping into the games from these towns was like traveling there from our small wood-frame home on the North Side of Pittsburgh, Pennsylvania.

It was a ritual of sorts, because the signals of these stations, as strong as they were after dark, didn't always come through loud and clear. Maybe it was the atmospheric conditions. I had to work some magic to make those stubborn signals sing. I would lower my head, and nestle my right ear as close as I could to the white latticework that covered the speaker of the trusty Emerson kitchen radio.

I actually rested my head on the shiny red Formica countertop, and I placed my hands against the warm body of the box, fired by the glowing tubes inside the back panel. Sometimes it seemed that if I held it, cradled it, and caressed it in a certain way, moving my hands a little or a lot, the machine would respond by allowing me to hear every word, every thought, every name, every play, just a little bit better.

I had been following the NBA season regularly, with the games on radio as my guide. But what was only a hobby rapidly became a passion as the Eastern Division playoffs marched toward their climax. I knew that the Philadelphia 76ers were giving the Boston Celtics a run for their money, but I also knew the inevitable would take place. Nobody beat the Celtics in the playoffs—nobody. They were certainly the best, the champs, the kings of pro basketball. But there was an arrogance about them that spawned a genuine hatred. I had it big time. I despised the Celtics because they always won, somehow, some way. They were especially invincible on their home court, the Boston Garden, the lucky-charmed, parquet chamber of horrors that left so many teams brokenhearted over the years. In particular, I knew all too well that Boston *never* lost a seventh game of a playoff series there.

Unheard of! Impossible! No way!

But it seemed like Lady Luck was spinning Philadelphia's way this time. Maybe it would be different this year. The 76ers had played

Boston tough all series long, forcing a decisive seventh game. In the battle of the giants, Philly's Wilt Chamberlain of the Sixers was dominating Boston's Bill Russell.

On the night of this final game of the Eastern playoffs, I went in search of Boston's WHDH Radio, home to the Celtics broadcasts and their on-air cheerleader Johnny Most. I had found my way to this signal before, but the station really didn't come in all that well or that often. As usual, the reception wasn't very good from Boston, and for long periods of time there was nothing but ear-stabbing static. I tried my usual human antenna trick, moving my hands, turning the radio on its side and upside down, carefully twisting the right hand dial back and forth, hoping to find that elusive signal. But it only worked well enough to keep me up-to-date with the score every few minutes.

Until near the end of the game.

Suddenly, as if the clouds stepped aside, the radio waves carried Most's raspy descriptions loud and clear. His next words sent panic into the hearts of Boston fans and prompted prayers of hope from 76ers fans like me.

"He lost the ball off the support," Johnny croaked, in surprise and dismay. "Russell lost the ball off the support, and Boston's only leading by one point! The Celtics are claiming that Chamberlain hit him [Russell] on the arm. And the ball goes to Philadelphia with five seconds left."

Then there seemed to be an eternity of silence. Fifteen seconds went by, and I thought for sure the signal had gone out at the damnedest time. But it wasn't that at all. Johnny Most was stunned silent. He couldn't believe what had just happened. He couldn't believe the Celtics might lose. Might lose a game seven. Might lose it in the Garden. Was that Celtics' four-leaf clover finally wilting?

As Most apparently regrouped, he cued his color sidekick, a fellow from WHDH named Jim Pansullo, to set the game situation for the listeners.

Pansullo chimed in, "110 to 109. Now, the tension is really there . . . and this change of events has hit us right in the nose."

I was dreaming, not with my face in the pillow, but with it still firmly fastened to the countertop, ear to the old Emerson, waiting for what I knew would be the winning basket by Philly.

True, the outcome was still in doubt, but at least the audio was clear, as Most snatched the microphone back from his broadcast buddy.

"Greer's putting the ball in play. He gets it out deep and *Havlicek steals it!* Over to Sam Jones. *Havlicek stole the ball, it's all over*," he screamed. "Johnny Havlicek is being mobbed by the fans. It's *allllll* over. Johnny Havlicek stole the ball. Oh, boy, what a play by Havlicek at the end of this ball game!"

Yeah, what a play. Boston wins again. Chamberlain loses again.

But those were just fleeting thoughts.

Because on this night when the entire professional basketball world was nearly shocked by an upset of mammoth proportions, I knew that Boston could and would be beaten by this Philadelphia team. It was just a matter of time, and I wanted to be a part of it, in my own little way.

So, this is the story of how that team and a kid from Pittsburgh found excitement, drama, and joy at the other end of the Turnpike more than three decades ago.

Today, the spirit of that team has risen up, calling to me to tell the story of their pride and power; to tell the story of a pro basketball team that had no peer then—or now; to tell the story of that glorious, unforgettable *Season of the 76ers*.

ONE

The Spirit of 76

The NBA was a broken record from 1959 through 1966. In fact, instead of being called the National Basketball Association, it should have been renamed the National Boston Association. The Boston Celtics were the New York Yankees of professional basketball, winning 8 straight titles and 9 out of 10. Plain and simple, the Celtics were the NBA.

But this book is not about the Boston Celtics. This book is about the man and the team that finally beat Boston when nobody, nowhere, nohow, thought it could be done.

The man was Wilt Chamberlain. The team was the 1966–67 Philadelphia 76ers.

The 76ers personified "power basketball" in that era. They actually created the term and defined it. Wilt Chamberlain was no longer just an automatic scorer and rebounding machine. Oh, he could still do those things whenever he wanted to, but his power increased dramatically with his willingness to surrender the ball to his teammates in the name of victory.

The first true power forward in pro basketball emerged on this team. Luke Jackson was lethal working next door to Wilt.

Add the shooting and poise of Hal Greer and Chet Walker, the instant energy of Billy Cunningham and Wally Jones, and the steady, stirring leadership of head coach Alex Hannum, and the power of this team was palpable.

It translated into 68 wins, the most ever in the NBA at that point in league history. It resulted in the demolition of a dynasty.

Had the 76ers existed in the 24-hour sports, mega-media world of today, their story would have been wall-to-wall every day on the television sports highlights shows. Their exploits would have been showcased and heralded by the national papers, the big-time magazines, the major broadcast networks, and the cable sports channels. They were rewriting the record books each time they took the floor. They were the team that dared to make a run at the super Celtics. They were David to Boston's Goliath. They were giant killers—and giants in their own right.

Unfortunately, the media spotlight never shone on this team. In a sense they became somewhat forgotten, or at least overshadowed. Perhaps it was because they only won one NBA title. Perhaps it was because Boston quickly regrouped and won two back-to-back championships in 1968 and 1969. Perhaps it was because of the dominance in the '80s of Larry Bird's Celtics and Magic Johnson's Lakers. Perhaps it was the Michael Jordan–Chicago Bulls double hat trick of NBA crowns in the '90s.

But the 76ers' story should not be forgotten.

Ever.

For it is a triumphant tale of courage and camaraderie, force and finesse, destiny and dominance. Their ultimate victory over the Celtics and then the San Francisco Warriors brought Wilt and

the 76ers their first rings. It pumped new life into what had become
a stagnant, Celtics-controlled NBA.

Ironically, that new life was jump-started by a sudden, tragic
death. And that's where the story of the 1966–67 Philadelphia 76ers
really begins.

Ike Richman died in the middle of his dream.

His dream was to bring professional basketball back to the city of Philadelphia, defeat the mighty Boston Celtics for Eastern Conference supremacy, and then capture the National Basketball Association championship.

In the spring of 1963, the first part of it came true. He and partner Irv Kosloff bought the floundering Syracuse Nationals NBA franchise and moved it to Philly as the new 76ers. But Ike Richman wouldn't be around to blow out the final two candles on the cake. In the winter of 1965, as he sat at the press table adjacent to the 76ers' bench during a game in the hated Boston Garden against the hated Boston Celtics, Ike Richman collapsed and died of a massive heart attack. He died right there—in front of his coach, his players, the opposition, and the Garden faithful.

A moment earlier he was screaming at the referees like he always did. "He's traveling." "It was charging." "It was the other way." He was yelling at the 76ers' players, too. "Keep your hands up . . . lotsa hands, lotsa hands." The Garden fans near courtside were all over him, heckling and telling him to shut up once and for all.

A moment later, he fell onto the shoulder of a reporter sitting next to him. Richman's eyes were closed, and he was gasping for breath.

Sixers coach Dolph Schayes began hollering, "Get a doctor, get a doctor." Play was stopped. Boston coach Red Auerbach and his trainer Buddy Leroux raced from the other end of the court. They helped lay Richman on the floor behind the Philly bench. Leroux joined 76ers trainer Al Domenico in trying to revive Richman as Celtics team physician Dr. John A. Doherty arrived in about 30 seconds.

But all of their help came too late. The doctor said Richman had no pulse, no blood pressure, no signs of heart activity. They tried cardiac massage, oxygen, and adrenaline shots. Nothing worked.

That fast, Ike Richman was gone.

The crowd was stunned and silent. The 76ers were in shock. The scoreboard stood frozen with the two teams tied at 13.

But that was more than an unlucky sign—it was unthinkable.

Philadelphia natives Wilt Chamberlain and Wally Jones didn't just play for Ike, they were part of his family. They had lived at his house. Ike gave Wilt a chance to come home again to shoot for that elusive championship. Ike literally saved Wally from himself, rescuing him from a self-imposed exile in the Pacific Northwest, where he had escaped to hide from a variety of personal demons. Now, they watched horrified with the rest of their teammates as Ike was carried out on a stretcher, never to return to their sides.

At halftime, Domenico entered the locker room and told the players what they already knew. He had spoken to Ike's wife. Ike was gone. Domenico told them, "If you never win another ball game, win this one for Ike." There were tears and vacant stares, and when the team went back out for the halftime warm-up, players wandered aimlessly around the court, still unable to shake what they had just witnessed.

But when the second half whistle blew, the 76ers quickly found themselves and their spirit—or maybe Ike's. They went on a scoring tear and avenged Ike Richman that night, beating the Celtics for the first time ever in the Garden, and doing it decisively. Ike would have really savored the win, but even more so, he would have loved what his team was about to become, and how triumphantly they would make the final two parts of his dream come to pass.

In the spring of 1967, the 76ers trounced the Boston Celtics in the Eastern playoffs and captured the league crown in six games over the San Francisco Warriors. And, when it was all over, the titles won and his loser label lost, Wilt Chamberlain knew exactly what to do. Fittingly, Wilt gave the championship game ball to Ike Richman's widow. Ike's dream was finally complete. If only he had lived to see it all.

Wilt Chamberlain was born in the long shadow of the Liberty Bell. But his champion Philadelphia 76ers were not.

In fact, you have to travel about 260 miles to the northwest to find the team's birthplace. It's Syracuse, New York, located at the crossroads of Interstates 90 and 81. It's a city whose basketball history began by way of a bowling alley boss, Danny Biasone. He owned the Syracuse Nationals franchise of the then-fledgling National Basketball Association during the late 1940s and early 1950s.

Owning a team in that new, financially unsuccessful league was, as they say in bowling, a difficult spare. Games then were largely yawn-inducing, fan-unfriendly exercises in dribbling, passing, and two-handed set shots from way out.

But Biasone had a better idea and fathered a concept that made the league different, faster, more fun, and more exciting. He invented the 24-second clock, a timing device visible to the players on the floor, which forced them to move the ball up the court more quickly, run their plays, and get off shots before losing possession when the buzzer sounded after 24 ticks. The rule, which would change pro basketball forever, went into effect in the 1954–55 NBA season. As fate would have it, the first team to win the league championship with the 24-second clock clicking every day was Danny's boys, the Syracuse Nats.

But the clock was counting down on Biasone in other ways.

Slowly but surely, pro basketball was moving on to bigger and better places. Minneapolis lost its franchise to Los Angeles. Rochester gave up the Royals to Cincinnati. By the 1962–63 NBA season, only 102,000 people filed through the turnstiles in Syracuse to see the Nats, led by third-year coach Alex Hannum and local hero Dolph Schayes. They finished 16 games over .500, but the team was losing money and Biasone was shopping the club.

Enter Isaac "Ike" Richman.

He was a gregarious Philadelphia lawyer who, when the glamorous West Coast beckoned in 1962, helped Philadelphia Warriors owner Eddie Gottlieb sell the team to San Francisco interests, reportedly for the then–unheard of price of $875,000. Some said the league let Gottleib make the move and make the money as a reward for being one of the original founders of the NBA.

Richman's son, Mike, now a judge in Montgomery County, Pennsylvania, said his dad was an integral part of the Warriors, before and during the team's transition. What he didn't know was that by helping Gottleib, he would ultimately become the owner of his own NBA franchise.

"We all went to the games," Richman said, "and he traveled out to San Francisco a couple of times." Richman was Gottleib's attorney, but Gottleib was family to the Richmans.

Mike still has many pictures of Eddie hanging in the lower level of his suburban Philadelphia home. "What a great man," Richman called him.

Gottleib is considered by basketball historians to be one of the game's leading early promoters. He invented the short-lived territorial draft rule, convincing the league to allow him to clamp on to Wilt Chamberlain of Philly's Overbrook High School even though Wilt was playing college ball in distant Kansas.

Gottleib's brainstorm ensured that the Warriors could make Wilt their property in 1959 when the physical phenomenon became eligible to enter the NBA. It also kept Wilt out of the clutches of Red Auerbach, archenemy of the Warriors.

But despite Wilt's hometown drawing power, scoring prowess, and early dominance of the sport (including the famous 100-point game in Hershey, Pennsylvania, in 1962), and despite Philly's rich basketball roots, a group of California investors lured Gottlieb and the NBA to the Bay Area, giving birth to the *San Francisco* Warriors. Whatever goodwill Gottlieb had garnered by bringing Wilt back was gone in a second.

Die-hard Philadelphia basketball fans resented Gottlieb for taking their team away from them—the team of Joe Fulks, Paul Arizin, Tom Gola, Guy Rodgers, Wilt, and others. Besides, the city had a time-honored, much-revered hoops tradition that dated back to pre–World War I. The Philadelphia SPHAs were one of the barnstorming ball-clubs of the early days. The Warriors cut their teeth in the Basketball Association of America—forerunner of the NBA—winning the first BAA title in the 1946–47 season with Eddie Gottlieb coaching. The Warriors won the NBA title in 1955–56, making them the only team besides the Minneapolis Lakers to capture two championships in pro basketball's first decade. At the college level, the famous "Big 5" teams of LaSalle, St. Joseph's, Villanova, Penn, and Temple gave Philly a top-shelf basketball reputation.

However, when the Warriors went west—taking Wilt Chamberlain along with them—there was no professional basketball played in Philly during the entire 1962–63 season. It was a void that needed to be filled fast, and the story goes that Gottlieb helped fill it. Even while running the Warriors after the deal, he was apparently an intermediary in getting basketball back to the City of Brotherly Love, clueing in the local lawyer who helped him complete the Warriors transaction.

"Eddie Gottlieb told my father the Syracuse team was for sale," remembers Mike Richman. "My father wanted to buy the team. He was a lawyer and doing pretty well, but financially he needed a lot more involvement," Richman added.

Enter Irving "Irv" Kosloff.

Irv Kosloff was a longtime friend of Ike Richman. They were both graduates of Southern High School's class of 1930. While Richman became an attorney, Kosloff entered the city's business world. The relationship continued and prospered as Richman represented Kosloff and the Roosevelt Paper Company that he started and built. Kosloff and Gottlieb were also good friends, and Kosloff loyally followed the Warriors as well. But it took all of the aggressive Richman's persuasive powers to get the cautious Kosloff to put up the money needed to buy the Nats.

"It was an important period in my business career," Kosloff recounted in a 1990 interview with his grandson David for a master's thesis entitled, "The Philadelphia 76ers, 1963–1967, The Business of a Championship."

"I was busy with the company, which was growing outside the city.

"Philosophically, I was a great believer, and still am, of having a concentrated approach. Of having all of my eggs in one basket where I can see them," explained Kosloff, who passed away in 1995.

His grandson wrote: "Given his predilection for maintaining a focused approach to his business, it seems that Kosloff would have terminally rejected Richman's sales pitch. Instead he wavered and finally consented to a proposal that seemingly went against one of his most fundamental principles."

Kosloff's son, Ted, who still runs the now New Jersey–based company his father founded in 1932, remembers vividly when the deal came down.

"I was a junior at Penn State," said Kosloff. "It was Mother's Day weekend in 1963, and my dad came up. We played golf with a friend of mine from Syracuse. Then that night, dad went home, and he gets a call that the Nats were for sale."

In the published interview, the elder Kosloff picked up the story from there: "The drive up to State College [Pennsylvania] and back in those days was devastating. All I was thinking about was getting home and going to bed. The next morning I rose early and drove into the office. When Ike called me on Monday morning with the idea that we purchase the Syracuse Nationals and move them to Philadelphia, I was taken by complete surprise. I was not for it at first. We had never even discussed the possibility of buying a team, and now he was making this passionate presentation on a morning where I was still very tired from the drive the night before. I turned him down. I turned him down three or four times. He was a very strong seller. He finally got me one day on the phone and I said yes."

The deal was done. Danny Biasone had dealt his Nats to the NBA's newest kids on the block for "somewhere between $500,000 and $600,000," according to Ted Kosloff. Ike Richman would be the franchise's front man and Irv Kosloff the so-called silent partner.

Ike and Irv's team now needed a nickname, so the next order of business was to conduct a contest for the fans to pick it. Four thousand entries poured in, containing 450 different names. A special board of judges (probably restricted to Ike and Irv) was commissioned to choose the winning entry.

"We were driving in my father's tan Cadillac up to Kutshers [a New York State resort] for the annual NBA charity game at the country club when he told us," recalled Mike Richman. "He just said it was catchy, fast."

A 48-year-old New Jersey man, with his eyes focused firmly on Philadelphia's historic Independence Hall, took the honors. Walter

Stalhberg, a quality control statistician from West Collingswood, New Jersey, was one of nine people who submitted the name "76ers." But each entrant had to do more than just suggest a name, they had to explain it, justify it.

Stahlberg put it this way: "No athletic team has ever paid tribute to the gallant men who forged this country's independence, and certainly, Philadelphia, shrine of liberty, should do so."

Kosloff and Richman agreed, saying, "The Spirit of '76 could very well be the spirit of the team that will represent the city this year after being situated in Syracuse for many years. The Nats were loaded with spirit. We expect a hustling club again this year, and the new nickname is certainly appropriate and symbolizes Philadelphia alone."

Although Mike Richman remembered that Stahlberg's winning name won him a lifetime pass, the newspapers said he won an all expenses paid trip to California to see the 76ers play the former Philly—now San Francisco—Warriors. Stalhberg was quoted as saying he attended some Nats games in Syracuse the previous season, becoming familiar with the team while his daughter attended college there.

What about a new logo for the newly named team? No contest needed.

"My father's cousin, Mel, was in the packaging business," Mike Richman related. "He envisioned it with the 76, the flag, the patriotism that was involved. He designed it." The "7" had a sweeping style with two bright red pennantlike shapes forming the number, which stood to the left of a fancy, straight-up-and-down, dark blue "6." Atop the "7"—arranged in a circle—rested 13 blue stars, commemorating the 13 original colonies (see page 257).

Richman added, "At the time, they had just completed the Schuylkill Expressway and my father got so excited when he saw it was Interstate 76. He wanted to find out who was responsible for that to make sure he was properly rewarded."

While the team and logo were brand-new to Philadelphia basketball fans, the coach and players were not. In fact, they were inherited, and worse, they were the enemy. Dolph Schayes, the offensive star who torched the Philly Warriors year after year, was named the 76ers' first coach.

Oddly enough, Alex Hannum, who coached the Nats for the previous three seasons, didn't come along, even after he had posted an overall winning record of 127-112 and led the team to a 48-32 mark in the pre-move season of 1962–63, the second most wins in club history. But early on, Hannum made sure he wouldn't have to stay in upstate New York for too long, even though he was having success there.

"I was coaching Syracuse, and we were hanging on by our fingernails against great teams every night," Hannum recounted from his Coronado, California, home. "Every game was a tough one against Boston, Cincinnati with Oscar [Robertson], and L.A. with [Elgin] Baylor and [Jerry] West. We were competitive every game we played. I got my baptism in Syracuse. Most fun I ever had.

"When I signed a deal with Danny Biasone, I said, 'If I can, I'd like to go back to the West Coast,' " Hannum added. "During the second year in Syracuse, Philly moved to San Francisco. I asked Danny if I could talk to Eddie Gottlieb, who was running the club in San Francisco."

Gottlieb was interested but told Hannum he was not first in line.

"He told me, 'Alex, love to have you, but I have coach Frank McGuire as my first choice. And if he doesn't take it, I have a local celebrity, Bob Feerick. You are my third choice,' " remembered Hannum. "He hired Feerick, but then I got a call after they had a disastrous year in 1962–63. I took the job, coached Wilt, and went to the finals," said Hannum.

Once again, the San Francisco connection to Philadelphia's future basketball success played out. First, the city lost the Warriors and Wilt in one fell swoop. Then, the coach the 76ers should have had that first year in Philly bolted for the Bay Area to team with Chamberlain for the first time. Together they went to the NBA finals there against Boston, tuning up for another title clash not far in the future.

So the 76ers coaching job went to Schayes, the man who was synonymous with Syracuse basketball. He led the team in scoring for 13 consecutive seasons, free throw percentage for 10 straight, and rebounding for 8 in a row.

After 15 years on the floor, he moved to the head of the bench, despite the fact that as a rookie he had declared that while he loved playing the game, when he was through, that would be all. Coaching, he said, had too many headaches.

Those words turned out to be prophetic.

The 76ers started out with Schayes and several talented on-court veterans like Hal Greer, Chet Walker, Johnny Kerr, Larry Costello, Dave Gambee, and Paul Neumann. But there was no star player. Success in Philadelphia—artistic and financial—would not be a slam dunk. The team went from 16 games over .500 in Syracuse to 12 games below in Philly. They lost to Cincinnati in a five-game playoff and had only the college draft ahead to salvage the season.

Published reports had Ike and Irv dropping somewhere between $25,000 and $50,000 in year one, with attendance well below expectations. For example, only 5,800 fans turned out for one of the highlight games of the year in November 1963, when the Warriors and Wilt returned to Philly for the first time. The 76ers won a tough overtime battle, 106–102. By Valentine's Day, 1964, it was quite clear that there was no love affair between this team and its new city. That night marked the 26th consecutive non-sellout since the franchise had arrived.

There was an added factor to this popularity problem, and that was the Philadelphia press. For reasons still unclear to this day, two of the major newspapers, the *Daily News* and *Inquirer*, instituted a press blackout of sorts against the new team.

Irv Kosloff said the reporters from these two papers were covering a Philly game against the Knicks in New York early in the season when, mysteriously, they were all called back to Philadelphia. Following that incident, Kosloff attested that these papers never wrote about the team except for three lines after a loss and only two after a win.

"Pre-Wilt days, the *Inquirer* wouldn't print anything," said Mike Richman. "The Sixers would go out and beat the snot out of the Celtics. You pick up the *Inquirer* the next day—box score! Drove my father crazy, probably contributed to his early demise. Nobody at the games. They would get meager crowds. It almost drove the team bankrupt," Richman remembered.

"The *Inquirer* and *Daily News* were owned by Walter Annenberg," said Richman. "Annenberg wouldn't see [Ike]. No matter who he called, Annenberg would have nothing to do with him." Richman offered an explanation, saying that Annenberg was angry at his father because he believed Richman was trying to steal the popular sportscaster Les Keiter from Annenberg's Philadelphia-owned television station to be the new general manager of the 76ers.

"Many a night I can remember my father sittin' there pullin' his hair out, what little he had left, over that," Richman laughed. "Don't know what brought it back, but as fast as it went on, it came off and they started writing."

Dolph Schayes offered a different theory. Schayes suspected that the *Inquirer* refused to cover 76ers games because Eddie Gottleib was still involved with the franchise.

After investigating the issue in his thesis, David Kosloff concluded: "Since Gottleib had just sold the Warriors to a group of investors in San Francisco, it would have been somewhat shady if he were to have been involved with the new team as well. The fact that *Inquirer* owner Annenberg had been a minority owner of the Warriors with Gottleib gives some credence to Schayes' proposition. It might be possible that in order to thwart what they perceived to be a scam job on the city, Annenberg and others used the press blackout to deprive the new team of much needed publicity and legitimacy. This, of course, is just a theory offered by Schayes and may not be wholly accurate. However, it is certain that the press blackout was a premeditated act and not just a short-lived whim."

Thus, the combination of former foes on the court, no publicity, and a rash of injuries sent the 76ers into a tailspin that lasted the entire season.

"The public wants a winner. But you can't win consistently when you are deprived of first-string players [through injury]," said Ike Richman in a 1964 newspaper interview. "I realize the fans don't want to know why a team isn't winning. But all we want is acceptance," Richman added. "You have to figure at least two years [for acceptance]. I feel we have a solid core of one thousand loyal fans. Next year this should increase to about two thousand five hundred for every game. Then we should be on our way," Richman predicted.

Richman didn't know the half of it.

The fortunes of professional basketball in Philadelphia were going to get a whole lot better, and very soon. Yes, there would be enough frustration to go around for everybody before the big payoff. There would be plenty of pain before the pleasure. But the 76ers were on brink of something big. Ike Richman would help orchestrate the biggest parts of it before he left this earth, but his partner Irv Kosloff would carry on. One at a time the men who would make pro basketball history were being assembled and sent forward toward that special season of the 76ers.

T W O

Starting Lineup

The championship 76ers were certainly not built like the NBA title teams of today. Today, big money owners spend fortunes to buy the best free agents, essentially trying to buy a world title right along with them. Free agency was as far away as the moon back in those days. Draft choices cost little to sign, and only a handful were good enough to hang on. Now, draft picks are plucked from high schools, man-children made into instant millionaires and branded as the future of the franchises that select them.

Not so the 76ers.

They were a strange and amazing amalgam of a team. Among the ingredients were Hal Greer, Chet Walker, and Dave Gambee, players leftover from a dying, relocated franchise; Wally Jones, who was snatched from basketball's "lost and found" department; Larry Costello, rescued from the retirement rolls; two rare originals— Luke Jackson, an Olympian who emerged from an obscure college in Texas, and Billy Cunningham, a fresh-faced Brooklyn boy plucked out of a college basketball shrine; Matt Guokas and Bill Melchionni, a couple of long shots drafted from local college courts; and

Wilt Chamberlain, the incredibly talented, temperamental super-star who had been put on the trading block. Ultimately, they would be brought together by the man who abandoned the coaching job when the Syracuse franchise first moved to Philly and instead migrated to San Francisco to coach basketball. But now, Alex Han-num had come back east to rejoin his old players from the Nats and the new players that Richman and Kosloff had handpicked.

THE ROOKIES

Philadelphia has always been a hotbed of basketball, and the fans have always loved their hometown heroes.

When the 76ers latched on to a couple of local boys in the 1966 NBA draft, they were making all the right moves.

Plenty of Philadelphia fans were still miffed when the 76ers passed on Villanova's Jim Washington a year earlier to draft the unknown Billy Cunningham out of North Carolina, even though Billy turned in a marvelous rookie season. But this time around, the 76ers stayed in their own backyard.

Matty Guokas was the biggest college basketball star in town, playing guard on Jack Ramsay's team at St. Joseph's. He was the ninth overall pick, forgoing his senior year to come out early for the NBA draft. He was a newlywed, so there was marital and money motivation.

He got a bonus and a no-cut contract.

There was added pressure on Matt Guokas to make good because he had Philadelphia basketball bloodlines. His father, Matt Sr., played a backup role for Philly's original champions, the 1946–47 Warriors of coach Eddie Gottleib. It was his only year in the league.

"He's better than I ever was," said Guokas Sr. of his son.

But there were early doubts about Matty. Even though he had a good jump shot and lots of basketball smarts, his thin frame caused many to think he couldn't stand up to the league's physical rigors. "I think he has all the tools to be outstanding. But I'm not putting any monkey on his back," said Hannum at the time.

From Villanova and Jack Kraft's program came the 6' 1", 170-pound guard Bill Melchionni, picked ninth in the second round. Melchionni brought a 27.6 college scoring average to the 76ers. He had also broken the scoring record of another local hero, LaSalle's Tom Gola. Melchionni's 801 points nipped Gola's mark by a single marker.

Bill Melchionni initially went overseas to play ball. Born in Pennsauken, New Jersey, near Camden, Melchionni attended Bishop Eustace High School and then went on to Villanova. He had played with Wally Jones of the 76ers as a sophomore on the 1963 Wildcats.

"I was to be part of a State Department tour behind the Iron Curtain going to Poland, Hungary, and Russia," Melchionni remembered. Clyde Lee of Vanderbilt University, Lou Hudson of Minnesota, and Jim Barnett of Oregon were among the high NBA draft choices who made the trip.

"We got to Frankfurt [Germany] and the Russians pulled the plug on the tour because of [U.S.] involvement in the Vietnam War.

"Then I had overtures to play in Italy. My grandfather was born there. They wanted me to give up my citizenship and come over there. They were going to send us [me and my fiancée] on a honeymoon cruise on the Mediterranean.

"I wasn't serious about it. I came back from the tour, not interested in staying in Europe."

In the meantime, Alex Hannum had called.

"In August [1966], I went to Irv Kosloff's house to watch a Phillies game," Melchionni recounted. "He told me he wanted to offer me a ten-thousand-dollar contract with a two-thousand-dollar signing bonus. He fell asleep during the game. I woke him up by clearing my throat. He offered me the deal."

Melchionni got married just a few days later and went to the Poconos on his honeymoon. The couple made a side trip to Kutshers to watch the Maurice Stokes charity game involving some of the 76ers. The seriously ill Stokes was a former forward for the Cincinnati Royals and proceeds from the game helped pay for his long-term care.

The outdoor game was rained out and several of the players, who had come in from around the league to participate, had to go.

Melchionni was asked to take a spot on the West squad, coached by Hannum. They vied with Red Auerbach's East team in the makeup game.

Billy played about 18 minutes, nailing four field goals and a couple of steals. He upstaged his rookie partner Guokas, who went scoreless.

"It was my first exposure to those guys," said Melchionni. "I didn't know if I would ever make it.

"I learned from the vets how to pace yourself in practice," he laughed. "I learned a lot watching them play and practicing against them. I realized how much better we were than everyone else."

THE VETS

Larry Costello had traded in his two-handed set shot for chalk and blackboard after the 1964–65 season with the 76ers. The nine-year NBA veteran became badly hobbled by a bum hamstring and decided to hang 'em up after the 76ers lost the "Havlicek stole the ball" game in Boston.

A new life beckoned.

He took a teaching and coaching job at a Minoa, New York, high school, finally giving himself and his family a real life after years of toil and travel, first with the Philadelphia Warriors, then with the Syracuse Nats, and then back to Philly with the transplanted 76ers.

But the injury sent him to the sidelines seemingly for good, even though he kept his hand in during the 1965–66 season by playing weekends for the Wilkes-Barre team in the Eastern League.

Then Alex Hannum called.

They were old battlers together in Syracuse, when Costello played for Hannum.

They were two of a kind—tough-minded and thoroughly dedicated to the game of basketball.

During the early 1950s, Costello was a star at Niagara University. He topped the team in scoring in his sophomore year en route to becoming the school's all-time scoring leader. "Costy" took Coach Tap Gallagher's Eagles to the National Invitational Tournament in his junior and senior season. Costello parlayed great hands, great speed, and unyielding tenacity into a pro career, beginning with the 1954–55 Philadelphia Warriors. After a stint in the Army, Costy rejoined Philly for the 1956–57 season until he was sent to Syracuse two years later.

That's where Hannum and Costello clicked when Hannum took the Syracuse coaching reins in 1960. Although Hannum jumped to coach San Francisco in 1963–64 and Costy went to Philadelphia with the Nats' franchise move, they were destined to be reunited.

After Franklin Mieuli gave Hannum the heave-ho in 1966, Hannum was the top choice for the Philly job. He wanted Costello's savvy and determination on his new team.

Hannum asked Costy to make a comeback and join the 76ers for the 1966–67 season.

It would have been easy for him to say no. But basketball was too much in the blood.

"I talked it over with [my wife, Barbara] and the people at the school and made the decision," said Costello. "I was giving up something good up there, but I wanted to come back. Maybe it's the desire to play on at least one pro championship team. I've never been on one," Costello said back then.

Costy believed him when Hannum said this was the team that would do just that.

Playing for Syracuse for six years, Costello had endured his share of frustrations at the hands of the Boston Celtics. Finally, he would have the chance to turn the tables.

"Costello did a big job for me in Syracuse," said Hannum at the time. Hannum turned out to be Costello's pro coaching tutor as well.

"He is a leader who has all the moves and knows the game from the inside out. He can get the ball to the open man, and he can put it in the basket. Even though he didn't play in the NBA last season, I'm sure he'll be in shape and ready to go at top speed when the season begins."

Costello was optimistic about his leg, believing it was actually better than ever. He appeared to be right. When he checked into training camp, he was at fighting weight, 186 pounds. That was two pounds lower than his weight at retirement. He survived Hannum's preseason rigors.

"My reflexes are taking time," he said. "I tell my legs what they're supposed to do, especially when we are in defensive drills, and they are a little slow in responding. I can feel myself getting used to everything.

"The leg didn't bother me a bit last season [in the Eastern League], and it feels great today, too," he said. "I gave it a good test, and I think it's completely healed."

Costello earned a starting guard slot next to longtime Syracuse teammate Hal Greer. The younger guards found him a great teacher and a tough taskmaster.

"I roomed with Costello," remembered Bill Melchionni. "He made me do exercises in the hotel room [when the team was on the road]." The rigorous regimen wore Melchionni out.

"I went to Alex and asked if I could room with Billy Cunningham," said Melchionni. "I asked Costy if he minded. He didn't."

And Wally Jones learned a lot from Costy, too. Hannum was sure Costello's influence played a big role in Wally's tenacious defense.

"Costy was like military for me," Wally recalled. Jones would wind up playing for Costello when he called the shots as head coach of the Milwaukee Bucks in the early 1970s.

Leaving behind the high school classroom and high school gym when he did was clearly the correct call for Larry Costello.

It changed his life forever.

Dave Gambee and Alex Hannum just missed connecting with each other for the first time during the 1958–59 NBA season. The 6' 6" forward was drafted by the St. Louis Hawks out of Oregon State University. Hannum had coached the Hawks to the NBA title the previous season, beating the Celtics (with Russell injured) in six games. He figured to be back at the Hawks' helm the next year, but it didn't work out that way. Hannum apparently couldn't survive another year with Hawks owner Ben Kerner.

"Kerner and he had a parting of the ways," recalled Gambee.

As it turned out, Gambee barely got on the floor that season under coaches Andy Philip and Ed McCauley. He had appendicitis after only two games and sat out for the rest of the campaign. "They let me sit out, practice with the team, and they paid me and everything," said Gambee.

But in his second season, the Hawks shipped him to the Cincinnati Royals. A year later, he was traded to Syracuse. Alex Hannum was his new coach.

"He really was the kind of coach that if you put out for him, he would do all he could for you," said Gambee of Hannum. "He stood behind you, a professional's professional, a motivator, about as good a coach as I could ever play for. He gave me my first opportunity to play.

"Except for the winters being so cold, I liked Syracuse."

He liked it even more in the 1961–62 season when he broke into the Syracuse starting lineup. Nats star Dolph Schayes was injured, and Hannum gave Gambee a shot at forward.

"We'd run, work hard on defense. Just not quite enough to get the job done," said Gambee, referring to repeated playoff defeats at the hands of the Boston Celtics.

With the Nats and the 76ers, Gambee earned a reputation as a scrappy backup forward, often called on to match up against the opponent's best shooter.

"I played [John] Havlicek," said Gambee. "A great athlete, never stopped moving, ran all the time, perpetual motion.

"I was counted on to play defense. If they put me in the game I didn't have to figure out what I was supposed to do. When they needed to rest somebody, I played."

He was an old-school, accurate, underhand free throw shooter and a late-game mop-up man. He was often kidded by his teammates for his good looks. They called him "Julius La Rosa" and "Tony Curtis" because of his resemblance to the old television crooner and the Hollywood actor. But Gambee wasn't just another pretty face. The 76ers elected him to the important job of player representative, and he was directly involved in what would later become contentious labor negotiations between the players and the NBA.

From Texas to Tokyo—that was Lucious "Luke" Jackson's story in 1964. The 6' 9", 235-pound center from small Pan American College was one of more than 5,000 athletes from 93 nations who competed in the '64 Summer Games. He starred on the United States Olympic basketball team.

The Americans won the gold medal but their team performance was overshadowed by Bob Hayes, who won the 100 meters and the nickname of "the fastest man alive."

But it was basketball that was on Luke Jackson's mind in Tokyo. It was also on the minds of the two bosses of the Philadelphia 76ers.

Ike Richman and Irv Kosloff journeyed to Japan for themselves to get a long look at Lucious. The team badly needed rebounding strength, and Jackson had risen to the top of the stats with Jim "Bad News" Barnes of Texas Western and Willis Reed of Grambling. The 76ers had the fourth pick in the draft. Ike and Kos wanted to make it count.

"I thought of myself as one of the top five players in the country," Jackson remembered. "At the '64 Olympic Games was the first time I had contact with anybody from the NBA. In fact, I have a picture of Ike and Mr. Kosloff watching. Right after the games were over we had some conversations in the hotel in Tokyo. I had been hearing that Boston was going to draft me. I never had any dreams or thoughts about playing in the NBA, but when the opportunity presented itself . . .

"Ike told me they were going to draft me."

The New York Knicks took Barnes as the top pick. The 76ers opted for Luke at number four and the Knicks captured Reed at number seven.

"Ike was like my father," said Jackson. "He got me on the road, took me under his wing."

No one was more devastated than Luke when Ike Richman collapsed and died courtside in the Boston Garden during that late 1965 game against the Celtics. "His death was horrible," said Jackson. "He had come into the dressing room before the game and told us we were gonna kick their butts. I remember when he collapsed, the score was 13-13. We wanted to win it for Ike. Playing for him was like family."

Until the Chamberlain trade in early 1965, Luke and center Johnny "Red" Kerr were the 76ers' big men. When Wilt arrived, Luke became a full-time forward and was destined to be the NBA's first prototype power forward. In his first season with Wilt playing alongside, Luke averaged almost 15 points and 13 rebounds a game, his best individual year as a 76er. After that season Kerr became expendable and the 76ers sent him to Baltimore to get hometown hero Wally Jones.

"I played a lot inside, then when Wilt finally came I had to move. He was the big guy. If he was there we could do anything.

"Alex was a man's man, the only coach I really enjoyed playing for. He said, 'I won't accept less than one hundred percent.' "

Luke Jackson always gave him more.

Hal Greer was the greatest basketball player in the history of his alma mater, Marshall College (now Marshall University), where he was the school's first black athlete.

He played forward, center, and guard for the Thundering Herd.

"My senior year I played opposite Wayne Embry," said Greer of the big guy who went on to play for Cincinnati, Boston, and Milwaukee. Greer led the Mid-American Conference in rebounding one year until Embry caught and passed him with a late-season rush. In an NBA playoff game in April 1965, Greer amazingly out-rebounded Embry again, 29–25.

"Guards don't out-rebound centers, but it was a crazy series," wrote *The Bulletin*'s George Kiseda.

At Marshall, of course, Greer was remembered most of all for his scoring. Just like with the Syracuse Nats.

Hal "Bulldog" Greer toiled for four years in Syracuse before moving vans came and moved him and the rest of the Nationals to Philadelphia in 1963. The last three seasons there he averaged 20 points per game. Dolph Schayes had moved past his prime as the Syracuse superstar, and Greer took up the mantle. The blue-collar fans there liked his work ethic and his shooting.

Things started out differently in Philadelphia. Nobody seemed to care about the new guys in town. Nobody at all.

"Our first year the fans almost boycotted," Greer recalled. "The arenas were so vacant you could hear us callin' the plays out. The papers didn't support us, the fans didn't, nobody supported us. It was so funny because we almost never played before an empty audience in Syracuse. We were glad to get out of Syracuse, it was not as big a metropolis as Philadelphia was. And I always said when I started in the league that if I was to be traded anywhere, it would always be Philadelphia. I just liked the people of Philadelphia, and I enjoyed every time we played there, so it was a good situation.

"[The fans] didn't support us that first year because they were upset that the Warriors had moved out of town. They were left with the enemy, so to speak. But after one or two years, they kinda warmed up, and it was a great situation. It was a positive thing for me."

Not so positive was Greer's perceived lack of respect around the league. Even after five straight All-Star Game appearances prior to the championship season, Greer still operated in the shadows of the NBA's legendary guards, Oscar Robertson, Jerry West, and even Sam Jones of the Celtics.

"I think I'm better than the fourth guard," Greer told reporters. "You gotta realize that Oscar is the greatest. Jerry West is right behind Oscar, but I think I should be up there. I think I'm on a par with West."

And what about the comparisons with Sam Jones?

"We're about even, I guess," Greer added. "He's on a team where they work for him. Our team is balanced. We're a team all the way. We don't work for one guy. Sam doesn't really have to work for his shots. They work for him. He's strictly offense. I'm offense plus I move the ball, too. I move the fast break."

And the 6' 2", 175-pound Greer often did it all in plenty of pain—the pain of arthritis in his right shoulder, his shooting shoulder. Sometimes before games he couldn't get his arm up more than three quarters of the way.

Trainer Al Domenico concocted a home remedy to keep one of the league's best middle-distance shooters gunning—hot sand.

"My grandmother used to sit on the beach in an old black bathing suit for two or three hours a day with her hands in the sand," said Domenico. Her doctor had recommended the sun-baked sand to help her arthritic fingers.

There was no beach near Convention Hall, so Domenico did the next best thing. Before each game, he would boil a sand bag in a contraption called a hydrocollater. Domenico said it operated like a coffee percolator.

After the water boiled, the sand bag was removed and applied to Greer's sore shoulder for up to a half hour. Then Domenico would massage the shoulder with analgesic balm for another 15 to 20 minutes. More often than not, the therapy was enough to get Greer in gear.

It was Al and Hal's little secret.

"Sometimes he had bad games and nobody knew the pain he was in," Domenico remembered.

Before Chet Walker came to Syracuse as a rookie for Danny Biasone's Nationals, his previous trips to New York State—specifically, New York City—had been nothing but trouble.

It shouldn't have been that way, but it was. After all, sophomore

Chet Walker and his Bradley University teammates had come to Manhattan to play at Madison Square Garden in the 1960 National Invitational Tournament. Back then the NIT had as much prestige, if not more, than the NCAAs. New York City was still the mecca of college basketball, and there was Bradley—after playing so well in Peoria and the Missouri Valley Conference—front and center at the NIT.

For Chet Walker, it was the pinnacle of his personal life and basketball life. He was a quiet, sensitive young man, born in rural Mississippi. His mother, tired of years of verbal and physical abuse handed out by her husband, picked up and moved her family to Benton Harbor, Michigan, in the early 1950s. That's where basketball took hold of Chet, allowing him to blossom.

"It's always been hard for me to open up," wrote Walker in his autobiography, *Long Time Coming*. "Even when I competed in basketball, the most public of sports, I held my cards close to my vest, kept my own counsel."

The racism he saw made him more guarded. Like all of the black athletes of his day, prowess on the basketball court did not always translate into equal treatment and equal accommodations.

But it was in a New York City hotel room—on the day of a key NIT semifinal match with St. Bonaventure—where Chet's first New York experience took a bizarre twist.

Walker and teammate Al Saunders were taking it easy when they heard a knock on the door. It was a hotel bellhop bearing two glasses of orange juice. He told the players the juice was compliments of their coach, Chuck Orsborn. The thirsty Chet chugged it down, but a suspicious Saunders didn't, reasoning that the coach had never done such a thing in the past.

Chet's chugging turned into a gulp, and a call to the coach confirmed the worst. He hadn't sent any juice to the room. Within minutes, Walker was doubled over in pain. The frantic coach and athletic director called the police and came running to help their star. Hotel security and the cops were ready to write it off as a practical joke, especially after some quick tests showed nothing obvious in the drinks.

But no one was laughing. Walker was in severe pain, and his team needed him for the big game. This was Bradley's big chance and Walker was the team leader. The pain and nausea kept sweeping over him, literally making him feel like he was about to die. But this game meant more to Walker than anything else. He was going to play.

The New York papers latched on to the story and one of the headlines read, "Bradley University Star Poisoned." There was no proof of that yet, but there was evidence enough for the point spread on the game to drop like a rock. Bradley was favored by seven, but not for long. After news of the orange juice incident spread, the Bonnies were suddenly the pick.

Word travels fast.

If people were now betting that Walker was too sick to play, it was the wrong wager. Fighting a cold sweat, dizzy spells, and frequent trips to the bench, Walker dazzled the Garden crowd with 27 points in just 23 minutes, leading Bradley over the Bonnies 82–71. Afterwards, he barely made it back to the hotel room where his ordeal began just hours earlier.

His weakness continued for two days more, when Bradley was pitted against Providence and their star Lenny Wilkens for the NIT championship. Again, Walker put his health aside and powered his team to an 88–72 title victory.

Recounting the incident in his book, Walker believed his doctored drink was no accident. He felt the bellhop was carrying out a mission from the gamblers that dominated New York City and college basketball at that time. Walker remembered how the bellhop waited around making idle chatter, asking how he and his teammate were feeling, as if he wanted to make sure both players finished their drinks before leaving.

It appeared to Walker that no one wanted to take his stomach trouble seriously. As it turned out, he had suffered permanent damage to the blood vessels in his kidneys. And, as it turned out, Walker's hunch about gamblers doctoring his drink had merit.

A year later, he was called to New York a second time, this time for a date with District Attorney Frank Hogan, whose office was probing the likes of Jack Molinas and other suspected sports gamblers. College basketball in New York City exploded into the headlines in the 1950s after players on the City College of New York basketball team conspired with gamblers to fix games from 1949 to 1951. Players shaved their point-scoring or made other deliberate mistakes during games, which enabled the gamblers who bet the point spreads to control the outcomes and victory margins of the games. The scandal tainted the college game, particularly in New York City, for more than a decade.

Walker was asked if he knew Molinas or any of the other college basketball players who had been previously linked to the point-shaving scandal. They even asked about the orange juice. They also asked him about an arrest for gambling when he was a teenager busted for playing a penny-ante game on a street corner. They asked about regular season games that Bradley played in its NIT championship year in which the team went in a heavy favorite, only to win by a tight margin.

Finally, the grilling ended.

Walker breathed a big sigh of relief when they let him leave. He breathed an even bigger one when his coach told him he was cleared.

His roommate Saunders wasn't so lucky. He was suspended from school merely for admitting that a gambler had contacted him, nothing more. It all left its mark on Walker.

Fortunately, his third visit to the Empire State went a lot better, even from the moment he got off the plane at the Syracuse airport.

Club owner Danny Biasone was there to do the greeting. "How are ya, kid? Welcome to Sireecuse!"

Walker had signed a contract for $12,000, but there was no big bonus money. It was just $2,000 and Chet generously gave it to his two brothers as a long-overdue thank-you for their support and love over the years.

Walker bought himself a car and Coach Alex Hannum made sure the rookie used it to drive the veterans to practice. Walker averaged 12 points in his rookie year under Hannum, but the boss was not that pleased.

"After the season was over, I had a talk with Chet," said Hannum. "I told him that a season which would be great for some people might not be great for him. Are you going to accept the challenges, to demand more of yourself, each night, night after night?" Hannum told him, "To be a star is to be willing to accept responsibility." Basically, Alex just wanted Chet to shoot more. "I tell him that if you help yourself, you help the team by doing what you can do best."

Walker took Hannum's advice to heart, even though Hannum left the Nats to coach in San Francisco. Chet and the rest of his teammates made the jump to Philadelphia and Walker adjusted his game, ringing up 17 points per contest during the first year in his new surroundings.

Billy Cunningham's journey to Philadelphia began in Brooklyn with a man who had ties to both Wilt Chamberlain and the City of Brotherly Love.

Frank McGuire, coach of the North Carolina University Tar Heels, recruited Cunningham from his Brooklyn, New York, high school in 1960. He found Billy through a family connection.

"My sister's best friend was [McGuire's] niece," said Cunningham. "She told him about me, and he recruited me. I signed a commitment to North Carolina at the end of my junior year.

"But when I got there in 1961, McGuire had left to coach the Philadelphia Warriors, so I ended up playing for Dean Smith."

"The most important thing was that the team came number one," recalled Cunningham, who was 6' 4" and still growing.

His new team was about to be the Philadelphia 76ers and the Frank McGuire connection surfaced again.

This time, McGuire put in a good word about Billy to 76ers co-owner Irv Kosloff before the 1965 college draft.

"Ike Richman had never seen me play," said Cunningham. "Irv Kosloff had spoken to Frank McGuire and Frank recommended that they draft me.

"I wasn't even aware the NBA draft was going on," laughed Billy. "I found out I was drafted by Philadelphia when a Philadelphia sports-writer called me in my dormitory room."

Philadelphia was a town that liked its basketball heroes home-grown and Villanova's 6' 8" Jim Washington seemed to be a logical draft pick for the 76ers.

But Ike Richman and Kosloff picked the smaller Cunningham, with Kosloff casting the tie-breaking vote when Richman and Dolph Schayes disagreed about which man to take.

"As expected, the local papers were very critical of this decision," recounted Irv Kosloff's grandson, David.

"Sportswriters like Claude E. Harrison, Jr., of the *Philadelphia Tribune* stressed the fact that the 76ers had done the same thing the year before. While he agreed that Lucious Jackson was an excellent selection ahead of the 'great Villanova playmaker' Wally Jones, he seriously questioned the team taking Ira Harge instead of the immensely popular Jones.

"After having taken care of their rebounding needs with Jackson, Richman told reporters that he chose Billy Cunningham because 'we need a big guard who can stop Oscar Robertson and Jerry West.' "

Cunningham was unaware of any controversy over his selection. He didn't know much about Villanova and even less about Jim Washington.

"They tried to make Billy a guard, but Boston kept stealing the ball," said Wally Jones, describing the 76ers' ill-fated attempt to justify their draft pick.

"They thought I could play guard when I got there," said Billy. But Cunningham was destined to play two roles. He moved up to forward and into the sixth man slot, previously pioneered by Boston's Frank Ramsey and John Havlicek. His jumping ability earned him the nickname "Kangaroo Kid" and his penchant for instant offense helped lead the 76ers to the Eastern Conference regular season crown in his rookie year, a year that saw him average 14 points and 7.5 rebounds a game off the bench.

But Cunningham couldn't match his regular season performance in the 1965–66 playoffs, going cold with the rest of the 76ers in the embarrassing 4–1 conference finals loss to Boston.

"We were disappointed in ourselves after ending up with the best record and losing to Boston," said Cunningham.

"There was not a lot said about it, but it resulted in a deeper commitment from this team. From my standpoint, it was quite a learning experience about how to prepare yourself."

Billy Cunningham turned out to be the right draft pick for the 76ers for all the wrong reasons. His brilliance as a player helped lead the 76ers to their first title. His talents as a coach resulted in their second crown 16 years later.

• • •

Wally Jones had, indeed, hoped to start his pro basketball career with his hometown 76ers, but destiny carried him elsewhere. Destiny also brought him back.

He officially began his professional basketball career with the Detroit Pistons, who chose him in the third round of the 1964 draft out of Philadelphia's Villanova University.

Wally had put together a pretty good sophomore season for the Wildcats, but slacked off some after that. Still, he was an All–Big 5 selection for three straight years. The 76ers could have easily drafted Jones, but they picked big man Ira Harge out of New Mexico, a pick that never paid dividends.

"I would have liked to stay in the city to play pro ball," said Jones. "I met Mr. Schayes a few times during the season, and he didn't say anything to me or ask if I wanted to play for the 76ers, so I didn't have my hopes too high that they would draft me."

The Pistons decided to give him a look. Or so he thought.

He never played a game for them.

"Before I knew it, I was traded to Baltimore." The Pistons peddled him to the Baltimore Bullets in a pre-season trade after talking briefly with the 76ers about dealing Jones back to his hometown. The Pistons wanted Larry Costello even up, and the 76ers weren't interested. So it was on to Baltimore for Jones.

"I didn't even have a car when I signed," said Wally. "Sihugo Green and Gus Johnson took care of me. Bailey Howell taught me how to look good with the old pick and roll, he communicated with me, made me look good."

But in Baltimore, the reality was that he rode the bench a lot more than he liked and got homesick for nearby West Philly.

"I just wasn't used to that," said Jones. "It was real hard to take. I was getting so I didn't care anymore."

Though he made the all-rookie team and picked up a playoff check,

Wally didn't like the money the Bullets were offering after the season ended.

He also found himself in mounting domestic difficulties, something he didn't talk about then and still doesn't discuss today. Jones was unhappy and unstable, desperate and drinking, and he decided it was best if he just took a walk.

And not just around the block to clear his mind.

In the summer of 1965, Wally Jones effectively disappeared.

He didn't even know that Baltimore had traded him to the Philadelphia 76ers for Johnny Kerr.

"I went into hiding to escape problems," he recalled.

Jones was hiding out from personal and professional pain in the Pacific Northwest, and for a time even in Canada.

Meanwhile, back in the City of Brotherly Love, Wally's soon-to-be new father figure, 76ers owner Ike Richman, was trying to pick up the scent of the prodigal son and sign him to a deal.

Richman added big bucks to his long-distance phone bill trying to find the elusive Jones. He got the police and private investigators involved. He even put an ad in the paper. No one remembers if it was in the "Lost and Found" section.

Wally was in Seattle, riding out what he characterized as a "very distraught time."

"I had stopped playing, and I wasn't going to play any more basketball."

At the request of Ike Richman, Wally's old West Philly runnin' buddy (and then-Lakers guard) Walt Hazzard was turned into a bounty hunter of sorts.

Hazzard, who later influenced Jones to convert to the Muslim religion, and Jones played together on the Overbrook High School basketball team. The team also included future pro Wayne Hightower and local legends Ralph Heyward and Richie Richman.

"Hazzard finds me in Seattle," said Jones, "the only person in the world who knew where I was. He told me, 'Go on back, you need to play.'" Lakers coach Fred Schaus fronted Jones an airplane ticket.

Back he went.

"Ike Richman had me stay at his house. He would not let me be around anybody else," Wally recounted. "He wanted me to get my head together. He knew that I was mixed up. He kept me at his house and took care of me."

"One day he shows up on my father's front steps with nothing but the clothes he was wearing," said Mike Richman, Ike's son.

"That's all he had, that's all he owned. We took him out and bought him clothes, bought him a hairbrush, bought him a toothbrush, and he stayed at my father's house until he got cleaned up, got himself somewhat back in shape."

"That started another phase of my life," said Jones. "Al Domenico came to Ike Richman's house every day and got me and trained me. I was about two hundred some pounds from alcohol consumption, from Thunderbird and all that stuff. I was destroying myself.

"He said, 'We want you here.'

"Al Domenico ran me to death, sometimes over at Franklin Field, to get me ready for exhibition games. I was making about twenty thousand dollars."

So Jones was back in Philadelphia, where he grew up in a big basketball family, with eight brothers and sisters. "We were raised in an environment where we played for churches. They weren't always the same denomination," said Jones. He was a product of the tough West Philly neighborhood. His older brother introduced him to the game of basketball. It was part of survival. "We had gangs. I was in gangs. They were protection for your community, but again, we were lucky we couldn't get a gun."

He sharpened his skills on the city's basketball playgrounds and at

Overbrook, where John Chaney (now the successful coach at Philly's Temple University) was his health teacher and junior varsity coach. He learned a lot about basketball from Chaney.

"He would beat [me and Walt Hazzard] one on two!"

Wally went to Temple Prep, then received a scholarship and enrolled at Villanova. "I picked Villanova [over Temple's offer] to get out of the city. I know it's only ten miles out, but when you grow up in West Philly, ten miles makes a mighty big difference when it comes to grass and trees." On the basketball front, "Coach Jack Kraft taught me the mental part of the game," said Jones.

Physically, Wally developed a unique shooting style off the dribble and from the foul line that attracted a lot of attention. Andy Musser, radio voice of the 76ers, called his jump shot the "jackknife" because his legs kicked out in front of him, almost meeting his arms in the follow-through, like the two blades of a jackknife. Stan Hochman, columnist for the *Philadelphia Daily News*, wrote: "He has this way of shooting like someone bouncing on the edge of a diving board while waving good-bye to the lifeguard." Jack Kiser of the *Daily News* described Wally's foul shot as "a wounded duck trying to gain altitude." Wally would extend his arms outward in a flying motion and be almost on tiptoes when he put up his free throws.

It was a sight to see.

His shooting style may not have always looked pretty, but it was pretty effective, especially when Wally went streaky from the floor. He would get into a groove, his confidence high, and nobody could shut him down for a while. He also loved to play that tough "D." Alex Hannum was happy to have him, though not completely sure about him at first.

"I had heard some funny things about this guy, Wally Jones, before I came here," said Hannum. "I wondered what kind of player I was getting. The day he reported to camp, he was ready to play. He gives the team zip on the court and always has been a good defensive player. Now I know that Wally is worth his weight in gold . . . as comedy relief for the team and as a solid player."

Hannum also invoked Costello's name again as the best influence on Wally. "Costello is one of the fiercest defensive men I've ever seen in pro basketball, and I think Wally has found out he must have the same approach to attain the heights that are within his reach," said Hannum.

Speaking of height and reach, there is the arrival of just one other player to talk about. He had already set the NBA on its ear in his first five seasons. He had achieved the impossible—scoring 100 points in a single game. He had averaged 50 points per game for an entire season and hauled down 55 rebounds in one game. His dominance had forced the league to changed its offensive rule book. He was already a Philadelphia sports legend. And he wanted to beat the Boston Celtics worse than anybody else in Philadelphia.

He was ready to come home again to try to do just that.

He was Wilt Chamberlain.

In one brilliant stroke, Ike Richman brought old friend and client Wilt back to his birthplace and set the stage for the basketball giant to put aside his scoring prowess and completely adjust his game as only he could. Wilt was poised to finally fit that long-elusive championship ring on his finger.

THREE

Reconstructing Wilt

The Sporting News
1966–67 Player of the Year
Wilt Chamberlain

The greatest point producer in basketball history, Chamberlain deliberately sacrificed what could have been his eighth straight scoring title in the interest of team play. As a result of his leadership, the 76ers set an NBA mark for victories with a 68-13 record and won the Eastern Division championship. His inspirational performance led his fellow performers to name him Player of the Year in a poll conducted by The Sporting News.

Under a picture of Chamberlain, those words are inscribed on a plaque that hangs on the living room wall in the Mount Laurel, New Jersey, home of Vinson Miller, the best friend Wilt ever had. The award is a polished, engraved, and lasting testament to the way Wilt reconstructed his game for the 1966–67 championship season of the Philadelphia 76ers. But before Wilt's *re*construction, there was his construction, and nobody knows more about that than Vince Miller.

Miller lived in North Philadelphia as a child, and his father wanted a move up. "My father bought a home in West Philly," said Miller. "He moved his family to a better neighborhood."

It was Wilt's neighborhood. He was born on August 21, 1936, the fourth of nine kids for William and Olivia Chamberlain. William, who worked welding, carpentry, and electrical jobs to support the big brood, stood only 5' 8", so Wilt's height wasn't in the family genes. In fact, at birth Wilt debuted at 8 pounds, 10 ounces, and 22 inches, no immediate indicators of his growth potential.

The story goes that at only four years old, Wilt was already prov-

ing his penchant for making money. He picked up pennies by return-
ing empty milk bottles.

He went to Brooks Elementary at 57th and Haverford, and in the
third grade made his first friend for life.

"I went to Brooks and was thrown into Wilt's class," said Miller.
"Instant chemistry.

"I think it was because I was second tallest. In elementary school
you line up according to size, so we were lined up next to each other.
At an early age, though, we weren't into basketball. At that time we
were into track." But it was basketball that would put Wilt Chamberlain on "track" for greatness.

Philadelphia folklore has it that when Wilt was about 10 years old,
he and some buddies were playing a basement brand of basketball on
the bottom floor of an abandoned building. Wilt kept dipping his head
down to avoid the pipes hanging from above. His friends gave him the
nickname "Dippy" and it stuck. (Later, he hated the nickname "Wilt
the Stilt," which was slapped on him by a newspaper reporter.)

Wilt was doing an awful lot of head-dipping just about everywhere
back then. By age 12, Wilt already stood 6' 11" or 7', depending on
who was doing the measuring.

Chamberlain and Miller stayed side by side through their years at
Shoemaker Junior High and then at Overbrook High School, where
the gargantuan but graceful Wilt led Vince and his "Brook" teammates to three straight Public League championships from 1953
through 1955, city titles in 1954 and 1955, and an amazing three-year
mark of 56-3 (19-2, 19-0, and 18-1). Wilt had scored 90 points in one
game, 74 in another, and 71 in yet another. In his senior year, he averaged 44.5 points per game en route to a grand total of 2,206 points for
his high school career. He led the YMCA to a national basketball
championship, too.

The young Wilt was making sports headlines and drawing the undivided attention of basketball scouts, coaches, writers, and fans. Miller said Chamberlain quickly got used to the constant scrutiny and the perks it brought him.

"I knew Wilt when he didn't have a quarter," chuckled Miller. But that all changed in the summer between Wilt's junior and senior years at Overbrook, when he took a vacation job at Kutshers resort, the NBA's off-season mecca in the Catskill Mountains of New York.

"I didn't go with him," said Miller. "It was the first time we had been away from each other for two or three months, without seeing each other. He musta come back with maybe two grand, three grand for two or three months. That's a lot of money. He was a bellhop. Kutshers paid two dollars a day, but they gave you room and board. He said, 'Vince, [the customers] would call me to their rooms and ask for extra hangers and give me five dollars, two dollars, just to see me.' Or the ladies always wanted him to set up the mah-jongg tables."

" 'Wiltie, after lunch would you have our table set up there,' " said Miller, recalling his friend's words. "Four dollars, five dollars."

The Kutshers connection paid off in many ways for Wilt. Besides bringing extra hangers and setting up the game tables, Chamberlain played plenty of basketball. Celtics coach Red Auerbach piloted one of the all-star teams that played the annual charity games there and had Wilt go against some of the Boston players.

"I used to try to beat them to death so I knew that I could probably do fairly well in the pros even at that early age," said Wilt. But a college career came first.

And for the first time since Wilt's summer job at Kutshers, Vince Miller and Wilt Chamberlain would have to separate again. Miller was headed south to play college ball at a black school, North Carolina A&T. Wilt was headed to the heartland of America.

B. H. Born, a basketball star at the University of Kansas, also worked a summer at Kutshers. He took one look at Chamberlain and quickly phoned Phog Allen, KU's legendary coach. It wasn't long after that Allen visited Wilt's parents in Philadelphia. Soon Wilt was on the road to Lawrence, Kansas.

And the road was bumpy.

He pulled up to a restaurant in Kansas City, Kansas, on the trip out. The manager said he would be happy to serve Wilt in the kitchen. Discrimination didn't set well with the Big Dipper. Wilt told Phog Allen that if he couldn't eat in those places, he wasn't coming to KU to play basketball.

Chamberlain recalled: "Dr. Allen sat me down and said, 'Anywhere in the state of Kansas you want to go, you can do it. Anyplace that refuses you for being there, we will close that place up. I promise you.'"

Chamberlain signed on.

His freshman team played the KU varsity in a pre-season exhibition game. Wilt put on a personal exhibition, scoring more than 40 points, nabbing some 30 rebounds, and blocking 15 shots, as the freshmen won by 10 points.

It was an early warning sign from Wilt.

"I knew I had to show them either I could do it or I couldn't."

Coach Allen sent a warning of his own to the staid world of college basketball, saying the game was in trouble because of Wilt's arrival and declaring it "an emergency for the rules makers." The NCAA soon changed its rules about dunking and forced foul shooters to remain at the free throw line because Wilt kept following up his own missed foul shots for scores. Teams began using the slowdown game to keep the ball away from Wilt as much as possible.

"If we would have been allowed to play basketball we would have won a couple of championships," said Wilt. Though Chamberlain racked up 30 points and 19 rebounds a game in his two years at KU, he and his Jayhawks teammates won no titles, losing the memorable triple overtime game to North Carolina and Coach Frank McGuire in the 1957 NCAA tournament finals.

Wilt was used to winning title after title up until then. That bitter defeat would haunt him and be a precursor of more frustration on the basketball court when championships were on the line. Wilt later called it the "toughest loss of my life."

It led Chamberlain to abandon his senior year at KU to sign a professional contract with the Harlem Globetrotters. He had that taste for money again.

"He got a ten-thousand-dollar bonus to sign," said Miller. "He gave it to me to hold while he put on a Globies uniform to pose. He took it out again in the car on the trip home, and we held it."

Chamberlain loved to spend his money on cars. He drove around in several flashy ones while at Kansas, and the NCAA did some investigating. But the university was only penalized for buying him tires, not cars.

"His first love was Oldsmobiles," remembered Miller. "His first car was a 1947 or '48 slant-backed Olds. But he graduated to a Bentley when he was in the NBA. He paid twenty-two thousand dollars for it, I think. But the guys gave him the needle about it. [Cadillac] El Dorados were going for eight thousand. They said he could buy three El Dorados for what he paid for the Bentley. But Wilt wanted the best. That Bentley lasted, and, at one time, was worth about a half million dollars."

His first NBA contract was for $65,000, according to press reports. Eddie Gottleib, the clever Philadelphia sports entrepreneur who owned the Warriors, used his territorial draft rights gambit and the persuasive powers of Ike Richman to snare Chamberlain.

"One particular evening my father said, 'I need you. Drive me to 4700 North Broad Street,'" remembered Mike Richman, Ike's son. "We drive down there, we're sittin' in the car, sittin' in the car, and a big white Cadillac pulls up. He says, 'Wait here for me.' He got out and left, got into the white Cadillac and drove away. I waited about an hour, two hours. He comes back, gets in the car, and says to me, 'I just worked as hard as I ever worked before in my life. I just convinced Wilt Chamberlain to leave the Globetrotters and come play for the Warriors.'

"Wilt said in the paper that he never met anybody like this in his life. The man could talk the birds out of the trees—Ike Richman. And from then on, whatever it was, they did together. They became very good friends."

Gottlieb and Richman had stolen Chamberlain away from the envious Red Auerbach and the Boston Celtics. "[Auerbach] always needled Wilt after that," said Miller. "They parted ways after that, but they were pretty close when Wilt was younger."

The gloating and diminutive Gottlieb posed for pictures with the giant Chamberlain towering over him, using his back to sign the historic Philadelphia contract. Both men were ready to take on Auerbach, the vaunted Celtics, and the entire NBA, for that matter.

Chamberlain impacted the pro game immediately, scoring 37.6 points per contest and grabbing almost 2,000 rebounds in his rookie season of 1959–60. But Auerbach and Boston weren't budging, beating the Warriors and Chamberlain in a six-game playoff series for the Eastern championship. And, just as the NCAA quickly acted after Wilt's debut at Kansas, the NBA instituted several major rule changes between Wilt's first and second seasons. The league widened the lane, added the three-second lane violation, and banned offensive goaltending in an attempt to put the clamps on Chamberlain.

It didn't do a damn bit of good.

In 1960–61, Wilt did himself better. He hiked his scoring average to 38.4 points per game and picked up more than 200 additional rebounds for a grand total of 2,149. And he was just getting started.

The next season, the Warriors brought in the coach who had beaten Chamberlain in the famous championship game against Kansas. Frank McGuire took over as Philly's head man, and though he may have been Wilt's nemesis in the 1957 title game, he was destined to help the player achieve early immortality. McGuire's game plan was simple. He wanted Wilt to score even more.

The 1961–62 NBA campaign was Chamberlain's personal crown jewel for individual effort. Before he was finished that year, he averaged a stunning 50.4 points per game, a mark challenged only by him in succeeding years, but never surpassed by Wilt or anyone else. He also averaged an amazing 48.5 minutes per game, counting overtime contests. In all, he missed only eight minutes of playing time all season.

"I do remember the year I scored 50, my third year," Wilt told an NBA interviewer. "I remember in January one day I had about 55 points and I said to myself, 'You know what? I'm building a monster year. If I don't watch myself, I'll be averaging 55 points a game, and next year they are going to want me to average 65 points a game. What am I doing?' So, I really, honestly pulled back and stopped trying to score, though I did score 100 points about a month later."

The 100-point game was played on March 2, 1962, in Hershey, Pennsylvania. Wilt made 36 of 63 field goal attempts and 28 of 32 free throws as the Warriors beat the New York Knicks, 169–147. Warriors statistician Harvey Pollack scribbled the number 100 on a piece of paper for Wilt to hold up for the photographers.

There was no television coverage for the game and only 4,100 spectators showed up in person, but Chamberlain once estimated that "at least one-hundred-fifty-thousand people" had told him they saw his incredible effort.

"As time goes by, I feel more and more a part of that 100-point game," said Wilt. "It has become my handle, and I've come to realize just what I did. People will say to a little kid, 'See that guy right there? He scored 100 points in a game.' I'm definitely proud of it.

"I loved the fact that no one could really block my shot. I jumped so high that there was nothing they could do. When you have no fear, it's just going to make you much better at what you're doing. So, while they were reaching for the ball this way, I was going on top of them and just taking it out of their hands. It gave me a sense of superiority. What hurt me was that I wanted to be the consummate basketball player, and I wanted to be able to shoot the ball instead of just taking it to the basket and dunking it like I should have. I was shooting fadeaway shots, hook shots, finger rolls, whatever came to my mind that I thought would be pleasing. A lot of times it was a negative more than a positive. If I just went out and took it to the basket every time, I'd have averaged 70 or 80 points a game."

But while the personal achievements of that season made him proud, the team accomplishments left him longing. He and the Warriors lost again in the playoffs to Boston and Auerbach and Bill Russell, this time in a heartbreaking seven-game series. Sam Jones hit a jumper with two seconds left in the final game to lift the Celts to victory.

The Warriors were not only finished for the season, they were finished in Philadelphia. Eddie Gottlieb went west for the money and moved Wilt and the Warriors to San Francisco, leaving only Coach Frank McGuire behind. That was the bad news. The good news was that Wilt would soon meet another important mentor, a man who was in the construction business. Or, as it turned out in Chamberlain's case, a man who liked the *re*construction business.

Alex Hannum didn't get to the Warriors until a season later, so Wilt had to struggle through a terrible first season in San Francisco, going 31-49 in 1962–63 under Coach Bob Feerick. Again, Chamberlain's individual numbers were awesome—a 44.8 per game scoring average and another rebounding title, with Wilt besting Bill Russell again by more than 100 caroms.

But the team was going nowhere. It missed the playoffs. At least Chamberlain wouldn't have to face the Celtics again. But he wanted another shot at them and so did Alex Hannum. Alex was brought on board the next year to get it done. Hannum also wanted to get back to the Western Division, tired of fighting the uphill battle of coaching the undermanned Syracuse Nationals against the likes of the Celtics and Wilt's Philly Warriors. Eddie Gottleib finally recruited the ex-Marine. Now he would coach alongside Wilt Chamberlain instead of against him.

In essence, the reconstruction job on Wilt began in his first season with Hannum. Chamberlain's scoring average "dropped" to 36.9 points per game. For the first time, he penetrated the "assists" column, unheard of for a center, and certainly for a man of his size and scoring ability. He made the league's top five, totaling five helps per game and trailing only teammate Guy Rodgers, Cincy's Oscar Robertson, Boston's Bob Cousy, and Chicago's Si Green. But why was Wilt suddenly changing his game?

The story, portending a similar confrontation that was still several years away, went like this:

When Hannum first arrived in San Francisco, Chamberlain was pouring the ball in the hole better than ever, and he didn't understand why Hannum would want him to change. Supposedly Hannum locked the clubhouse and had it out with Wilt, face-to-face.

"You been fighting me as a coach all the way. Now fight me as a man," Hannum was alleged to have yelled at Chamberlain. Wilt was said to have made a couple of fists, but backed away saying, "I can't fight you, Alex."

No one can corroborate the specific story, but the results are self-evident. Vince Miller can attest to Alex and Wilt butting heads.

"Alex was a Marine—they called him 'Sarge'—barrel-chested, in shape. He stood up to Wilt. But they had no dislike for each other," said Miller. "The mere fact that when Alex went into the Hall of Fame, who was the one that went up there to present him? That says a lot right there. If there was anything stronger than just natural basketball knocking of the heads, Wilt would have never done that."

Head-butting aside, Hannum had convinced Chamberlain that he could win more championships playing a complete game rather than a totally individual one. Hannum believed in the team concept, not the game plan of one player scoring at will to lead a team to victory.

"Wilt scored that way because [Frank] McGuire wanted him to," said Hannum at the time. "I don't think it will ever be done again. The Celtics changed the game by winning with defense. They showed that a big shot-blocker [like Russell] could keep you in the game. Oh, sometimes there is a weak man in there against Wilt, so we give him the ball.

"Against Detroit the other night, Wilt kept giving up the ball from the pivot, and we got a lot of really easy baskets. Of course, I understand this is easier to do when you are winning the way we are. Wilt doesn't mind giving up the ball because he sees the results. But suppose we were losing. It's only natural for him not to want to give up the ball to a guard who's shooting 40 percent when he can shoot 70 percent.

"He does what he's told. He's told to score points, he scores points. He's told to pass off, he passes off."

Wilt would only say, "I always do what coaches tell me to do."

So, with Hannum's attitude and the change in Chamberlain, the Warriors blossomed, holding opponents to a league low of 102.6 points per game en route to a 48-32 season in 1963–64. They squeaked by Hannum's old St. Louis Hawks by two games to capture the regular season crown in the Western Division and nipped them in a seven-game final playoff series for the right to meet the mighty Celtics. Boston hadn't lost a playoff series since the Hannum-coached Hawks beat them in 1958. Chamberlain had never won a playoff series against them. There were plenty of story lines to go around. But, in the end, it was the same old story for Wilt. The Celtics embarrassed the Warriors in five games.

Conditions deteriorated quickly the next season, beginning when Wilt failed to make training camp due to an illness. The won-lost record suffered, and attendance waned right along with it. Hannum found out that the Warriors' new owner and his boss, Franklin Mieuli, wanted to salvage his profits, if not the season, by dumping Chamberlain. Hannum railed against it, but the end came just after the All-Star Game in mid-January 1965 in one of Alex's favorite towns, St. Louis. Wilt was going back to his hometown of Philadelphia to join Ike Richman and Irv Kosloff's 76ers, the Syracuse transplants Hannum once coached.

The co-owners had initially wanted to acquire Wilt's teammate Nate Thurmond to give the 76ers a much-needed big man in the middle. They made a strong run at a trade for Thurmond on the night of the 1964 NBA draft, but it didn't work out.

Then, in the aftermath of the All-Star Game, the Warriors told Ike and Irv that Wilt was available.

"First, we wanted him as a drawing card in Philly," said Irv Kosloff back then. "Secondly, we wanted him to win. Wilt was not only a spectacular player, he was a spectacular presence."

The Warriors wanted to rid themselves of Wilt's big salary after losing money in his previous year, despite the fact that they went all the way to the NBA finals. There were also some rumors afoot that the Warriors were worried about Wilt having some type of heart condition.

But Kosloff and Richman decided they would bite the financial bullet to bring Wilt home, and they dispatched team physician Dr. Stan Lorber to examine Chamberlain. Lorber gave Wilt a clean bill of health and the trade was on.

"I can't confirm or deny if my father brought the team here with his eye on Wilt. But I remember how excited he was when he made the deal to bring Wilt back," said Mike Richman. "There's a story that he did it on the steps at Stan Musial's restaurant in St. Louis and made the deal with Franklin Mieuli. Father called Vince Miller, who was teaching shop at a high school, and he made up all these signs, 'Welcome Wilt,' and the first game he played when he came back to the 76ers was at the Arena.

"Wilt only wanted to live in New York. He didn't want to live in Philadelphia and that irritated my father, 'cause he felt the commuting was interfering with his ability as a ballplayer. So he made Wilt move into our house, and he was living in our house in Elkins Park," laughed Richman. "A neighbor told us, 'My wife said call the police, there's a big black guy hangin' around Richman's house.' People still remember."

After the trade, a euphoric and upbeat 76ers coach Dolph Schayes told the local papers, "I think I'm dreaming."

When reporters persisted about Wilt's track record of being difficult to manage, Schayes replied, "There's a myth that he is uncoachable. It's ridiculous. I think quite a bit of Wilt as a person. He is very coachable. He will build our morale on a team with very high morale. He's still a young man who wants to play on a championship team. I feel he has a good chance to be a champion this year."

Eventually, Schayes wound up eating just about every one of those words.

Wilt finally arrived in Philadelphia after taking a full eight days to settle his personal affairs in San Francisco. In the meantime, the

76ers were playing shorthanded because the players they had traded to the Warriors (Connie Dierking and Paul Neumann) were already gone. But any rancor over his delayed debut was gone when he tallied 22 points and 29 rebounds in his first game, leading the 76ers to a 111–102 win over his old Warriors. He got a two-minute ovation from the home crowd of 6,000. Ike Richman told a reporter that only about 2,000 would have showed for the game without Wilt's presence. Ticket manager Mike Ianarella exclaimed, "My sales went up four hundred percent. I am selling tickets to guys who haven't been here since 1961."

"It was the warmest ovation I've ever had," said Chamberlain. "I'm proud to be a Philadelphian." And Philadelphians were proud, too, when in Wilt's third game the 76ers beat Boston to end a 16-game Celtics win streak. Even though the game was played in Syracuse, 76ers fans seemed to sense that their team was now a legitimate threat to Boston.

It all seemed like "home, sweet home." But things quickly soured. Wilt was immediately uncomfortable with his new coach.

The trouble seemed to start at the free throw line. Schayes was a great foul shooter in his day, and, of course, Wilt wasn't.

"He made a statement after my second year in the pros, 'Anyone can make foul shots if they just practice,' " Wilt wrote in his book, *A View From Above*. "He was making a definite dig at me, intimating that I was not working hard. When he became my coach, he took up the gauntlet; we spent many an hour shooting foul shots. I shot very well in practice, but stunk out the joint in most games. Under his tutorship, I had my worst foul-shooting year, percentage-wise."

Asked about Wilt's relationship with Schayes, Vince Miller described it in one word: "Rotten." It worsened in the 1964–65 play-offs. Again, Wilt and his team matched up against the Celtics. The

76ers were down 2–1 in the series when *Sports Illustrated* hit the newsstands with a front-page picture of Wilt and a story called "My Life in a Bush League."

Chamberlain criticized Schayes in the article, saying that he was "almost too nice a guy" to be a coach. "Schayes is so tender-hearted," said Wilt, "that someone sitting on the bench can look over at him with those big wet eyes, and he'll put them into the game, even if the man replaced is having a big night. We could have won at least seven or eight more games than we did this season with fierce, eat-'em-up coaching."

Chamberlain tried to downplay the aftershocks of the article. He disavowed it, claiming he had nothing to do with the title, and that he wasn't trying to belittle Schayes. Vince Miller recalled Wilt's frequent tussles with the media and said, "Wilt taught me this. Any bit of publicity is good, whether it's bad or good. He would say things just to keep his name in the paper whether he meant it or not. He worked the media."

Although Dolph stayed mum on the article, a few of Wilt's teammates reacted strongly.

"It's a good article, if you like science fiction," chided backup center Johnny Kerr. He called the article "poor timing" and branded the knocks at Schayes as "out of line" and "undeserving."

"I don't think it's a player's place to be talking about his coach like that, especially at a time like this when we should all be pulling together," complained Hal Greer. "It could hurt our chances. Why did he do it?"

Dave Gambee recalled: "The key was Wilt, and the situation was the feelings between Wilt and Dolph. It could've been the greatest idea in the world, but if it was Dolph's, Wilt wouldn't do it. What Dolph wanted to do, Wilt didn't want to do, As long as Dolph was there, Wilt wasn't going to be there mentally."

Despite his anger, Greer went out and saved the day for the 76ers in the next playoff game, sinking a mid-court desperation shot to force overtime against Boston. The 76ers won 134–131 to tie the series at 2-2. But it was Greer who would be forever linked to the play that further divided Wilt and Schayes.

Just six days later, Greer was the trigger man on the historic inbounds play where "Havlicek stole the ball" on Greer's weak lob to Chet Walker. Chamberlain and the 76ers had lost yet another last-second, heartbreaking seventh game to the Celtics.

After the 76ers clubhouse had mostly cleared out in the aftermath of the bitter loss, Schayes and Wilt were on opposite sides of the room. Chamberlain reportedly walked over to Schayes, extended his hand, and said, "It was a great effort, Coach, it really was." Was he being uncharacteristically gracious or disingenuous? Probably the latter.

In his 1996 interview with the NBA, Chamberlain laid the blame on Greer and Schayes for the decisive, errant play: "Every time I see John Havlicek, I say, 'How lucky can you be?' The guy makes an inbounds pass that my grandmother could have made better. If the ball would have come to me, I wonder what the difference would have been."

Across the corridor on the night of that game, Bill Russell realized just how close he and his Celtics had finally come to losing to a Wilt-led team.

"I was starting to look pale," joked Russell. He quickly added that Chamberlain did not deserve the rap of "loser" after dropping another playoff series to Boston. "So far, we've set a sports record nobody has come close to. How can you blame him? How can you say he's a loser?"

Regardless of their feelings as they left Boston after that fateful game, Chamberlain and Schayes were forced to coexist for another shot at the Celtics in the 1965–66 season. It was a season that focused Wilt's resolve for the future.

First came the tragic loss of Ike Richman at courtside in Boston. Chamberlain, his teammates, and the huge Garden crowd saw it happen. His attorney, his agent, his landlord, his close friend was suddenly stolen away.

"I was a senior in law school, and I was in town working for [Dad's] law firm," recalled Mike Richman. On the day of the game, he had invited his son to lunch. "He was a meat eater, but he said, 'I don't feel that good, just give me a tuna fish sandwich or something.' " Ike asked his son if he wanted to come to Boston with him, but Mike turned him down.

"I was down the shore for the weekend," said Richman. "[The game] was televised but I happened to be at somebody's house who didn't have a converter to get UHF stations. I called a friend to see if [my dad] had checked into the hotel.

"He said, 'Mike, you better call your mother.' I said, 'What are you talking about?' He said, 'Just call your mother.' That's how I found out about it."

The 76ers went on that night to beat Boston for the first time ever in the Garden. It made Chamberlain want to beat them once and for all—not only for himself now, but in Ike's memory. The following year, the 1965–66 season, it looked like Wilt was going to make that happen.

For the first time in 10 years, after nine straight Eastern Division regular season championships, Boston was dethroned by Philadelphia. The 76ers posted 11 straight wins down the stretch to finish 55-25, one game better than Boston. Many basketball observers thought this was Philly's year to end Boston's reign for good. But Boston prevailed once again, in overpowering, embarrassing fashion.

The 76ers had a first-round bye, and they just went stale. Boston seemed to sharpen themselves in a tough five-game struggle against Cincinnati, and they came into Philadelphia with revenge on their mind for the regular season failure. Boston posted a 19-point blowout in game one and made it a 21-point margin in game two. The 76ers were reeling, but they regrouped to win game three 111–105 at home. They came close to evening the series in Boston in game four, but fell frustratingly in overtime, 114–108. The Celtics finished off the 76ers on Philly's home court, taking game five by eight points and the series, 4–1.

Wilt had fallen short again.

Exit Dolph Schayes.

In a March 1967 article entitled "The Startling Change in Wilt Chamberlain," *Sport* magazine's Leonard Shecter wrote:

> Schayes got fired because, well, it was apparent one of them had to go, and how do you fire Wilt Chamberlain? Before Chamberlain got Schayes fired he embarrassed him. He forgot to show up at practices. Schayes would call a practice and in the clubhouse Chamberlain would complain of persecution to the club owners. "That's bush, Ike," Chamberlain would yell.
>
> At the very end, when they were blowing the playoff to the Celtics, Chamberlain missed a practice and Schayes said, "Well, he could have practiced foul shooting." And then Wilt missed a lot of fouls and lost a game. Add to that the times Chamberlain would come off the court during a time-out and sit on the bench, leaving Schayes to give instructions to four players standing around him instead of five, and you have a fairly ugly situation. Schayes went back to Syracuse a wiser if more bitter man.

Enter Alex Hannum.

He had been unceremoniously fired by the Warriors. He got an immediate feeler from Irv Kosloff. "He and his son made a combined business and basketball trip out to see the Los Angeles–Boston playoff game," Hannum recalled. "We had dinner, but they were talking ifs. I told them that I was interested but under no circumstances would I talk about a job as long as no job was available. Mr. Kosloff called me back after he had informed Dolph and asked me to take the first plane east. So I went back there on a red-eye and sat down with Irv at his company and came back to coach. We came to terms quickly. I knew this team could win it all.

"Look, he's my friend. He's a great guy, and he'd make a terrific college coach," added Hannum at the time about his predecessor Schayes. "But I don't think he's suited to be a professional coach. He's got all the patience in the world. I don't. A player needs something said to him, I say it. Right now. That's why in time-outs I meet with the players on the court, not on the bench. I don't want people to hear me and misunderstand."

There was press speculation that Chamberlain gave his seal of approval to the 76ers before Hannum was offered the job.

"It's ridiculous to think we clear anything with Wilt or that Wilt had anything to do with the coaching change," insisted owner Kosloff, speaking to reporters.

After Hannum took the job he immediately called Larry Costello, the old Syracuse Nationals guard and warhorse he once coached. "The first thing I did was I got Larry out of retirement, and then I called Wilt. Then I flew to San Francisco and talked with him. I let him know my ideas and consolidated his and mine."

The Sarge and Dippy were together again. The man who loved the construction business was back to finish the reconstruction job he had started on Chamberlain back in San Francisco.

"When Alex came in, he wanted to interview everybody," recalled Miller, who scouted off and on for the 76ers back then. "He sat everybody down and wanted to know what your responsibilities were."

Miller believes Hannum must have thought, " 'This man is close to

Wilt and knows what he's doin' and he has an eye for basketball.' He kept me around." He hired Miller as "special statistician," with the job of keeping accurate records of the plays the official scorer didn't keep track of, like missed offensive rebounds, bad passes, or other types of turnovers. Chet Walker called him a "hell of a man with the little black pencil."

The question was whether Hannum really had hired Miller to collect stats or to be a day-to-day buffer for Wilt. "Alex never really tried to use me to find out things about Wilt," Miller insisted. But he did turn out to be a liaison with Irv Kosloff.

"Kos would often have secret meetings with me to find out what was goin' on or how things were." The newspapers slapped the handle of "Secret Agent 0076" on Miller, borrowing from the popular James Bond craze of the time.

In addition, Hannum wanted Chamberlain to stop commuting from New York and take up residence in Philadelphia like everybody else. Wilt had a posh place near 97th and Central Park West, where he lived with his two Great Danes, Odin and Thor (and reportedly a Swedish maid-in-residence). Miller was a regular weekend roommate, and he and Wilt spent many an evening together at Chamberlain's Harlem nightclub, Big Wilt's Smalls' Paradise. Chamberlain loved New York, so getting him to set up housekeeping in Philly was a struggle. Miller said the 76ers finally decided to put Wilt up in Hopkinson House, a classy high-rise apartment building in the city. Miller became Chamberlain's full-time roomie there. Now, Hannum had Wilt right where he wanted him. Miller may not have been a secret agent for the coach, but he was at least Wilt's watchdog, home and away.

"I was very understanding of Wilt's position with the team, that he was something special," said Hannum. "Everyone understood that my greatest desire was for the team to win."

And if Greer thought himself to be the big star in Philly, that soon changed when Wilt arrived. Nobody was a bigger man in that town than Wilt, literally and figuratively.

Greer was skeptical of the Dipper.

"I didn't know Wilt, but I read all those stories about him. I thought he was an individual player—all for his points. Then I got to know him. He wanted certain things to happen, and I wasn't happy with it for a while. But I got used to it, and I knew we needed him to win."

While Chamberlain got all of the publicity, Greer had to look hard for his mentions.

"The stories are all Wilt," whined Greer back then. "Mayme [his wife] and I talk about it a lot. I tell her he's better news and people want to read about Wilt."

Alex Hannum helped Hal understand.

"I know he sat down with me," said Greer. "He told me about some of the problems Wilt was going through with all the other teams that he was with." Hannum pledged that he would not let those problems happen with Wilt and the 76ers.

"He actually told me, suggested to me, to just play it cool. Wilt's a special person anyway. As big as he was, he demanded special treatment. We didn't want to call him special, we tried not to make him special. But being the big figure he was, he demanded it and that's what happened."

Hannum recalled: "There was no 'my way' philosophy. I told them we had to do this thing together. There was only one Wilt and we all recognized that. He had different sleep habits, personal habits, playing habits."

From time to time there would be friction between these two strong-willed, powerful personalities, but Hannum's previously interrupted reconstruction of Wilt was now ready to resume in earnest.

"He was bored scoring forty, fifty points a night," said Miller. "He was already learning to change his game. Alex convinced him to go all the way with it."

In the *Sport* magazine article, Leonard Shecter offered a different insight:

> Certainly, throughout his life, little has been denied him. From the time he was 15 he has been babied, wooed, flattered. It is difficult to say whether it is a sudden maturity or merely more pressure from the little boy who dwells inside that big body that is forcing Chamberlain to do whatever is necessary this season to help his team win the NBA title.

FOUR

One Year Wondrous

A fire in San Francisco and some fiery words in Sacramento started the 76ers' march to their first NBA title.

San Francisco was Wilt Chamberlain's home, and his home went up in smoke on Tuesday, August 30, 1966. Initial press reports put the damage total to his second-story flat at $35,000. But Chamberlain said the loss was much higher, in both dollars and emotion.

The fire broke out 17 days before the opening of the 76ers' first training camp under Alex Hannum, and when Hannum called the first practice in Margate, New Jersey, on September 15, Wilt was AWOL.

"I talked to Wilt last week," Hannum told reporters. "He really sounded down over the fire at his apartment. Apparently, his insurance coverage was not what it should have been, and many of his household goods were not protected."

But was it the aftermath of the fire that kept Chamberlain away from camp, or was it a lingering contract dispute with team owner Irv Kosloff? Reports had surfaced prior to camp that the three-year $370,000 contract signed by Wilt the previous season was no longer binding. The story was that the final two years were linked to Chamberlain getting a financial stake in the 76ers, something Wilt said was promised him by 76ers co-owner Ike Richman before he died in December 1965.

Such a deal was against NBA rules anyway, but it was a moot point. The original ownership pact between Richman and co-owner Irv Kosloff put all the shares in the survivor's basket if either died. Chamberlain seemed to be the odd man out.

"There's no truth to it," said Kosloff about the rumors that Chamberlain no longer had a firm contract with the 76ers. But Alex Hannum was all too aware of Wilt's unpredictability, and he knew he had to prepare the team for the possibility Wilt might not show for a while, or never show at all. Luke Jackson was immediately installed at center.

In the meantime, with no place to live because of the fire, Chamberlain had left San Francisco to stay with his parents in L.A. Wilt believed he had made it clear to team management that the fire would make him late for training camp. But Kosloff had a different understanding. The 76ers tried repeatedly to contact Wilt, but because he had left town, he was nowhere to be found.

"I wasn't missing, I knew where I was," Chamberlain sarcastically whined later.

"I wasn't hiding, it would be ridiculous for me to try and hide. I was out on the playgrounds. When I read in the paper that I was missing, I thought it was a joke.

"Everything I owned—my clothes, all my new furniture, everything—went up in smoke," Wilt explained. "It wasn't covered by insurance because of a foul-up and it cost me around two hundred thousand dollars, not to mention the time I spent redecorating it. It shook me up."

It was the first crisis faced by the brand-new general manager of the 76ers, Jack Ramsay. Ramsay was the successful, longtime coach at Philadelphia's St. Joseph's College. But he had been bothered by an eye ailment and was in the market for a career change and more money. The 76ers offered him the general manager's job and gave him a three-year deal at $25,000 per year, according to press reports. He joined the organization just prior to the start of the 1966–67 championship season.

"It was all a misunderstanding," Ramsay said of the tug-of-war with Chamberlain. Ramsay said that the 76ers hadn't known that Wilt had gone to Los Angeles, and that when he returned to San Francisco he got all of the messages left by the team.

"He called us, and Mr. Kosloff told him we expected him to be here," Ramsay added.

Regardless of whether he was pouting over his contract or just putting his private life back together after the fire—or perhaps a little bit of both—Chamberlain, a good 30 pounds heavier, finally joined the club in Allentown, Pennsylvania, on September 15, walking into the arena in street clothes about halfway through the second quarter of an exhibition game against the New York Knicks.

The big guy was back.

Ten days later, the 76ers broke camp and headed for a 10-game exhibition swing through the West. The team was shaping up nicely, but Chamberlain was testing Hannum, even though the pair's prior relationship was well established.

During a stop in Sacramento, Chamberlain faced fire again—this time from the tongue of Hannum. Shades of that "unsubstantiated" confrontation in their early San Francisco days.

"One time Alex and Wilt almost went at it," recalled Billy Cunningham. "Alex told everyone to leave the locker room. They went nose to nose. No blows were thrown, but it cleared the air."

"They were comin' at each other," remembered Wally Jones. "Alex wouldn't back down to anybody."

The papers got hold of the confrontation, too, and pronounced it a key event of the pre-season.

"The most important part of the 76ers' pre-season training didn't take place on any court, in any game or during any practice," wrote *Philadelphia Bulletin* reporter Bob Vetrone in the October 12, 1966, edition. "It was in a dressing room in Sacramento, Calif. [*sic*], in a discussion—to put it mildly—between Wilt Chamberlain and Coach Alex Hannum. When it was over, Hannum had established in the minds of the other players that he is the boss and will be during what promises to be an eventful National Basketball Association season."

So, as opening night of that season drew near, the 76ers were whole. They had a new, tough-minded, Celtics-killing coach, fresh hometown faces to blend with the talented veterans, and a reconstructed Wilt Chamberlain poised to lead the team to that elusive first championship.

OCTOBER 1966

The biggest opening night crowd in the short history of the 76ers came to Convention Hall on October 15, 1966, to see the first game of a season full of high expectations.

Chamberlain literally found the spotlight right away, getting a standing ovation of nearly a minute as the crowd acknowledged his power to take this team to the title.

And once the game against the New York Knicks began, it didn't take long for Wilt to draw all eyes again. After a foul, he lumbered to the free throw line to show Philadelphia the latest cure for his long-standing free throw problems.

Actually, he had unveiled it during a pre-season game in Albuquerque, but on this night Philly fans would get their first look.

He lined up at the left of the foul line instead of dead center, using a variation of the fadeaway shots that served him so well over the years. He put them up overhand, line-drive style. There were a few beauties, but mostly bricks. Wilt made just four of nine attempts. It was certainly no quick fix and after just a few weeks Wilt gave up the angle shot and changed back to underhand.

But the Knicks were the main focus on opening night, bringing with them veterans like Dick Barnett and Walt Bellamy, up-and-comers like Willis Reed and Dave Stallworth, and the rookie phenom Cazzie Russell of Michigan. Russell sat out with an injury, and the rest of the Knicks were no match for the 76ers, who won the game 128–112. It extended the 76ers' regular season consecutive win streak—dating back to the final 11 games of the 1965–66 season—to 12.

Wilt scored 28, pulled down 21 rebounds, and handed out a game-high six assists. This despite going to the bench in the second period with double damage. He took a finger in the left eye from the Knicks' Howie Komives and also hurt his right knee.

That opened the door for what Hannum called "the Jackson Offense," with Luke Jackson playing center. Hannum said it gave the team a more dramatic fast break, praising Luke's play but perhaps tweaking Chamberlain just a little.

Villanova alums Wally Jones and Bill Melchionni teamed up to form what Hannum nicknamed "the Wildcat Press," named for their alma mater's mascot. The tandem guards put up eight points during their stint together, pleasing the hometown crowd.

In game two, one of the other Philadelphia freshmen made an impression against the stubborn St. Louis Hawks. Matty Guokas sparked a second period 76ers comeback, setting up his mates for key buckets, clearing the boards from a guard slot, and hitting a late, fallaway, left-handed foul line bank shot to give the 76ers a lead they would never relinquish.

He even mixed it up with a grizzled NBA veteran. Hawks player-coach Richie Guerin complained that Guokas held him. Guerin got in Matty's face, but the rookie showed poise, walking away and later downplaying the confrontation.

"It was no big thing, just something that happens on the court," Guokas explained. "[Guerin] was talking to me like I was a young kid, and he was the veteran who'd been around for a while. Heck, I wasn't mad. I guess maybe he was trying to teach me something. Giving me something to learn."

Perhaps it was Hannum's tutelage of the rookie that was already paying off.

A hometown hero emerged again in game three against his old club, the Baltimore Bullets. Wally Jones put together a 13-point, six-assist game in a 141–112 rout on the road.

On the team bus back to Philly, Jones kept up the tempo, balancing Chet Walker's portable record player to keep the Top 40 tunes from skipping on the bumpy ride back home. Wally played deejay all the way back with banter befitting a mid-60s rock jock.

"Every team should have a Wally Jones," praised Hannum. "He may not be the greatest player going, but he's good for a team." Wait until Hannum saw what Jones would do in a critical game against the Celtics many months later.

Game four of the season was a good one again for Melchionni. The 76ers beat Baltimore once more, 130–110, and Billy pumped in eight points, handed out a pair of assists, and, despite his short stature, even pulled down some key rebounds.

The winning streak moved to 15 straight.

On that same October day, the 76ers also got a glimpse of their future. Kosloff and Ramsay announced that the team would play in

Philadelphia's brand-new sports arena next season. The Spectrum, at South Broad and Pattison, would take the place of Convention Hall.

Located at 33rd and Spruce, Convention Hall was better suited to political meetings than professional basketball. All of the seats seemed close to the court, almost dwarfing the arena floor. It was a perfect place for the passionate Philly fans, well known for being among the most knowledgeable, but toughest, anywhere. Convention Hall was nicknamed "the snake pit." The raucous, rowdy atmosphere made visiting teams recoil. And while it was no Boston Garden, most teams were far happier leaving the Hall than entering it.

Just two days before Halloween, the 76ers put on a performance there that left the rest of the NBA scared and shaken. The Celtics, with Red Auerbach as the GM and Russell as player-coach, paid their first visit of the year to Convention Hall. They left humbled and humiliated.

Hannum had played down the entire event. "There's no big deal about this game," he declared, knowing full well he was fibbing. "It's just another one. It's nice we have a streak going, but we know we're up against the best. Both teams, I'm sure, will go at it with a great deal of enthusiasm. We have no special plans for the Celtics, though," Hannum insisted.

No special plans except to thoroughly destroy them.

The 76ers crushed the Celtics 138–96 in a stunning victory that put the league on notice about the power and talent of this 76ers team. They played in front of a record-setting crowd of 11,914.

"The 76ers did their Halloween celebrating early last night," wrote Bob Vetrone in the *Bulletin*. "They showed up at Convention Hall dressed as Murder, Inc. Taking out six months of frustration from last season's ill-fated playoffs, they killed the world champion Boston Celtics."

The crowd went crazy. When the lead got to 20, they roared to make it 30. When it reached that mark at 115–85 late in the game, they screamed for 40. The 76ers won by 42, and extended the unbeaten streak to 16.

"Our second and third periods, when we really tore it up, was the best a 76ers team has ever played," Chet Walker declared. Chamberlain notched 13 points, 31 rebounds, and 9 assists. Greer led the 76ers with 26 and said, "When everything goes our way, when we play together, we'll kill anybody."

Earlier, the Convention Hall crowd picked up that same theme.

"Kill . . . kill . . . kill," they screamed.

Red Auerbach had watched the bloodletting from the stands, but left early and abruptly, supposedly to catch a plane.

No victory cigars on this night.

It had been the worst defeat in the Celtics' proud history.

"What do you want me to say," said Bill Russell afterwards. "We just got beat. Beat bad. Beat every way you can get beat. Philly was sky-high for this one, and we just couldn't do anything right after that first quarter. It was like a snowball going downhill, the more it went the better they got and worse we got."

Hannum, while finally admitting the game's importance, continued his understated approach later in the locker room.

"We had a good night," he said. "Everything went our way, and that's great because this was a big game for us. But the score doesn't indicate the difference in the caliber of the teams. Boston has too much pride and talent to take this without a comeback. They kept playing us tough into the fourth quarter. You know they'll be ready when we go up there Saturday."

But before that rematch, some time for fun.

"Wilt had a Halloween party at his house, his high-rise in Philly, and it was a costume party," laughed Hannum. "I went as a ballerina wearing a tutu. Wilt was an Arab sheik. Other guys wore disguises, I didn't know who they were. That showed the feeling of Wilt toward that team."

OCTOBER RECORD (5-0)

76ers	128	N.Y.	112	1-0
76ers	119	St.L.	110	2-0
76ers	141	Bal.	112	3-0
76ers	130	Bal.	110	4-0
76ers	138	Bos.	96	5-0

STANDING: 1ST PLACE 1 GAME AHEAD OF BOSTON

NOVEMBER 1966

November saw the 76ers push their winning streak to 18 straight with wins over the Hawks and San Francisco. The victory over the Warriors gave the 76ers a new NBA record for consecutive wins, breaking the mark of 17, jointly held by Boston and the old Washington Caps. (Note: The Celtics and Caps won consecutive games in a single season, rather than over two seasons, like Philadelphia. As a result, the 76ers had an asterisk in the record book next to their 18 straight wins.)

San Francisco, featuring the deadeye shooting of Rick Barry and rebounding power of Nate Thurmond, gave the 76ers major trouble. So much so that early in the second half, Hannum had to abandon his plan of Chamberlain as playmaker, pushing his team to send assists *Wilt's* way and turn him big scorer again.

It worked. Wilt slammed home 24 points in the second half, finishing with 30 overall, plus 26 rebounds and a dozen blocked shots to spark a 134–129 win.

"He was our last hope," smiled Hannum. "Our other things weren't going well at all, so we *had* to go to him. We were dead if he didn't come through, but he did. Magnificently."

The previous day's triumph over St. Louis came in Pittsburgh, one of two second homes for the 76ers during that regular season. They played 17 "neutral" court games, six in Pittsburgh, and two in their original home of Syracuse. They also made game stops in Cleveland; Memphis; Fort Wayne and Evansville, Indiana; and played a couple of doubleheader games in New York and Boston. All told, the 76ers played only 30 games in Philadelphia during the championship season, less than 40 percent of the 81-game schedule.

November would also bring the 76ers their first losses of the season.

Boston ended the winning streak and got revenge for the 42-point annihilation by putting the clamps on the 76ers' sharpshooters. The Celtics won 105–87 at the Boston Garden, handing Philly its first regular season setback since March 1, 1966, and tying the 76ers for first place with an identical 7-1 record.

Wilt scored big with 26 but was out-rebounded by Russell.

Greer and Walker couldn't shake loose, and Boston won easily.

"Look, we know we've got to win as many as we can against Philly because it doesn't seem like anybody else can beat them," Russell reasoned. "We've got to stay with them in our individual series, and had they beaten us this time, goodness knows when they would lose one."

"We knew this was going to happen sooner or later," said Coach Hannum. "You can't go on winning forever. This gives me something to talk about when I get with the boys again in practice."

By game 10, the 76ers found themselves in second place for the only time that season. A win over Chicago (in which a frustrated Chamberlain returned to his underhand free throws) put them at 9-1, but the Celtics leaped ahead with a 10-1 mark. The very next night,

November 12, the teams switched places for good when the 76ers topped Oscar Robertson and the Cincinnati Royals while the Celtics fell to 10-2 with a loss.

The 76ers stretched their record to 15-1 on November 19, outscoring Cincinnati by 24. But five days later, the Royals handed the 76ers their only other defeat in November, 111–106. Cincinnati shot 37 of 38 from the free throw line and overcame a 16-point third quarter deficit to beat the 76ers.

Apparently some free throw shooting advice by an elderly woman didn't help Chamberlain all that much in the loss to the Royals. A local newspaper account said the woman confronted Wilt in a midtown Philadelphia supermarket the day before and told him, "Mr. Chamberlain, I know you can shoot fouls. Just don't listen to anybody and everything will be OK."

Then, she simply turned and walked away.

The next night Wilt was 8 for 16 from the line, only a touch above his average.

Missing free throws had made Wilt infamous, but making field goals had made him famous.

Wilt surpassed the 22,000 mark in career points in the next to last game of November, a 137–116 win over St. Louis. No one else was even close to him. Alex Hannum had changed Wilt a lot, but the scorebook was never too far from the big guy's sights.

NOVEMBER RECORD (15-2)

76ers	120	St.L.	108	6-0
76ers	134	S.F.	129	7-0
76ers	87	Bos.	105	7-1
76ers	118	Det.	100	8-1
76ers	126	Chi.	113	9-1
76ers	112	Cin.	98	10-1

76ers	132	Chi.	126	11-1
76ers	113	N.Y.	109	12-1
76ers	117	N.Y.	108	13-1
76ers	145	Chi.	120	14-1
76ers	134	Cin.	110	15-1
76ers	106	Cin.	111	15-2
76ers	140	S.F.	123	16-2
76ers	129	Bal.	115	17-2
76ers	131	Det.	123	18-2
76ers	137	St.L.	116	19-2
76ers	128	Det.	119	20-2

STANDING: 1ST PLACE 3½ GAMES AHEAD OF BOSTON

DECEMBER 1966

Christmas actually came a little late for the 76ers in December. On the 28th, they moved their record to 34-3 with an important 113–108 win over the Celtics in Philadelphia, dropping Boston seven games behind the 76ers.

Despite snow on the ground and more in the forecast, a crowd of 12,711 jammed Convention Hall, the largest crowd ever to watch a live basketball game at any level in the history of Philadelphia sports.

They watched the Celtics build a 13-point margin early. The 76ers managed to shave two points by the end of the first quarter to trail by 11.

"I thought we'd never get started," said Hannum. "Then Billy Cunningham got running, and soon we were all running, and I felt better," Alex cracked. The 76ers charged back in the second quarter, outscoring the Celtics by 17 and taking a 59–53 halftime lead.

With Chet Walker having a sub-par night, Hannum went deep in the bench late in the third period and called on veteran Dave Gambee to match up against Boston's John "Hondo" Havlicek. Gambee smothered the Celtics star the rest of the way while adding nine points off three Chamberlain assists. One was a length of the court pass from Wilt to Gambee that led to a basket and a 14-point 76ers lead.

"I felt like John Brodie," Chamberlain chuckled, referring to the talented quarterback of the San Francisco 49ers.

While Wilt was showing his San Fran fandom, Gambee shot back Philadelphia style. "I felt like Pete Retzlaff," he said, referring to an Eagles star pass receiver.

Asked later if Chamberlain was really playing any differently this year, Russell answered, "Wilt is playing the same way he's always played—great. Don't let anybody kid you."

Wilt wasn't kidding two days later when he got angry over Red Auerbach's selection as the coach of the East squad in the upcoming NBA All-Star Game. With Auerbach now the Celtics GM, Wilt didn't want him back on the bench for any reason.

"We won the regular season Eastern Division title and the rules say that our coach is supposed to have that honor," chided Chamberlain. In an ironic twist, Chamberlain actually touted Dolph Schayes, the man he had almost single-handedly ousted.

"Dolph Schayes was our coach, and if they're going to bring anybody out of retirement to coach the team, why don't they bring Dolph back? He earned the right to coach the team, not Red," argued Wilt (Hannum was his next choice).

Wilt even put it in letter form for Commissioner Walter Kennedy and wanted his teammates to sign it.

> Dear Commissioner Kennedy:
> We the undersigned want you to know that we do not believe that Red Auerbach, general manager of the Boston Celtics, should be the coach of the Eastern All-

Stars in the game . . . in San Francisco.

We feel that because we finished first in the Eastern Division last season, the coach of the Eastern All-Stars should be the man who coached us.

In light of the fact that Dolph Schayes is now supervisor of officials for the National Basketball Assn. and because it might be awkward for him to return to the coaching ranks, we believe the job should at least go to the man who is now our coach, Alex Hannum.

We can't understand the reasoning behind the selection of Mr. Auerbach by you and the league's Board of Governors.

Signed

[The players of the Philadelphia 76ers]

The league had announced in November that Auerbach was chosen "after due consideration." But the league handbook, issued at the beginning of the season in October, already had Auerbach listed as All-Star coach, meaning that it had been a done deal. Even Auerbach himself mentioned it in his autobiography, which had to have gone to the printer months earlier.

Another player in the sideline soap opera was Franklin Mieuli, controversial owner of the San Francisco Warriors. The inside story was that he did not want Alex Hannum, the coach he had fired just nine months earlier, to return to San Francisco, coach the All-Stars, and, in Mieuli's mind, spoil the party. Mieuli lobbied for Auerbach and got his way. (Mieuli had another trick up his sleeve to rankle Chamberlain. He did not want the man he traded in 1964 to come back to town and receive the 1966 MVP award on the Cow Palace court, so the league delayed it until later in the year, a move that infuriated Chamberlain.)

Despite the fact that the deck was stacked from all sides, Wilt still had to have his say.

The Celtics did their talking earlier that December, beating the

76ers in Boston in the third meeting of the teams. Havlicek poured in 34 as Boston raced to a 17-point lead by halftime and won it 117–103.

The loss was the 76ers' only defeat during December. They posted an amazing 15-1 record, averaging 124 points per game.

The 76ers closed out the month and the year in Fort Wayne, Indiana, former home of the Pistons and frequent site of NBA neutral court games. In fact, the 76ers breezed by the Pistons, 137–113. It was one of those classic team efforts when everything was clicking.

"That team is just too much," whined Pistons coach Dave DeBusscherre. "They can kill you with their muscle and their shooting and now they're killing you with their passing. It just ain't fair."

Billy Cunningham and Bill Melchionni even brought some of that teamwork back to the motel after the game. Determined to play a practical joke on trainer Al Domenico, they folded him inside a mattress, threw a sheet and blanket on top of him, and threw the underwear-clad medical man out into the five-degree weather. Then they phoned the front desk and said a stranger had stolen their bedding. Meanwhile, Domenico spent the next few minutes wrapped in the sheet and blanket, pulling the mattress along and knocking on every player's door until he got some help. Luke Jackson finally took pity and let him into his room.

It was a New Year's Eve party—one day early. But as merry as the holiday season was, there would be some bumps in the road as the toughest stretch of the season closed in.

DECEMBER RECORD (15-1)

76ers	138	L.A.	130	21-2
76ers	137	Bal.	120	22-2
76ers	129	Chi.	119	23-2
76ers	117	Chi.	103	24-2
76ers	112	N.Y.	107	25-2
76ers	133	St.L	123	26-2

76ers	103	Bos.	117	26-3
76ers	127	N.Y.	112	27-3
76ers	124	St. L.	113	28-3
76ers	120	Det.	105	29-3
76ers	129	L.A.	123	30-3
76ers	116	S.F.	114	31-3
76ers	118	L.A.	107	32-3
76ers	134	Cin.	118	33-3
76ers	113	Bos.	108	34-3
76ers	137	Det.	113	35-3

STANDING: 1ST PLACE 6½ GAMES AHEAD OF BOSTON

JANUARY 1967

It was an hour from game time at New York's Madison Square Garden on January 4, 1967, and Wilt Chamberlain sat in a motel restaurant across the street. The experts say an athlete should have his last full meal about four hours before playing.

But not Wilt.

After sneaking some salad away from a sportswriter, Wilt dug into his own eats, a bowl of soup, a steak, a soda, a dish of Jell-O, and some orange juice.

Maybe Wilt should have listened to the experts. He flubbed his first three shots once the game against the Knicks got under way. Indigestion may have been the culprit, but in fact the entire 76ers team was out of sorts, falling behind twice by 12 points and once by six before catching up near the end. Wilt deliberately missed a foul shot with the 76ers down by five with just over a minute to go. He raced in to grab his own rebound and stuffed it down. That gave the 76ers a spurt down the stretch and they went on to tie the game in regulation on a clutch three-point play by Hal Greer. The 76ers won it 148–142 in overtime for their 10th straight win.

But the Knicks turned the tables on the 76ers just two nights later at Pittsburgh's Civic Arena. Chamberlain had a miserable night, scoring only 13 points, and the Knicks out-rebounded the 76ers with Walt Bellamy and Willis Reed doing the damage. The final score was 112–104.

"It was the best night Bellamy ever had against me," Chamberlain told reporters.

Hal Greer blamed the arena's "cold floor" and Hannum blamed the schedule maker. The Knicks had the day off after the tough overtime loss to Philly, while the 76ers played and defeated the Chicago Bulls. But whatever the reason, the loss snapped the 76ers' 11-game win streak.

However, as quickly as one streak ended, another began.

The 76ers reeled off eight straight, starting with a costly overtime home win against Baltimore. Veteran guard Larry Costello, with 10 years of floor leadership behind him, stole the ball from the Bullets' Kevin Loughery. Costy tossed the ball to Hal Greer, but the off-balance Loughery fell into Costello from behind. He was hurt so badly he couldn't even shoot his free throws on the foul call. The ligaments in one of his knees were shot. He was placed in a thigh to ankle cast, and his recovery time was uncertain. Wally Jones would be getting a lot more playing time, and, as it turned out, the Costello injury may have been a blessing in disguise.

The Baltimore game also help to forge Vince Miller's nickname of Secret Agent 0076. The score was tied 111–111 with just 18 seconds left in regulation. During a time-out, Hannum was setting up defensive strategy when Miller, who had been seated at the press table near the Bullets' bench, ran toward the 76ers' huddle. The Bullets claimed Miller was eavesdropping. "It's bush, that's what it is," screamed Herb Heft, president of the Bullets. "All the fellow does is squat near our bench and listen in on our huddle and then report to Hannum. Make no mistake, I am going to make an official protest with Commissioner Walter Kennedy."

"No, I didn't think the bugging of the huddle was the reason we lost," added Coach Shue. "We were beaten because we couldn't maintain the rapid pace. However, I still consider the spy thing bush. Anytime a rival official has to listen in on huddles to win, all you can say is that it is a bush club."

Despite Shue's insistence that Miller's data didn't make the difference, the 76ers felt just the opposite. Miller had told Hannum, "They are going to set up Loughery for the final shot. He is to come off a [Bob] Ferry screen." Using their newfound intelligence, the 76ers bottled up the play, forcing the Bullets' Don Ohl to take an off-balance jump shot from 20 feet out that hit high off the rim and came down to Wilt's waiting hands.

In addition to the Bullets, the Hawks, the Knicks, and the Lakers all fell to the 76ers during their new nine-game win streak. In fact, the 119–108 win over L.A. marked the 76ers' 36th straight regular season home victory, and stretched their record to 45-4, 10 games in front of the second place Celtics, the biggest bulge of the year on Boston.

Five games earlier, smack dab in the middle of that winning streak, the 76ers routed the Celtics on the parquet floor, and in front of a national television audience. It was a chance for the 76ers to show everyone—especially the Celtics players—that they could beat Boston big on their home court.

"We had to show 'em that we can win up here, and I think we showed 'em," said Chamberlain, all the time complaining about a torturous 10-hour train, cab, and bus ride from Philadelphia because of a fogged-in East Coast. But despite only getting an hour's sleep, Wilt scored 19 and added 25 rebounds. Luke Jackson managed a little more sleep and it paid off. He went on a 12-point run early in the fourth period, extending the 76ers' lead to 17 points, putting the game out of reach and finishing with a game-high 28 points.

Hannum was more humble about the win than Chamberlain.

"We won a few up here last season, then got beat bad in the play-offs, so what we do today isn't going to help us in March or April."

On January 23, the 76ers flew into Memphis, Tennessee, for another of their infamous neutral court games. The game itself wasn't memorable, although the 112–105 win gave the 76ers an unprece-dented 46-4 mark. But something else that happened on that road stop has stayed with Billy Cunningham to this day.

He remembered a visit to a Memphis Toddle House with Chet Walker and Luke Jackson. The waitress offered to serve Billy but not his African-American teammates.

"These two men got up, shaking their heads," said Cunningham. "I remember the anger in myself toward the woman. It was an eye-opening experience. To be there and to be a part of that was some-thing I have never forgotten."

Southern cities were the worst for black players of that era. They could stay in the hotels, but couldn't eat in them.

St. Louis was another tough town.

Al Domenico remembered being chased out of a corner bar there when Jackson and Wally Jones could not be served. "I even knew the guy and had drunk beer with him," Domenico recalled. "He says, 'I'm not serving these guys. Let me see their age cards.' " Incredulously, Al said, "Their age cards?"

They all walked out together.

Back in friendly Philadelphia, the 76ers were ready to put their 36 consecutive home win streak on the line against none other than the Celtics.

Boston was ready and vengeful after the 15-point thrashing at home nine days earlier. Sam Jones quieted the huge Convention Hall crowd with 38 points, leading Boston over the weary 76ers, who took the court after a 12-hour round-trip flight to Memphis.

Despite their sluggishness, things looked good when Hal Greer threw in a 40-footer to put the 76ers ahead 89–87 at the end of the third quarter. But in the last three minutes of the game the 76ers finally faded. Boston outscored them 10–2 down the stretch to win 118–106, cutting one game off of the 76ers' 10-game division lead, ending the long home winning streak, and squaring the regular season battle between the two teams at three wins each. The 76ers were 46-5.

"I look at that record and think it's a typographical error," said Bill Russell. "But I know it's not." Asked if he thought the 76ers were the best ever, Russell was cautious. "They might be. I wouldn't want to say anything to give them a boost. One thing they got is four or five players who can get an awful lot of points. Cunningham, Greer, Chamberlain, Walker can put the ball in the hoop consistently. Last week Jackson came up and killed us. They have diversified scoring. Somebody's bound to have a good night every night. If they get two or three of them, they get all the points they need right there."

At a pre-game buffet, GM Red Auerbach told reporters, "This is a fantastic team. When someone will stop them, I don't know. It's a type that can overpower anyone. One or two players can have a bad night, and you can still beat most teams in the league just on that power. [The Celtics] never had that.

"On the other hand, they haven't had any bad breaks. When everything is going good, everyone loves everyone else. But when a couple of things go wrong, it's entirely different.

"There's still a long way to go, too," said Red. "Like I used to tell my team, the most marvelous season can be forgotten unless you come up with all the marbles."

Translated, Auerbach was reminding the 76ers that they still needed to beat the Celtics in the playoffs. Never an easy task for any team.

Hannum responded this way: "When I think of Boston, I think of a little boy walking home through a cemetery all alone. It is dark and he hears noises. It sounds like that little boy is starting to whistle."

The war of words never ended.

After some much-needed rest, the 76ers did bounce back three nights later to take the Royals at home, 110–107, but the month would end on an unfamiliar low note, with the 76ers' second loss in three games. The team wasn't used to this kind of treatment. St. Louis finished them off at Kiel Auditorium, 114–108, with the help of three technical fouls on the 76ers. The loss cut their lead over Boston to just seven games.

The 76ers were glad to say good-bye to January, but little did they know how strange February would be.

JANUARY RECORD (12-3)

76ers	148	N.Y.	142(ot)	36-3
76ers	136	Chi.	115	37-3
76ers	104	N.Y.	112	37-4
76ers	121	Bal.	115(ot)	38-4
76ers	117	Chi.	108	39-4
76ers	125	St.L.	107	40-4
76ers	110	Bos.	95	41-4
76ers	119	N.Y.	111	42-4
76ers	113	Det.	105	43-4
76ers	127	Chi.	102	44-4
76ers	119	L.A.	108	45-4
76ers	112	St.L.	105	46-4
76ers	106	Bos.	118	46-5
76ers	110	Cin.	107	47-5
76ers	108	St.L.	114	47-6

STANDING: 1ST PLACE 7 GAMES AHEAD OF BOSTON

Note: *Despite his protestations, Wilt Chamberlain did play in the NBA's 17th annual All-Star Game on January 10 in San Francisco's Cow Palace. And he did play for ex–Celtics boss and nemesis Red Auerbach. Chamberlain started and played 39 minutes, more than any other player on the East squad, scoring 14 points and getting 22 rebounds, despite complaining of a painful Achilles tendon problem. Some skeptics attributed Wilt's pain to having to play for Auerbach. But Wilt and Red chatted at a practice session, and Wilt assured Auerbach he would play. 76ers Hal Greer and Chet Walker joined Wilt on the team, Greer as a backcourt starter and Walker as a backup. The West All-Stars beat the East team 135–120. Auerbach was ejected in the third quarter after getting two technical fouls.*

FEBRUARY 1967

It was bad enough that the 76ers started the month with two straight losses, one by 10 to the Lakers in L.A. and another by 17 to the Warriors in Oakland. That was three straight defeats, and four losses in their last five. They had suddenly lost their touch and a bit of their poise, and they faced 11 more games on the road (including five more neutral court contests). They would see home court only twice during the entire month.

"I guess we were getting complacent, and that goes for me, too," said Hannum. "Winning had come so easy I guess we were getting lax. We better shape up or we're in trouble."

But something more troubling was in the air.

While the talk began that the 76ers might finally be coming back to the league, there was also talk that Chamberlain was going to another one.

The American Basketball Association was suddenly making noise. It was a new league ready to take on the big boys of the NBA.

And one of the NBA's first big boys would help them to do it. George Mikan, former star center of the original Minneapolis Lakers, was named the league's first commissioner.

And the league had its eye on yet another center.

Wilt Chamberlain.

John Murphy, an Oakland businessman and co-owner of that city's soon-to-be ABA franchise, told newsmen that Chamberlain "has committed himself to us." He added that Wilt "will more than likely come in as a part owner of one of the teams."

Suddenly, all the early season concerns about Chamberlain's contractual ties to the 76ers emerged again. That dispute was all about the supposed guarantee that Wilt would get a share of the 76ers. Deep down, Wilt was a businessman, and the new league might actually be able to give him what the 76ers could not.

One report had it that several prospective ABA owners were actually shown a contract with Chamberlain's signature on it.

It was creating a major distraction for the sagging 76ers. And although Wilt was denying to the press that there was any signed contract, he wasn't shutting the door on anything.

"No, I have not signed such a contract," Wilt protested. "If somebody is showing any contract around, it certainly doesn't have my true signature.

"I'll talk with anyone who presents me with an opportunity to better myself. But talking and signing are two different things."

A Philadelphia sportswriter asked Chamberlain, "Is there any chance you won't be playing for the 76ers next year?"

Wilt answered, "All things are possible, I just take things one year at a time."

The reporter shot back, "Considering that fact, then, why did you sign a three-year contract with the late Ike Richman, your good friend?"

Wilt responded, "That's your answer—our friendship. But you don't *know* I have a three-year contract. That's what the club announced, but the club announces a lot of things. A couple of months after the season, some news will be forthcoming to clear all those things up."

Despite the drama and distraction, the 76ers rebounded with a 140–127 win over San Francisco (the injured Larry Costello had planned to return to action in this game, but he re-injured his knee in practice and was back on the disabled list again). Wally Jones led the 76ers with 33 points and won praise from Warriors coach Bill Sharman.

"Wally Jones is a good ballplayer, and I never realized it till tonight," said Sharman. "I knew he hustled well, but I never gave him his due before. Like a lot of others, I was misled by all that extra motion he puts into his play. When you give your pre-game talk you talk about Wilt and Greer and Walker and Cunningham and Luke, but you don't talk about Wally because you don't figure him to be a threat. That's why I put Rick Barry on him. I wanted Rick to be fresh on offense, so I figured I would give him the easy defensive job, but what happens? You can tell a good shooter by the way he shoots his foul shots and Wally shoots good foul shots, excellent foul shots."

Jones would make another strong impression on Sharman and San Francisco come playoff time.

Philly's next victim was the L.A. Lakers, 130–123. That vaulted their record to 49-8, six ahead of Boston.

After a slight respite, the ABA/Chamberlain soap opera resumed when the team landed in Pittsburgh the next day to meet San Francisco.

Wilt was visited by Art Brown and Max Zaslofsky from the ABA's New York franchise.

"I don't think you could say I showed any interest," Chamberlain declared. "I don't make deals when I'm already involved in one. I'm giving all my attention to what I'm doing. I have listened. I can't say whether I have rejected or not rejected anything."

According to owner Brown, president of a freight company and president of the prospective New York team, that "anything" was a $50,000 salary and a 20 percent interest in the team. There were reports Brown offered Wilt $250,000 in annuities, but no one could confirm the story.

And that wasn't the only distraction on the Pittsburgh stop. A major snowstorm hit the city that day, turning the basketball game into a bit of a barnstorming event.

First, 76ers equipment manager Larry Jacobs was supposed to bring the team's home white uniforms to Pittsburgh from Philadelphia, along with 12 basketballs and the 24-second clocks, which the Civic Arena didn't have. But the weather canceled Jacobs's flight, and 76ers GM Jack Ramsay and trainer Al Domenico had to go to work fast. Domenico found some white uniforms at a nearby sporting goods store and bought them all. Then he borrowed some basketballs from Point Park Junior College. Meanwhile, Ramsay jumped on the phone and raised Danny Biasone, the father of the league's 24-second clock, and Danny drove his old timepieces down from Syracuse.

One of the referees got snowed out, too, so the league hired Chuck Heberling, an NFL official who had worked some college basketball in Pittsburgh.

Heberling ended up making a controversial continuation foul call that favored the 76ers and caused Warriors coach Bill Sharman to play the game under protest. It mattered not, as Philly won 126–123.

It was the 76ers' turn to play under protest five days later, on February 12, when they marched into Boston on Bill Russell's 33rd birthday to play the seventh game of the regular season series with the Celtics.

With about eight minutes left to play in the game, and the Celtics up 100–97, Boston sent in Don Nelson to replace forward Satch Sanders, and the ball was put in play. But Sanders was slow getting off the court, and the 76ers screamed that the Celtics had an extra man.

"There were 13,909 here who saw the sixth man," yelled Hannum. "Everybody saw him but the refs. This is a violation of the rules and calls for a technical foul. It is not a judgment call or a rule interpretation ruling. An injustice has been done, and I have every reason to believe our protest will be upheld," Hannum insisted.

A technical would have given the 76ers a free throw and extra possession, and it might have made the difference in a tight game.

The 76ers hoped that the protest somehow would change the game's outcome. Boston won 113–112.

"They'll never put up the five hundred dollars [needed to file a protest with the league] because they know they'll be throwing money away," chided Red Auerbach. "A protest hasn't been upheld in twenty years."

Auerbach was wrong about that fact. Eddie Gottleib's Philadelphia Warriors won a protest in 1952.

But Red was right about this one.

Although the television videotape, rushed from Los Angeles to New York for viewing by Commissioner Kennedy, did show that the Celtics had six men on the floor for four seconds, Kennedy denied the protest, ruling that neither of the two officials saw the secret Celt.

Sixth man controversy aside, the game was vintage Philly–Boston. Chamberlain and Wayne Embry got into a fight early in the fourth quarter.

"Wayne had his arms all around me there," Wilt pointed out. "You just can't take this stuff. If you do you're gonna get knocked on your posterior."

Newspaper accounts called it "Wilt's angriest moment of the year."

Earlier in the game, with the 76ers trailing by seven, Chamberlain took his frustration out on one of the hoops, breaking it on a slam dunk. The referees said Russell had blocked the slam, and Wilt screamed that it had to be goaltending on Russell because the ball was already headed downward into the bucket.

The referees weren't listening. They were more interested in getting the basket repaired.

"Despite the loss, Boston won't catch us," growled Hannum.

"We have a tough schedule with only five of our last nineteen games at home. But we have a great team, and we can do the job. I expect to win the Eastern Division by at least five games. Nuts to the schedule, we have worked all season long to get six games ahead of Boston by good play on the floor and that's the way we'll stay there. I don't care whether the games are at home or on the road, we'll win it."

Russell got a birthday cake from some fans and took a jab at the 76ers.

"A real birthday present was beating Philadelphia."

Red Auerbach joined in.

"I notice that nobody in Philadelphia is shooting his mouth off as in the past about beating the Celtics," said Red. "[The 76ers are] starting to feel important . . . Sure they're hopped up, but we still lead the [season] series 4–3.

"No, we're not conceding anything. We're seven behind them in the loss column, we have two games left with them, and if we take those, it'll be five. The percentage isn't with us, but it isn't over until it's mathematically over," Red reminded.

Philly knew Boston would not go easily. The 76ers stood at 52-10, just five and a half up on the enemy.

The two heavyweights were on a collision course.

And, apparently, so were two others, Wilt Chamberlain and the then–Cassius Clay.

So began the story of February's other major off-court distraction for the 76ers.

The story surfaced just after the 76ers beat Cincinnati 131–123 on February 13. It was the day before Valentine's Day, and although Chamberlain later became well known for his inclinations toward making love, it was making war on the reigning heavyweight champ that was on his mind. There was talk that a fight could be scheduled shortly after the basketball season.

"I'm ready and willing to listen to all offers," Wilt said, "but I haven't had any offers yet."

Actually, reports about Chamberlain quitting basketball for boxing surfaced first in the early summer of 1965. He told reporters that he was thinking about becoming a boxer but had made no firm decision. By that August, Wilt summarily stuffed the story, saying he was sticking with roundball. But now, the talk was hot again with Wilt and Clay the focus.

It had been Cus D'Amato's idea to get Chamberlain pointed toward pugilism in the first place while Ike Richman ran the 76ers.

"Ike listened to my idea and to what I had to say to Chamberlain and said he was very impressed," said D'Amato, who was manager of two-time former heavyweight champ Floyd Patterson. "As a matter of fact, I remember him asking me, 'How would you like to manage my team?' I told them both what I thought Chamberlain could do and couldn't do in boxing, and that it would be a mistake to exploit his size and reach only. There's much more to it than that . . . size doesn't mean that much in boxing."

D'Amato now fed the rumors once again and offered to teach Wilt boxing for nothing more than expenses.

"I'm completely confident that Wilt Chamberlain could beat Clay and become champion if I handled him," said D'Amato.

"Chamberlain won't do it in one fight. This man has to be taught. I think he learns quickly and learns well."

But the crusty Cus hastened to add that he didn't think Clay would take the bait.

"They have criticized this man Clay so often, and, in my opinion, so unjustly, that I don't think his handlers will risk his being criticized further by having him meet a man without any previous experience."

Chamberlain always loved to compete against anyone—in any type of game, at any time, at any place—so his idea of fighting Clay was not far-fetched at all.

It caused a major media buzz.

UPI columnist Milton Richman wrote: "Chamberlain in his own mind can do everything better than the next guy."

Sport magazine's Leonard Shecter wrote: "The one thing Chamberlain despises most is to be considered a freak. That's why he contemplated leaving basketball to become a professional decathlon star. That's why he considered becoming an end for the Kansas City Chiefs, and why he considers becoming heavyweight boxing champion of the world . . . to prove he isn't a freak. He has a strange drive that leads him not only to believe he is the best basketball player in the world, but the best chess player, the best track man, the best cook."

Even Hannum chimed in: "I'd hate to fight him. I personally have never seen an athlete like this guy. Anything he made his mind up to do he'd do expertly. At one time at Kansas he unofficially tied the world record for the sixty-yard dash. He can palm a bowling ball and hold it out with his arm extended."

Trainer Al Domenico predicted a Chamberlain victory in a title tilt with the champ. "He'd win, he's the strongest man in the world. He can lift Luke Jackson with one hand."

Clay's manager, Herbert Muhammed, rejected a proposed contract for a June 29 fight, according to an article in the *New York Post*.

Reporter Milton Gross wrote:

> Muhammed made the rejection dramatically when he had a ladder brought to the hotel room where he, Clay, and former football player Jim Brown (who would have managed Wilt) were discussing the fight.
>
> "This man is 7-2, he weighs 290 pounds," said Clay's boss. "He's up there . . . let me see you hit him."
>
> Clay yelled, "I'm gonna give him a good whupping."

Wilt would later answer, "So, he's gonna give me a good whupping, eh? That I'd like to see."

Houston's Astrodome was mentioned as the fight's location, with predictions of a sellout and a purse projected in the millions. Money always attracted Wilt.

While the hype continued, the 76ers carried on.

Before the month was out, they would win six straight, including a 149–118 win over Baltimore that threw Chamberlain into yet another war of words.

Wilt had come into the game against the Bullets in Pittsburgh with 13 straight field goals. As the blowout progressed, he had added another 16 hoops in a row, upping the consecutive streak to 29, three baskets short of tying the record with four minutes left in the game.

Hannum pulled Wilt out of the game, apparently unaware of how close he was to the mark. But after a fast check at the scorer's table, Hannum popped his player right back in.

That brought Baltimore boss Gene Shue off the bench in a sudden hurry. "What's up here?" yelled Shue for everyone to hear. "What are they trying to prove?"

A nearby reporter quickly filled Shue in.

"What's the record?" Shue shouted. "Thirty-two, huh, well that [bleep] isn't going to get any more records tonight." Shue started screaming at his players as Chamberlain returned to the court.

"Foul him, foul the big guy, don't let him stop to get a shot up, we've gotta stop him from getting more baskets," Shue barked.

The Bullets swarmed Wilt when he got the ball, and he could manage only two more baskets, bringing his streak for the night to 18 consecutive field goals (a single game record, in its own right) and 31 straight overall, just one shy of the mark for consecutive goals regardless of the number of games. Even though Wilt had already set a single game field goal record, Shue still gloated about stopping Wilt from setting the bigger record that night.

"He didn't get the record, did he?" Shue asked sarcastically of reporters after the game.

"He needed four and got only two because we wouldn't let him get four. Nobody but nobody is gonna set a record against us if I can help it.

"Look, Hannum takes him out like he should when the game is over, then he sticks him back in just to get a record? Well, what the hell, I just don't like that kind of [bleep]. Let him get his record against somebody else," Shue added.

"I was told Wilt was going for the record, and I thought it would be nice if he could get it," replied Hannum. "I wanted him to have a shot at the record, but I told the boys not to change their style of play. Just go back out there and play normal, I didn't want it to be a phony record."

"If Shue hadn't known about me going for the record, I would have scored six or seven more baskets," said Chamberlain, who was far more upset about only being awarded one assist in the second half. "Besides, I've still got the streak going and have a chance of breaking the thirty-two."

In fact, Wilt did just that, setting a brand-new mark on the final day of the month with three more consecutive buckets in a 20-point win over Cincinnati. He had notched 35 straight.

As usual, Red Auerbach weighed in.

"The biggest joke in the history of all statistics is to count field goals by a man who is dunking the ball," fired Red. "I'm not knocking Chamberlain in particular, but just to turn around against a guy who is six-eight and go boom, that's not shooting.

"I can't take Chamberlain's record away, but to me it's silly. A dunk isn't a shot, and it's ridiculous to consider it one," added Auerbach.

"I think Red is a silly old man, and dumb, too, because he thinks he can get me riled up," Chamberlain retorted, saving the very last word for himself.

"I know what he's trying to do, but it won't work."

Meanwhile, Wilt's flirtation with the ABA seemed to be cooling off, presumably over how much money and how big a piece of the action Wilt would get. New York sources were saying that owner Art Brown and Chamberlain were no longer hitting it off.

"I am disenchanted with him," said Brown. "I wouldn't have him at any price."

For his part, Chamberlain was reportedly asking ABA officials to sound out the Oakland franchise about a meeting with that team.

For the moment, there were no red, white, and blue basketballs in Wilt's future. The ABA distraction was done, and Wilt was settling in for the stretch run.

One of the reasons the ABA officials felt they could get a hold of some of the NBA's top stars was their dissatisfaction with low salaries, bad schedules, and a poor pension plan.

How right they were. And it would all come to the fore in March, threatening to stop the 76ers' championship steamroller.

FEBRUARY RECORD (11-4)

76ers	133	L.A.	143	47-7
76ers	120	S.F.	137	47-8
76ers	140	S.F.	127	48-8
76ers	130	L.A.	123	49-8
76ers	126	S.F.	123	50-8
76ers	118	Cin.	106	51-8
76ers	148	L.A.	131	52-8
76ers	133	Bal.	139	52-9
76ers	112	Bos.	113	52-10
76ers	131	Cin.	123	53-10
76ers	127	Det.	121	54-10
76ers	127	Cin.	118	55-10
76ers	123	St.L.	122	56-10
76ers	149	Bal.	118	57-10
76ers	127	Cin.	107	58-10

STANDING: 1ST PLACE 6½ GAMES AHEAD OF BOSTON

MARCH 1967

The month began with 13 games to play for the 76ers and a 6½ game lead over Boston. They were ready for the final leg of the long season. Although nothing stood in the way of their second straight regular season Eastern Division pennant, a major obstacle began to threaten their drive to the ultimate victory in the playoffs.

The NBA players were talking *no* playoffs. They were talking strike.

News accounts early that March reported NBA players were dissatisfied with the league's pension plan. They were vowing not to participate in any playoff games unless team owners drastically changed the plan, saying they would not be put off any longer by what they believed were the league's stalling tactics.

Initially, the players wanted to strike a game scheduled for national television, but opted instead to potentially put the playoffs on ice—a move that could ruin all that the 76ers had achieved during their incredible season. Not to mention the money sitting in the pot at the end of that NBA title rainbow.

Dave Gambee, the 76ers' player representative, was worried, but tried to look at the issue as long-term gain rather than short-term pain.

"Our team naturally has the most to lose," Gambee explained. "If we go all the way in the playoffs, we get something close to ninety thousand dollars. Broken down, that comes to about seven thousand dollars a man. We're gambling that against a pension fund that could bring each man almost one-hundred-forty thousand dollars if he should live into his eighties," he added.

"I'm sure everyone would go along with the strike," said Billy Cunningham. "You vote for a representative, and you go along with what all the representatives vote. But this would hurt us more than some others since we've got a good shot at a lot of extra money."

In fact, money seemed almost more on the minds of the 76ers than the title shot.

"I guess the strike's good, but I could sure use the playoff money," said Hal Greer.

"We have to do something," added Wally Jones, "but does that something have to hurt our pocketbooks as well as theirs?"

"We had a meeting," said Gambee. "We were talking about what we should do. Wilt piped up, 'If you guys decide to strike, I'm behind you a hundred percent.' He was solidly behind it, and that made the whole thing legitimate," Gambee added.

One might think that Chamberlain would fight anything that might jeopardize his winning that first championship ring. Instead, he was preaching solidarity.

"What we're looking for is something the owners should have given us a hundred years ago. Maybe we are violating our contracts in striking the playoffs, but every player in the league feels it's worth a chance," reasoned Wilt. "The strike is the only lever we have against the owners.

"Do I feel as strong about the pension fund as others, the ones that don't make as much as I do?" he asked out loud.

"Yes, I do. So does everyone on my team, and we have the most to lose. As for me, it's not the money that's so important; Uncle Sam will get most of it anyhow. What we have to tell ourselves is that we may lose now, but we'll be making more later. We'll get more later by taking the chance. A strike could be a setback to the league for years to come.

"Why shouldn't I want to strike with the others? I am part of the whole picture. The Commissioner puts a deadline on us—'Let us know by Tuesday or we'll have to call off the playoffs.' They should have said, 'Let's get together and work this out.' "

"We want the playoffs, the public does, and the players do, too," countered 76ers GM Jack Ramsay. "I expect this matter to be settled before playoff time."

But Ramsay also articulated the owners' position.

"Back in '46–47 the owners took a big risk when they formed the NBA and tried to make a go," Ramsay explained.

"Guys who wanted to play basketball then didn't make demands about salaries or pensions before signing. Many teams didn't break even, but nobody volunteered to help them out of debt. Very gradually over twenty-one years—it's been a long haul—the NBA has reached a point where teams are more stable financially. Just because a corporation is finally showing a profit, should the money be immediately funneled back to the employees?" Ramsay questioned. "I don't think so."

"We're ready to negotiate, we want to negotiate," declared 76ers owner Irv Kosloff. "If our committee was called to New York, we'd be there in the morning."

He added that the deadline set by the owners could be moved. But he was concerned that pushing it back would not give ABC much time to set up its playoff schedule. "Television is very important to professional basketball," Kosloff reminded.

And beating the Boston Celtics was very important to the Philadelphia 76ers.

After losing the opening game of March 129–122 to Chicago in Evansville, Illinois, the 76ers reeled off five wins in a row, carrying their record to 62-11 and a seven-game lead over the Celtics.

Philly pulled into Boston on March 8 with a chance not only to break the Celtics' league record of 62 regular season wins, but also to clinch the East on the Garden floor.

Again, the game was classic Philly–Boston.

The 76ers were down 84–69 late in the third quarter, and they were still down 12 at the start of the fourth.

But the Celtics went cold, and the 76ers turned it on, fighting back to tie it at 100, when Hal Greer took matters into his own hands, hitting a twisting semi-jump hook that put Philly on top.

The 76ers thought they had it won, but the Celtics managed to tie the game in an agonizing six-second closing sequence.

The clock started as Larry Siegfried hit John Havlicek with the inbounds pass. Havlicek fired from the left corner, but it airballed, and Sam Jones caught up with it on the other side of the bucket.

Two seconds left.

Sam flung the ball skyward, but it bounced off the rim.

The buzzer was about to blow as Bailey Howell tipped the ball back up and in.

"That was the longest six seconds I've ever seen," Hannum remembered later. "I just can't believe a team could do that much in six seconds."

But the Celtics had done it; the game went into overtime.

The 76ers were not spooked by the "luck of the Irish" ending in regulation, nor were they bothered when Don Nelson opened the extra stanza with a three-point play.

Wally Jones calmly came down and jammed a jumper from deep in the right corner, then turned a three-point play of his own after getting bludgeoned by a Celtics defender on another jumper from the same spot.

"I actually didn't even see the basket after I got the ball," Jones described. "I shot from memory and didn't even have the satisfaction of seeing it go in."

But Boston wasn't finished.

A Bill Russell foul shot tied it at 113–113 with 21 ticks to go.

The 76ers had the final shot, and Hal Greer had the ball. He began dribbling out the clock as Chamberlain reminded him of the time remaining.

Greer came left toward the 76ers' bench with seven seconds remaining and started to make his final move—a quick turn to the right, throwing up a 25-foot jumper that swished.

The 76ers had done it. They had beaten the Celtics for the pennant on the fabled parquet. They had an eight-game lead with just seven to play.

"How sweet it is, how sweet it is," exclaimed the joyful Greer in the locker room after being hoisted onto the shoulders of his teammates at the buzzer.

"This is my second biggest thrill in basketball," he added, remembering that he'd scored 50 against the Celtics in his rookie year.

"I knew all along we were gonna clinch the title, but there was something extra special when it comes in Boston. Some people have been saying we were afraid of them, that we couldn't beat them up here, and this was the time to show everybody they were wrong," Greer continued, smiling but weary after playing all 53 minutes, some of them with painful cramps in his calf muscles.

"Wilt yelled out the seconds to me, and the bench gave me the signal with four seconds to go. I never thought the Celtics would tie it in regulation.

"Man, it is great to win here. We wanted it that way. No question, a great psychological boost for us. You know there was a playoff atmosphere out there tonight. It's always like that when we play Boston."

"He just played out of his skull," said Russell of Greer. "I didn't think we played well, and to be honest I don't think Philly did either. We knew Philly was gonna wrap up the title sooner or later, but we didn't want it to be here."

"Morally and mentally it did a lot for us to win it here," Chamberlain told reporters. "It definitely will give us an added incentive for the playoffs."

But Wilt was disappointed that Russell did not come to the 76ers' locker room to congratulate Hannum as the opposing coach.

"No, nobody came in to congratulate the coach, but I think he should have come in," Wilt bristled.

"We wanted this one more than any game all year. You could feel the tension in the locker room before the game, and we really didn't start playing our game until the fourth quarter. Wrapping it up on their court meant a lot more than winning it at home Saturday night."

That evened the season series between Boston and Philly at 4-4, with the deciding match set for the following Saturday at Convention Hall.

And Boston wanted to make a statement in the final meeting before the inevitable playoff confrontation.

Convention Hall was packed with 12,472, bringing the season home attendance total to a record 236,399. The old mark of 226,412 had been established in Wilt's rookie season, 1959–60.

But the Celtics sent the crowd home unhappy—very unhappy. A Russell jumper from 15 feet with two seconds left vaulted the Celtics to a 116–114 win, clinching the regular season series 5–4.

"If there's anybody on the court we wanna see take the shot in that situation, it's Russell," said Hannum after the game. "Even though he was hot in the second half [scoring 19 points], you have to let him have it."

But Hannum hastened to add, "Wilt played him all the way like I wanted him to play him. I wanted to stay back and let Russell shoot if he wants."

The 76ers had lost only two home games all year, both of them to Boston. The Celtics were trying to plant the usual seeds of doubt in the 76ers; that despite their record-shattering season, they were not a lock in the playoffs as long as the Celtics were still kicking.

But the 76ers were no longer the doubting kind.

The very next day the 76ers went to New York and took the Knicks by 11, as Greer and Cunningham combined for 68, atoning for their cold shooting against Boston the night before.

For Chamberlain it was a strange day.

He finally received the long-awaited Most Valuable Player award due him from the 1965–66 season. He was supposed to get it during the previous year's playoffs but was told the trophy wasn't ready.

Then he was supposed to get it at the 1967 All-Star Game in San Francisco, but again it was delayed, with Warriors owner Franklin Mieuli the vengeful culprit who did not want Chamberlain honored on his watch.

The NBA's public relations man, Haskell Cohen, said the league just wanted to showcase the MVP award separately from the All-Star Game.

NBA commissioner Walter Kennedy irritated Wilt when he said the league didn't owe him any explanation for not presenting the award in San Francisco. Wilt was told he would get the trophy during a televised game later in the season.

That sent him on a rant.

"They can mail it to me or present it to me at midnight under some bridge, but they will never present it to me on any TV program, and if they try, they will be embarrassed," fumed Chamberlain.

But the dispute was settled, and ABC-TV's Jack Twyman and newspaper columnist Murray Olderman made the presentation to a placated Wilt at halftime of the Madison Square Garden game.

Chamberlain seemed much more concerned about the news he had seen regarding Cassius Clay. A newspaper headline blared that Clay would be inducted into the Army in April, ending any hopes of the much talked about post—basketball season championship fight with Wilt. The word came just after the pair's famous joint appearance on ABC's *Wide World of Sports* with Howard Cosell, during which Clay taunted Chamberlain with mock punches and a slingshot signifying his David to Wilt's Goliath.

The pair made the most out of what would be their final confrontation.

"I'm out to get you," said Clay in front of a national television audience. Wilt flashed a smile and said sardonically, "How soon?

"I may not be experienced at fighting, but I'm an athlete. The element of surprise will be on my side," added Chamberlain. Clay demanded that the fight be held in New York's Shea Stadium, hoping to outdraw the performance there by the Beatles.

"That would be an outdoors match," Chamberlain retorted. "Why? Do you want more room to run from me?"

"I'll take on all challengers," the champ shouted back. "His hype don't bother me. I'll get Bill Russell and a few other tall boys as sparring partners."

But Clay, who became Muhammad Ali, was destined to fight his most important and most famous battle with the federal government.

A reporter asked Wilt if getting the MVP trophy made him feel any better after getting the bad news about Clay.

"No," Wilt answered. "The MVP trophy isn't worth two million dollars, is it?" He added he was "sick, real sick" over news of the impending induction.

"I was counting on that extra loot to help pay off some of my fines," Chamberlain chuckled.

Some extra loot from NBA owners also removed the only remaining obstacle in the 76ers' path to an NBA championship.

A last-minute agreement, hammered out in a March 15, 36-hour negotiating session just before the league-imposed deadline, ended the threatened cancellation of the playoffs and established a new, vastly improved pension package which NBA commissioner Kennedy called "a new plateau in player relations."

"I'm satisfied," said 76ers' boss Irv Kosloff. "There was a definite lack of communication for a long time."

"I'm happy the entire matter has been resolved," added the Royals' Oscar Robertson, president of the players' association.

The settlement cleared the way for the 76ers to put the finishing touches on their season in the sun.

The 76ers beat Baltimore 135–119 at home on March 18, which propelled them to a 67-13 record. For good measure, they went to Baltimore the very next day and beat the Bullets 132–129 in the season's final game. That made it 68 wins, an NBA record, against only 13 defeats, which translated into an incredible, league-record .840 winning percentage. The previous best was the Washington Capitals' .817 mark 20 years earlier. They finished eight games ahead of Boston.

The 76ers set new NBA marks for most points in one season, 10,143; best field goal percentage, 48.3; most 100-point games, 80; most road wins, 40; most free throws attempted, 3,411.

It was one team's amazing, season-long tour de force.

Unprecedented.

Unheard of.

Unbelievable.

"I'm as anxious as they are to get to Boston, but first we must take care of Cincinnati, and that may be easier said than done," cautioned Hannum. "You can believe me when I say they are ready for us. This Cincy team is blazing hot now. They've won something like six of their last seven. We've got to get serious about them.

"We've already proven we're the best ever, now it's up to us to prove it again, and I think we will."

"Comparing this year's team to last year's is like comparing a newlywed to a divorcée," Hal Greer joked. "This is a happy team, a real team where everybody pulls for everybody else and has faith in everybody else. If I can't get the job done, there always seems to be somebody else who can."

"Alex is the kind of guy you go through hell for," added an admiring, confident Luke Jackson. "I know in my case he has made this season a true pleasure. We're gonna get the championship for him and ourselves."

As for Chamberlain, he lost the scoring title for the first time in his pro career, finishing third. He posted 1,956 points for a game average of 24.1, his lowest average ever and down more than nine points from the previous year. But he still led in field goal percentage with .683 and won the NBA rebounding title again in a walk.

But the numbers story he was most proud of in the championship season was in the assist department. He tallied 630 assists, most ever for an NBA center, third in the league behind former teammate Guy Rodgers and Oscar Robertson, 216 more than the previous season, and almost four times more than in his rookie season seven years earlier.

As the sensational season of the 76ers unfolded, his exploits won the praise of archenemies and former teammates alike:

"He's doing a lot of things he didn't do before," said Al Bianchi, who played with Wilt in Philadelphia for a season and a half before retiring at the end of the 1965–66 campaign and going on to coach the Seattle Supersonics. "He's pitching the ball out on fast breaks, blocking shots, and he's not taking the fallaway jumper. That's the shot you're willing to give him. He's not scoring so much anymore, and I don't know if it's good, but they're winning. When I was with Syracuse, he'd get 70 points and we'd win by 30. If he had played the way he's playing now, well, maybe he wouldn't have won, but the games would have been a lot closer. Right now he's playing a more complete game every night. The name of the game is not scoring, it's rebounding and defense, and that's what he's doing now."

"He's a lot different," said Wayne Embry of the Celtics. "You have to think when you play him. Should you drop off on the guy coming through or should you stay with him? If you stay with him, he might pass off. If you drop off, he might fake the pass, take it in, and he's up there dunking. When he was shooting, what the hell, you just tried to keep him away from the basket. This way he's stuffing more on you, and there's nothing you can do about it."

"True," said Bill Russell. "He's tougher on you mentally now. And I think he's passing better than he ever did. That pass isn't as easy as it looks, you know. If you give it to them in mid-stride it's hard to handle. The timing has to be just right."

"Sometimes I just want to kick him in the shins," said one anonymous opponent. "The only thing that stops me is fear."

A reconstructed Wilt, indeed.

Reconstructed and ready for the playoffs.

Ready for Boston.

Ready to win it all.

But first, Cincinnati.

MARCH RECORD (10-3)

76ers	122	Chi.	129	58-11
76ers	136	S.F.	128	59-11
76ers	129	Det.	103	60-11
76ers	131	Det.	106	61-11
76ers	119	L.A.	117	62-11
76ers	115	Bos.	113	63-11 (ot)
76ers	114	Bos.	116	63-12
76ers	131	N.Y.	120	64-12
76ers	139	S.F.	110	65-12
76ers	138	L.A.	123	66-12
76ers	131	S.F.	145	66-13
76ers	135	Bal.	119	67-13
76ers	132	Bal.	129	68-13

HOME	AWAY	NEUTRAL
28-2	26-8	14-3

TWO 11-GAME WINNING STREAKS

SEASON SERIES

9-0	vs.	Detroit
8-1	vs.	Baltimore, Chicago, Cincinnati, L.A., and St. Louis
7-2	vs.	S.F.
4-5	vs.	Boston

1966–67 FINAL TEAM STANDINGS

East

	W	L	PCT.
Philadelphia	68	13	.840
Boston	60	21	.741
Cincinnati	39	42	.481
New York	36	45	.444
Baltimore	20	61	.247

West

	W	L	PCT.
San Fran	44	37	.543
St. Louis	39	42	.481
L.A.	36	45	.444
Chicago	33	48	.407
Detroit	30	51	.370

1966–67 INDIVIDUAL LEADERS

Scoring

	G	FGM	FTM	PTS.	AVG.
Barry, San Fran.	78	1011	753	2775	35.6
Robertson, Cinc.	79	838	736	2412	30.5
Chamberlain, Phil.	81	785	386	1956	24.2
West, L.A.	66	645	602	1892	28.7
Baylor, L.A.	70	711	440	1862	26.6
Greer, Phil.	80	699	367	1765	22.1
Havlicek, Boston	81	684	365	1733	21.4
Reed, New York	78	635	358	1628	20.9
Howell, Boston	81	636	349	1621	20.0
Bing, Detroit	80	664	273	1601	20.0

Field Goal Pct. (Minimum 220 made)

	FGM	FGA	PCT.
Chamberlain, Phil.	785	1150	.683
Bellamy, New York	565	1084	.521
Howell, Boston	636	1242	.512
Robertson, Cinc.	838	1699	.493
Reed, New York	635	1298	.489

Assists

	G	NO.	PCT.
Rodgers, Chicago	81	908	11.2
Robertson, Cinc.	79	845	10.7
Chamberlain, Phil.	81	630	7.8
Russell, Boston	81	472	5.8
West, L.A.	66	447	6.8

Rebounds

	G	NO.	PCT.
Chamberlain, Phil.	81	1957	24.2
Russell, Boston	81	1700	21.0
Lucas, Cinc.	81	1547	19.1
Thurmond, S.F.	65	1382	21.3
Bridges, St. L.	79	1190	15.1

FIVE

A Royal First Round

Oscar Robertson was having a good month. As president of the NBA Players Association, he had just led his negotiating team to a hard-fought pension plan victory over league owners at the bargaining table.

So, even though the 76ers had beaten the Cincinnati Royals and the "Big O" eight of nine during the season, and outscored them by an average of 11 points per game, Oscar might have been thinking his good fortune would carry over to the first round of the playoffs against yet another powerful opponent.

Outside of Robertson and the Royals, nobody thought that, including Philadelphia fans, only 5,097 of whom showed up for the first playoff game. Like everyone else, they were waiting for the main course, Boston. Cincinnati was an hors d'oeuvre.

Or maybe they were content to sit at home and listen to the games on 50,000-watt, clear channel WCAU Radio in Philadelphia, where the 76ers were heard during the ill-fated 1965–66 season.

"Sy Keil, who was a onetime salesman at CAU, left and got the rights and planted the games on WDAS," recalled then–WCAU sports director Andy Musser, longtime play-by-play voice of the Philadelphia Phillies.

"I don't know if he made the deal for just the regular season or if it was an oversight or what, but he was contractually free to put the games back on WCAU and WCAU was interested."

With the 76ers going for the championship and fan interest seemingly high for the playoff run (or at least for the upcoming series with the Celtics), the CBS owned and operated station gave fans near and far a chance to hear the big games, instead of struggling to listen on the weak-signaled WDAS.

Musser was excited.

"I was champing at the bit to do them when they came to me and told me about it," recalled Musser, who was quickly teamed with KYW-TV sports anchor Al Meltzer.

But whether or not fans were listening or watching at Convention Hall, the 76ers turned out to be ripe for the taking in game one. The Royals—nothing more than a sub-.500 club during the regular season—took them.

"We didn't do anything different in preparing for the game," said Royals star and Hall of Fame forward Jerry Lucas.

"We approached the game the same way as we approached others. Go to our power and take advantage of what was working on that particular night."

Ironically, it was the man who was a minor name in a major trade who was working that night. He had come back to Philadelphia to haunt the 76ers in the playoff opener.

Connie Dierking, traded by the 76ers to the Warriors in the deal that brought Wilt back home, was now the Royals' starting center, matched up against Chamberlain.

Dierking played way over his head, scoring 29 points and taking down 18 rebounds. He also played lucky, getting a gift basket early in the fourth period when a pass from guard Adrian Smith struck referee Earl Strom in the face; instead of bouncing into the backcourt, it richoteted to Dierking, who hit for two. Combined with 18 rebounds from Lucas, the Royals matched Wilt and Luke Jackson, who finished with 35 caroms.

Chamberlain tried to take the game on his shoulders, scoring 41, eight more than the hot-handed Robertson, who clinched the the win on a baseline jumper with 28 seconds left that put Cincy up 118–114. It was really the Royals all the way. They led by 2 after the first quarter, built the lead to 6 at halftime, extended it 11 by the end of the third quarter, and held on to win.

"We were thrilled and happy to win that first game," recalled Lucas. Now better known as "Dr. Memory," Lucas runs a California institute to help people improve their memories. It's no surprise that his images of that first game remain clear. He and Dierking were hitting from outside and driving Wilt crazy by luring him away from the basket. Amazingly, they also matched Chamberlain and Jackson on the boards that night.

Lucas wasn't a great leaper, but he had made a science out of rebounding since boyhood. "I did something unusual growing up," said Lucas. "For hours, I would purposely miss shots, shots from different angles, with different arc." He basically created a memory bank of where the ball was likely to go when shot at various trajectories from certain places on the court. He extended his studies to college and the NBA, analyzing his opponents' shots. "I developed a knack of knowing where the ball was going," said Lucas, who credits the scientific approach for his rebounding success.

"That first game was a big win for us and a devastating loss for them," Lucas remembered. "You don't want to start a five-game series that way."

Indeed, the basketball world was in shock.

Billy Melchionni was in tears.

"I cried when I drove away from Convention Hall that night," recalled the then-rookie sharpshooter from Villanova. He had been called up to active military duty and had to cut his season short to report to Fort Bragg, North Carolina.

"I knew we had a very good chance to win the title, and I didn't know how many other opportunities there would be. Having grown up in the area, playing for that team, having missed the most enjoyable part of the season, it was horrible. I was crushed."

So, the mighty 76ers had lost at home, to a team other than Boston, to a team they had utterly dominated all season long.

It turned out to be the wake-up call Philadelphia needed.

The 76ers turned it on in the next game of the best-of-five series, winning 123–102 behind a Chamberlain triple-double of 37 points, 27 rebounds, and 11 assists. Dierking played well again, but Wilt had taken control. Greer added 28 and Chet Walker 20 for the 76ers. Robertson tallied 29 for the Royals.

Greer took over in game three as the 76ers jumped out to a 13-point lead after a quarter. They built it to 15 at halftime and finished with a 121–106 win, behind Hal's 33. Robertson scored 25 but seemed to be losing his effectiveness as the series wore on.

By game four, it was clear that the physical power and speed of the 76ers had conquered the Royals.

Jerry Lucas seemed to run out of gas, collapsing in the first row of seats after chasing Hal Greer on a runaway layup. And the 76ers' defense collapsed on Oscar, holding him to just 12.

"Our whole team sloughed off toward Oscar," explained Coach Hannum. "Wally, Hal, and Matty took turns guarding him after Larry Costello was hurt. They all worked hard, and Oscar looked tired. We two-timed him. In fact, everyone guarded him at one time or another."

The final score was 112–94, with Greer tossing in a game high 30 and Chamberlain finishing with 18 points, 27 rebounds, and 9 assists.

The 76ers had eliminated the Royals 3–1.

"Alex understood the game and how to match up," said Robertson, reminiscing about the series some 34 years later at a Washington, D.C., area charity golf outing.

"They had a great basketball team, as great as any team alive."

"Alex was hard-nosed, tough, a man's man," added Jerry Lucas.

"They were a phenomenal team, one of the dominant teams of all time, incredibly powerful."

Meanwhile, that other dominant team, the Boston Celtics, powered past their first round playoff opponent, the New York Knicks.

Everybody knew it was going to come down to this.

Boston vs. Philadelphia.

Russell vs. Chamberlain.

It would all begin on the last day of March.

FIRST ROUND PLAYOFFS
76ers Win Best-of-Five Series, 3–1

Cinc.	120	76ers	116
76ers	123	Cinc.	102
76ers	121	Cinc.	106
76ers	112	Cinc.	94

76ERS VS. ROYALS—EASTERN SEMI-FINALS
Game 1, March 21, 1967, at Philadelphia

CINCINNATI

	FG-FGA	FT-FTA	REB	ASTS	F	PTS
Lucas	8-13	1-1	18	3	3	17
Hairston	7-13	3-6	5	1	5	17
Dierking	14-25	1-1	18	4	5	29
Robertson	11-20	11-11	3	16	5	33
Smith	8-14	4-7	5	3	3	20
Chappell	1-5	2-3	3	2	5	4
Robinson	0-1	0-0	0	0	0	0
Totals	49-91	22-29	52	29	26	120
	(.538)	(.758)				

PHILADELPHIA

	FG-FGA	FT-FTA	REB	ASTS	F	PTS
Walker	6-15	4-5	6	2	3	16
Jackson	6-14	3-4	13	2	1	15
Chamberlain	19-30	3-9	22	5	1	41
Greer	8-23	7-10	8	5	5	23
Costello	4-5	3-3	3	2	2	11
Jones	2-9	0-0	2	5	3	4
Cunningham	2-12	2-5	10	4	4	6
Guokas	0-3	0-0	2	2	2	0
Totals	47-111	22-36	66	27	21	116
	(.423)	(.611)				

	1st	2nd	3rd	4th	Final
Cincinnati	33	30	33	24	120
Philadelphia	31	26	28	31	116

Officials: Earl Strom, Manny Sokol
Attendance: 5,097

76ERS VS. ROYALS — EASTERN SEMI-FINALS
Game 2, March 22, 1967, at Cincinnati

CINCINNATI

	G-FGA	FT-FTA	REB	ASTS	F	PTS
Chappell	3-4	0-1	3	3	4	6
Dierking	8-17	5-5	17	3	4	21
Hairston	5-13	3-3	7	1	3	13
Lewis	0-1	0-0	1	0	0	0
Lucas	4-10	0-0	11	1	4	8
Robertson	9-17	11-11	6	9	2	29
Robinson	9-16	0-0	1	1	3	18
Smith	2-11	3-3	1	3	2	7
Ware	0-1	0-0	0	0	0	0
Wesley	0-2	0-0	1	0	1	0
Totals	40-92 (.434)	22-23 (.956)	48	21	23	102

PHILADELPHIA

	FG-FGA	FT-FTA	REB	ASTS	F	PTS
Chamberlain	16-24	5-9	27	11	4	37
Costello	2-3	2-2	1	1	0	6
Cunningham	3-10	5-6	6	0	4	11
Greer	12-24	4-4	3	3	5	28
Guokas	0-1	0-0	1	0	1	0
Jackson	0-6	2-2	5	1	1	2
Jones	8-16	3-3	4	3	4	19
Walker	8-17	4-4	4	3	2	20
Totals	49-101 (.485)	25-30 (.833)	51	22	21	123

	1st	2nd	3rd	4th	Final
Cincinnati	22	27	26	27	102
Philadelphia	35	23	33	32	123

Officials: Manny Sokol, Earl Strom
Attendance: 5,276

76ERS VS. ROYALS — EASTERN SEMI-FINALS
Game 3, March 24, 1967, at Philadelphia

CINCINNATI

	FG-FGA	FT-FTA	REB	ASTS	F	PTS
Lucas	6-21	1-1	23	1	4	13
Hairston	4-8	0-3	3	2	4	8
Dierking	6-19	0-0	8	3	0	12
Robertson	9-12	7-7	6	13	0	25
Smith	0-7	0-0	0	2	0	0
Chappell	3-9	0-0	4	2	2	6
Robinson	11-21	2-4	4	4	4	24
Wesley	1-6	0-0	7	0	4	2
Ware	5-9	0-0	1	0	1	10
Lewis	3-6	0-0	3	0	1	6
Totals	48-118	10-15	59	27	20	106
	(.406)	(.666)				

PHILADELPHIA

	FG-FGA	FT-FTA	REB	ASTS	F	PTS
Walker	7-17	10-11	8	0	1	24
Jackson	4-6	2-2	9	2	1	10
Chamberlain	8-13	0-2	30	19	1	16
Greer	15-31	3-4	7	5	4	33
Jones	2-4	0-0	2	2	4	4
Guokas	5-8	3-3	4	2	4	13
Cunningham	8-22	5-5	5	1	1	21
Melchionni	0-2	0-2	3	1	0	0
Totals	49-103	23-29	68	32	16	121
	(.475)	(.793)				

	1st	2nd	3rd	4th	Final
Cincinnati	26	23	22	35	106
Philadelphia	39	25	23	34	123

Officials: Richie Powers, Norm Drucker
Attendance: 8,987

76ERS VS. ROYALS—EASTERN SEMI-FINALS
Game 4, March 25, 1967, at Cincinnati

CINCINNATI

	FG-FGA	FT-FTA	REB	ASTS	F	PTS
Chappell	3-9	0-0	3	2	3	6
Dierking	4-14	0-0	9	4	4	8
Hairston	12-20	2-3	12	2	3	26
Lewis	1-2	0-0	0	0	0	2
Lucas	6-11	0-0	25	3	4	12
Robertson	4-15	4-8	1	7	2	12
Robinson	4-9	0-0	2	3	1	8
Smith	8-16	2-2	2	3	3	18
Ware	0-3	0-0	1	0	0	0
Wesley	1-2	0-0	1	0	2	2
Totals	43-101	8-13	56	24	22	94
	(.425)	(.615)				

PHILADELPHIA

	FG-FGA	FT-FTA	REB	ASTS	F	PTS
Chamberlain	7-14	4-13	27	9	1	18
Cunningham	1-11	5-7	7	0	2	7
Greer	14-27	2-2	5	4	3	30
Guokas	0-0	0-0	0	0	2	0
Jackson	7-13	2-5	10	3	2	16
Jones	7-19	4-4	2	3	2	18
Walker	10-21	3-3	9	1	2	23
Totals	46-105	20-34	60	20	14	112
	(.438)	(.588)				

	1st	2nd	3rd	4th	Final
Cincinnati	29	27	25	13	94
Philadelphia	31	34	23	24	112

Officials: Richie Powers, Norm Drucker
Attendance: 2,724

S I X

Boston Is Dead

The circus was in town.

The lions, tigers, and bears were booked under the big top at Convention Hall on Friday, March 31, 1967.

So, the first game of pro basketball's "Greatest Show on Earth"—the 76ers against the Celtics for the NBA Eastern Division championship—would have to move a few blocks away to the Philadelphia Palestra.

But for the 76ers, the place wasn't important. The time was.

It was time to put the Celtics away once and for all.

There were still ghosts around from the end of the 1965 playoffs, when "Havlicek stole the ball." They had to disappear.

There were also demons left behind from the 1966 playoffs. After edging the Celtics for the regular season title with a blazing 11-game win streak down the stretch, it was the same old story in the playoffs. Boston drubbed the apparently still outclassed 76ers in five ugly games.

Chamberlain blamed ex-coach Dolph Schayes for that one.

"A successful coach is one who gets the most out of his men," Wilt told the writers. "Schayes lost the respect of his players. We had the best club in the NBA, but the Celtics beat us in the playoffs because we weren't even a basketball team."

Owner Irv Kosloff blamed himself for bragging too soon. "Last year I predicted four in a row [over Boston]," said Kosloff. "Not only didn't we win four in a row, we didn't win it at all."

To be sure, there was no shortage of self-confidence on this team, but all of the 76ers had to be somewhat wary going into the title rematch with the Celtics. It was a numbers game.

Even though Auerbach was gone and Russell was doing amazing double duty as coach and player, the Celtics held a 5–4 edge in the regular season series against the 76ers, a mark that both haunted Philly and tainted their powerhouse season record. Despite their incredible stats and league dominance, the 76ers still could not master the Celtics as they had the rest of the league. The 76ers lost two home games all season, both to Boston. And the Celtics had atoned for their early season 138–96 embarrassment by the 76ers with an 18-point victory at Boston just a week later. They held the 76ers to only 87 points. It was the only time all season that Philly failed to score more than 100 points against an opponent.

Could history repeat itself? The 76ers had to make sure it didn't.

This was their best chance.

This was their time.

That went double for Chamberlain. Because every loss to the Celtics was more fuel for his critics. They kept writing and saying that he couldn't win the big ones. And the big ones were always against Boston, always against Russell, always in the playoffs.

Chamberlain had all the numbers against William Felton Russell.

Russell had all the championships.

Wilt and Philly's futility against the Celtics began in the Dipper's first season with the old Warriors, 1959–60. Boston won the Eastern finals four games to two.

Then in 1961–62, Wilt's 100-point season, the two teams had their first seven-game playoff showdown. The home court advantage was in full play, as Boston won four times in the Garden to Philly's three wins at home. The Celtics won the clincher 109–107 when Sam Jones nailed a jumper with two seconds on the clock.

Wilt and the Warriors went west the following season and missed the playoffs completely, but in 1963–64 with Hannum at the helm, Wilt in the middle, and rookie Nate Thurmond on the wing, San Francisco met Boston in the NBA finals. While hopes were high, the futility continued for Wilt. The Celtics dismantled the Warriors in five games to win the crown.

In 1964–65, with the new 76ers nestled in Philly and Chamberlain traded back to his hometown, the Eastern finals went to seven games once again. Again, the two teams exchanged victories on their home courts, with the 76ers winning game four in spectacular fashion when Hal Greer threw in that 35-foot bank shot at the buzzer to force overtime. The 76ers prevailed 134–131. The Boston papers claimed the Celtics were robbed by the timekeeper, because Greer couldn't have dribbled the ball and shot before the clock ran out with Boston leading. In fact, the *Boston Record American* put it in 60-point headlines: "Celtics Robbed by Philly Clock."

However, after further review on videotape, the pictures showed that Greer simply caught, spun, and fired, all in one memorable second.

Even Celtics great Bob Cousy had to admit it.

"I don't think there was any question about it," conceded the Cooz.

Eventually, judgment day came to the Boston Garden in the form of another game seven, the "Havlicek Stole the Ball" game.

Again the Boston–Philly confrontation would come down to the final few ticks, but this time on the Garden's antiquated scoreboard clock.

As time was running out, Russell's inbounds pass for the Celtics hit the guide wire above the basket support with Boston leading by just one point, 110–109. The 76ers actually had the final shot to win it all in the Garden and finally end the Celtics' playoff spell.

Coach Dolph Schayes set the play.

Greer was to toss in to Chet Walker from under the 76ers' basket. Hal would then cut off a pick set by Johnny Kerr, take a return pass from Walker, and knock it down. Wilt was stationed underneath as usual waiting for a rebound or tip-in.

It didn't happen the way it was designed.

Greer's pass to Walker was intercepted by John Havlicek, and the rest is not just history. It's legend.

"I didn't call the right play," said Schayes. He shouldered all of the blame. Chet Walker tried to pull some of it off.

"I should have had it," Walker claimed.

"I don't know where he came from," said Greer of Havlicek.

"He won the game," said Schayes. "He hit the key shots, and he made the key steal."

Havlicek the hero said, "I didn't think Walker was going to get it. However, after Greer used up three seconds, I knew he had to get rid of it, and I figured he had to throw it out long."

Smoking his traditional post-game cigar, Coach Red Auerbach actually found a few moments to be gracious amidst the gloating.

"They were great," said Auerbach of the 76ers. "We had to play our best to beat them."

Of Chamberlain, Red said that he was "absolutely great in this series."

"We should have won that series," remembered the 76ers' Dave

Gambee. "We were a better team. I don't think Wilt had his heart in it because of Dolph." Gambee implied that Wilt wanted nothing to do with the last play of the game.

"I've lost some dandies," whined Wilt. "They're still the world champions and we're still just a second place team." Wilt had been gracious to Schayes in defeat, but he wasn't happy.

Reporters asked if he was looking forward to another chance to top Boston next season.

To stir up some controversy, Chamberlain said no.

But, in fact, he led the 76ers to the regular season title in the East with that roaring run of 11 straight wins to nip the Celtics. But again, the Celtics won the playoffs, this time in an embarrassing five games. It spelled the end for Dolph Schayes, but brought the 76ers a new beginning with Alex Hannum and Wilt teaming up again in 1966–67.

"Boston was really tough," recalled Coach Hannum. "They had the right combination of everything." But Hannum's respect was tinged with anger and frustration.

"The dislike, in my opinion, came from Red Auerbach. A domineering type of person, arrogant, lighting up the cigar," Hannum barked.

The Celtics came with their usual group of Philly killers, all of them expecting to somehow eliminate the 76ers once again in the playoffs.

It was ritual.

Besides Russell, who still finished second in rebounding to Chamberlain and managed to add 13 points per game for Boston in the regular season, there was the venerable veteran forward Sam Jones, who loved to bury opponents with his patented bank shots.

Of Jones, Russell said, "In a seventh game of a championship series, I'll take Sam Jones over anyone who ever stepped onto a basketball court. When the pressure was greatest, he was eager for the ball." Sam could still shoot it, racking up a 22-point average in his 10th season.

Defensive ace K. C. Jones was there, too, in his ninth campaign of harassing the other team's best shooter. Hal Greer would be his target in this series. "Next to Russell, K.C. was the Celtics' most valuable player," said the Lakers great Jerry West, who tangled with K.C. on numerous occasions.

"I loved playing alongside Case," said Sam Jones. "That meant I didn't have to play against him. I'd look at the poor souls he was haunting and was thankful it wasn't me."

Satch Sanders was another defensive mainstay for the Celts. The 6' 10" New York University grad usually drew the high-scoring forward on the other team.

"When I think of Boston's great defense, I think of Satch Sanders," praised ex-Laker Elgin Baylor. "Satch was the toughest defender I ever went against, very aggressive and totally unselfish."

"He did more to help our team than anyone realized," added Celtics Hall-of-Famer Tom Heinsohn.

Bailey Howell had stepped into Heinsohn's old forward role, playing his first year for Boston after coming over from Baltimore. Known as the "garbage man," Howell made a point of sweeping up loose balls and stray rebounds and cashing them in for baskets. He ran at full tilt, all game long, and added 20 points per contest to the Celtics' offense in his debut season with them.

John Havlicek was the ultimate weapon in the playoffs for the Celtics. That ball he stole against Philly in 1965 still haunted the 76ers every time they saw this man of perpetual motion and heart.

"God, what a competitor," said Hal Greer, the man from whom Harlicek stole that ball. Havlicek had averaged 21.4 for the Celtics in the regular season, but he thrived on the playoffs. The 76ers had to watch him every second he was in there. Red Auerbach would say, "John Havlicek is what being a Celtic is all about."

"We had great respect for them," recalled Billy Cunningham. "You had to be at the top of your game to beat them. There was more incentive from our standpoint to beat them because of what they had achieved. We hadn't achieved anything. Best record didn't mean a darn thing. We knew about the big picture. We thought we were ready as a team."

I was ready, too. This was the series I had been waiting for as a young, gung-ho fan of the 76ers and a flat-out, passionate hater of the Boston Celtics. There was not going to be a repeat of the 1966 debacle against Boston. The 76ers were not going to go stale in the playoffs this time around. I was so sure of the 76ers in this series. But I was ever wary of Boston.

OK, I was a nervous little wreck.

But, as usual, I was going to lean on my old, trusty kitchen radio to get me through what was going to be a very important evening of basketball. The white Emerson was cranked and ready to go as announcers Al Meltzer and Andy Musser set the stage.

The Palestra was packed with Philly fans ready for the kill. It was no-man's-land for Boston backers, but that didn't bother a young Celtics fan named John Miller, who, decades later, would coach the women's basketball team at nearby LaSalle.

Miller grew up in Reading, Pennsylvania, a mere 50 miles from Philly. His friends and high school classmates avidly followed the hometown Warriors in the late 50s and early 60s, but never Miller. In 1964, when he traveled to Philadelphia to study the priesthood at St. Charles Seminary in Overbrook, he was again surrounded and hounded by Philly fans.

It was Boston that Miller worshipped.

"I just fell in love with Bob Cousy," Miller remembered. "I was ten years old in 1957 when the Celtics won their first title. As time marched on, I always followed and rooted for the Celtics. I just always felt they played the game like it was supposed to be played."

Although he eventually abandoned his goal of being a priest, he always preached the Celtics gospel to his entire family.

"We drove down from Reading, me, my two brothers, and my mother," Miller recalled. "We were scared we were not going to make the game in time. So we parked at Convention Hall, running toward the Palestra, about two blocks, and they are bringing in the elephants. We literally blasted through the elephants. We got to those seats just as the ball is tossed up for the opening tap, and the tap goes to the Celtics. The fans start to scream and people around us are going, 'Oh, no.'"

That feeling lasted for a while as the 76ers started slowly, and Boston raced to an early lead behind the scoring of Sam Jones. But with a little more than two minutes to go in the opening quarter, the 76ers began to take control. Sam gave Hal Greer too much room on defense, and Hal popped a 20-foot jumper to give the 76ers their first lead, 22–21. Then Cunningham took Bailey Howell inside, flashed across the lane with the left hand dribble, and flipped up a running hook that put the 76ers ahead by three. They finished the quarter up by a half dozen, 32–26.

Greer continued with the hot hand in the second period. On one play, he penetrated the lane on a drive, left his defender behind, switched the ball in the air to his right hand, and tossed in a short jump shot. Moments later, he took a jump ball won by Chamberlain and neatly nailed a 15-footer.

Wilt was working hard at both ends, rejecting jumpers by first Sam Jones and then Wayne Embry. And he was rebounding everything in sight. On offense, he was finding the open man almost every time. Wilt shoveled the ball from the low post to a cutting Luke Jackson for an open jumper. Then another time down the court, Greer dumped it inside to Wilt and cut for the hoop, ditching K. C. Jones in the process. Wilt fed Hal the return pass underneath. Russell countered quickly, forcing Greer to adjust his layup attempt. It missed, but Wilt snared the rebound and followed with a bucket. By halftime, the 76ers led by 17, 68–51.

The Celtics sliced three points off the lead in the third quarter but could get no closer, and the 76ers took the first game 127–113. They established their power and stopped the Celtics from getting any early ideas that this year against the 76ers would be like other years.

As for me, I breathed a big, long sigh of relief right into the speaker of the radio.

Chamberlain dominated Russell, finishing with 32 rebounds to Russell's 15. He added 24 points and handed out 13 assists to complete a classic Chamberlain triple-double. Greer was the scoring star, pumping in 39 points.

For game two, the scene shifted to the Boston Garden.

Come playoff time, the Garden seemed more cathedral than basketball arena. Above, nine championship flags were hung from the rafters, silent sentinels assigned to somehow protect the Celtics against all who would challenge them.

Side by side, one after another, in dark green lettering on a white background with a thin green border, they stood for a supremacy unmatched in professional sports.

BOSTON CELTICS—NBA—1957 WORLD CHAMPIONS
BOSTON CELTICS—NBA—1959 WORLD CHAMPIONS
BOSTON CELTICS—NBA—1960 WORLD CHAMPIONS
BOSTON CELTICS—NBA—1961 WORLD CHAMPIONS
BOSTON CELTICS—NBA—1962 WORLD CHAMPIONS
BOSTON CELTICS—NBA—1963 WORLD CHAMPIONS
BOSTON CELTICS—NBA—1964 WORLD CHAMPIONS
BOSTON CELTICS—NBA—1965 WORLD CHAMPIONS
BOSTON CELTICS—NBA—1966 WORLD CHAMPIONS

Below, the fabled parquet floor seemed to absorb a special energy radiating down from those flags of glory.

Good energy to the Celtics.

Bad energy to the other team.

Oh, that floor below.

The parquet was a crisscrossed patchwork fashioned out of Tennessee oak. The floor contained 247 panels, 5-foot squares of inch-and-a-half-thick wood. One thousand bolts held them together.

But NBA players had come to believe that this floor consisted of much more than just wood and bolts. It seemed a witch's brew with the spell cast in nearby Salem. It possessed an uncanny power to help the Celtics and hex the opposition.

"Long ago the parquet became part of Red Auerbach's psychological warfare against paranoid guests . . . blaming anything and everything on Red's obsessive dedication to gaining a Celtics' edge," wrote George Sullivan in his book, *The Boston Celtics: Fifty Years.*

"If teams felt that way, I used it for an advantage by playing with their minds," Auerbach said.

"It was either ice cold or boiling hot," remembered Al Domenico. "I used to go up before the team arrived to make sure the locker rooms were all right," Domenico added.

On the court, there were some suspicious activities as well. "The rims were loosened so the rebounds wouldn't bounce true," said the 76ers' feisty trainer. "Celtics fans used to throw light bulbs at the players."

And the torment for opponents wasn't limited to the Garden. It usually began at the team hotel.

"The fire alarms used to go off in the middle of the night at the Sheraton Boston," said Domenico, recalling vividly the lost hours of sleep the night before big games against Boston.

It seemed that there was no safe harbor from the Garden ghosts, even though some of the live cast of characters had changed.

Bob Cousy was long gone. So were Bill Sharman, Tom Heinsohn, Frank Ramsey, and Jim Luscotoff. Even Auerbach had finally departed, choosing to lead from the front office rather than courtside. But all of their dedication to basketball—winning, championship basketball—remained. One could sense it, feel it, in every corner of the sport's sacred ground.

So, it wasn't just the latest powerful edition of the Boston Celtics that the 76ers had to beat in this critical game two, it was an arena full of tradition, legend, lore, and maybe even some black (make that green) magic.

Despite the power of the leprechauns and the frustrating memories of playoffs past, the 76ers felt confident as usual heading north, because they had done a decent job in the Garden during the regular season, beating the Celts there twice in five tries.

And, probably for the first time ever, they really and truly believed they had the better team.

Obviously, it was a pivotal game for the 76ers, who badly wanted to break the Celtics' home serve. A win would tip the entire series in the 76ers' favor and put the Celtics in a situation they had never known—down 2–0 in a playoff series. That just didn't happen to the proud and mighty men in green.

In my mind, this game would decide the championship. A win by the 76ers would show the Celts in no uncertain terms that they were nearing the end of the line. As the game approached, my bad habit of nail biting was already in full motion. It turned out to be another tight contest, just like always.

The 76ers used their balanced scoring attack to steal this one away from the Celtics. The heroes were Chet Walker with 23 and Wally

Jones with 21. They picked up the slack for the sluggish Greer, who shot just 5 of 18 from the floor after his torrid first game, and ended up with 17. Jackson and Cunningham added 15 and 13, respectively, and Chamberlain contributed 15 of his own. His biggest stat was rebounds, pulling down 29 to neutralize Russell's 24. The Celtics led at halftime by three, but the 76ers came out smoking in the third quarter, outscoring Boston by 12 and leading 84–75 at the end of the period. Boston rallied a bit, but the 76ers won 107–102, and suddenly the Celtics knew that to stay in this series, they would have to go back to Philadelphia and take one at Convention Hall.

By this time, the circus was finally gone from Philadelphia, but the usual beasts would be in their seats at the snake pit, led by the irascible ringmaster himself, public-address announcer Dave Zinkoff. Zinkoff's sharp and wildly energetic voice fueled the 76ers' players and fans alike on many occasions. After baskets by Wilt and Hal, he would simply shout: "Chaaaaaaaaaaymberlain!" and "Grrrrrrrreeeeeeeeeeeer!" Years later he would do the same for a 76er named Julius "Errrrrrrrrving."

Even during breaks in the action, he would delight the crowd simply by announcing, "The 76ers . . . [long pause] . . . call time!"

Against the Celtics, Zinkoff was even more likely to get the crowd worked up. The Celtics and Red Auerbach didn't care for Zinkoff's antics very much, but there was nothing Auerbach could do about it. "Zink" would have a field day in this series.

The Celtics had won two regular season games in Philly, so there was little doubt that they could conquer the 76ers there, despite losing game one. The 76ers were determined not to squander their home court advantage.

As it turned out, it was a seesaw game most of the way, with neither team gaining a clear advantage. Boston took a two-point lead after the first period, but the 76ers were stronger in the second, tallying 35 points to the Celtics' 26 and taking a seven-point lead into the dressing room. Boston closed to within three by the end of the third quarter with John Havlicek and Bailey Howell leading the way. But then the 76ers' breakthrough came on a fourth quarter play triggered by a determined Dipper.

Chamberlain snagged a rebound and fired the length of the court, tossing the ball like a dart to the streaking Billy Cunningham. Billy took it in full stride at the left foul line, faked Russell, and laid it in. Then Greer, matched up against Havlicek, spun his way to the foul line to score a critical jump shot. The 76ers had taken over the game.

Near the end, K. C. Jones wrapped his arms around Chamberlain when he got the ball, fouling him in hopes he would stay true to form and miss his free throws, giving Boston a chance to stay in the game.

Wilt went to the line unnerved. He nailed two underhand tosses and the victory, 115–104.

Greer bounced back with a 30-point performance, with Wally Jones adding 21 and Wilt 20. But Chamberlain had won this game on the backboards. He had 25 rebounds by halftime and finished with 41, 11 more than Russell and a single game playoff record that still stands.

Wilt took this seesaw game and made it a personal statement game. He would not be denied against Boston this time. The Celtics had never been down 3–0 in any playoff series. Boston was at the brink of extinction. The chanting had already begun in Convention Hall: "Boston is dead." Wilt and the 76ers were going back to the Boston Garden to bury the Celtics for good in an unprecedented four-game sweep.

After the game was over, I switched off the radio and all I could think was, *Sweep*. How sweet a sweep it would be. How appropriate it would be to end the Celtics' reign in a crushing, devastating, history-making sweep. I was pumping my fist, ready to burst with joy, but trying not to wake my mom, who was asleep on the couch in the next room. I quietly shouted to myself, "We got 'em, we got 'em."

Not quite.

Not yet.

Things were stranger than usual at the Boston Garden on Sunday, April 9, 1967.

"There were death threats against me and my wife, called in to my wife on the West Coast," remembered Alex Hannum. "The FBI got involved. I had plainclothesmen with me. I needed a police escort in and out of the Boston Garden. Once the Philly people said, 'Boston is dead,' the Boston fans yelled 'You're dead' at me. A plainclothesman grabbed one guy who yelled it," added Hannum, who later underplayed the threats. "Boston fans were like that in a game, but a half hour later in the bar they would buy you a beer and not let you go home," he laughed.

And still more strangeness.

The game was to be televised nationally by ABC. And though professional basketball on television then was not nearly the event it is now, this matchup of two powerful teams, the collision of the two greatest big men in the sport, and the possible end of the Celtics dynasty made it another showcase event for the league and the network.

But ABC and the other two networks were in the middle of a labor dispute with the American Federation of Television and Radio Artists (AFTRA), the union representing on-air performers and newscasters.

The strike had already forced Walter Cronkite off the air at CBS, and at NBC the *Huntley-Brinkley Report* had been reduced to just

Huntley. Anchorman Chet Huntley opposed the strike and went on the air, while his partner, David Brinkley, honored the picket line.

On the sports front, CBS had to cancel a National Hockey League playoff game between New York and Montreal, and the strike caused disruptions of the network's telecast of the Masters golf championship.

Normally, veteran ABC voice Chris Schenkel and Jack Twyman, former star forward for the Cincinnati Royals, handled ABC's telecast of the *NBA Game of the Week*.

But not today, a day when the 76ers and the Celtics were likely to draw a strong Sunday afternoon audience and the network wanted its best talent at the microphones.

Instead, emerging from the television production truck and walking into the broadcast booth were Chet Forte and Chuck Howard, director and producer, respectively, of ABC's weekly games.

Forte was a control room ace and went on to build his reputation as the director of ABC's *Monday Night Football*. Though his voice was shrill, his basketball knowledge was solid. Playing at Columbia, he was named college basketball player of the year in 1956, besting Wilt Chamberlain, even though Forte stood only 5' 8" tall.

Howard had the better voice, and, like Forte, would also become a pioneer in network sports television.

It was an uncomfortable position for the duo, and it threatened to get even more uncomfortable when the electrical workers union at the Boston Garden offered to support the strike by turning off the house lights during the game. In the end, rather than tangle with an angry Celtics general manager, Red Auerbach, the union backed off and the game was uninterrupted.

For my part, I assumed my normal television viewing position, spread out on the living room floor in front of the set. I was praying for a sweep by the Sixers. I was fantasizing about going to school the next day with total bragging rights, and the chance to officially say "Boston is dead" to a couple of my Celtics-loving buddies who had taunted me for long enough.

But Boston would not go easy. The club's excited, egg- and light bulb–tossing fans were in their element, ready to derail any thoughts of a 76ers sweep in the hallowed Garden. By halftime, Boston moved to a 66–60 margin, despite an inspired performance by Luke Jackson, who scored 20 points and nabbed 7 rebounds in the first two quarters. The other 76ers played flat.

As they came back on the floor for the second half, the 76ers knew history would be made if they could rally and crush the Celtics in four straight.

Chet Walker got it going right away with a great two-fake move on Bailey Howell that led to a short banked-in jumper. But the 76ers still seemed lethargic early in the second half. Case in point was a play after the refs whistled Chet Walker for an offensive foul. K. C. Jones took the ball out for Boston on the sideline in backcourt. The 76ers' defense fell asleep and John Havlicek hustled behind it to take a quick pass in forecourt. He drove for an easy layup to keep the Celts ahead by six.

Then Wally Jones provided a much-needed spark. After getting no field goals in the first half, Wally made one of his patented moves on Howell. First, he dumped it in low post to Chamberlain, who flicked it right back to Wally. Jones then took Howell cross lane for a running hook that swished through and put the 76ers behind by just four, 72–68.

It wouldn't take long for Howell to get a measure of revenge. Howell collided with Wally under the Celtics' basket and drew the foul. The pesky defender had to leave the game with five personals. It left the 76ers' backcourt in trouble, and it brought Matty Guokas off the bench. Matty was only expected to buy the 76ers some precious time for Wally while he watched from the sidelines. No one knew then how important that substitution would turn out to be. Wally would not return to the ball game.

Meanwhile, Howell kept hurting the 76ers, running the Boston break to perfection for a drive to the basket, or pulling up for a jumper like the one he banked in for an 82–74 Celtics lead, a basket that really got the Celtics fans screaming. A Sam Jones bank shot pushed the lead to 10.

The 76ers then began to chip away, dropping the score to 91–88 with a 5-0 run as the third quarter ended. They were coming back, closing in on their dream of sweeping Boston with only 12 more minutes to go.

Chamberlain gave the 76ers a boost right away in the fourth period. He blocked a Havlicek shot and another from Sam Jones on the same play. Jackson came up with the loose ball and tossed it ahead to Guokas, who pitched to Greer for a foul line jump that made it 93–88 Boston.

But the Celtics built their lead again, stretching it to 10 at 101–91 when Sam Jones hit a foul line jumper that clanked on the front of the rim, bounced off the backboard, and fell through.

Chamberlain powered home a dunk with Boston leading 103–97, getting fouled in the process. He converted the three-point play, and the 76ers were three behind again.

Wilt made the difference once more after a miss by Sam Jones. Russell got the rebound, but Wilt leaped to block his follow shot. Chamberlain got the ball out to Walker, who tried to ignite the break. He found Guokas open about halfway down on the right side, but Matty badly missed his jumper. The ball squirted out to Hal Greer, who grabbed it and fired up a left foul line jumper to bring the 76ers within one at 103–102. Walker finally tied it on a free throw with 4:45 left.

That's when Matty Guokas began to make his move.

With the Celtics up 107–106 and 3:45 remaining, Sam Jones had a pass batted away in forecourt and Chamberlain snapped it up. He moved it sharply out to Guokas, who pulled up for a right side jumper to finally put the 76ers ahead 108–107.

After another Jones miss, Chamberlain rebounded and sent the outlet pass to Walker. He pushed it ahead to Greer, who found Guokas free on the left baseline for an 18-footer that gave the 76ers a three-point bulge.

But, as usual, the Celtics weren't finished.

Russell hit a short baseline jumper.

Don Nelson rattled in another from left of the foul circle.

Just like that, Boston was back in the lead, 111–110.

Luke Jackson answered for Philadelphia, pumping in a jumper from quarter court left for a 112–111 76ers lead with 2:00 left.

The Celtics were frenzied to get the rebound after Jones missed another jumper. Russell botched a tap. Embry did, too. Russell got it back, but was off target with a short baseline follow. Larry Siegfried picked up the loose ball and threw it to Havlicek, who had drifted into the clear at the left foul line. He drilled the jumper and the Celtics led again by one.

On the other end, the bulky Embry fouled the quicker Chet Walker, whose two free throws vaulted Philly back on top 114–113.

Walker and Jackson then doubled on Siegfried as he took the ball from Russell just inside the foul circle. As the two big guys closed in on him, Siegfried spied Embry all alone under the basket and hit him for an easy layup to put the Celtics back up by one with 1:15 left.

But before another shot could be taken, a Celtics fan took a shot at the 76ers bench, tossing a lighted firecracker at the team as they huddled during a time-out. Fortunately, it fizzled. The 76ers wished the same for the Celtics in the final minute, but it was not to be.

Walker took the inbounds pass and tried to shoot over Russell. The Celtics leader blocked it, as he had blocked so many shots over his long career. It was his specialty, and it always seemed to make a big difference in important games. This time, though, the 76ers got the ball back. But for only a moment. Luke Jackson grabbed it deep in the corner, but he made a critical error. Jackson had stepped on the end line. Celtics' ball.

Less than a minute remained as the Celtics worked the ball to Embry. He threw up a short jumper that missed, but the Celtics kept it alive and Sam Jones took possession. It was time for the veteran to teach a lesson to the rookie who had been guarding him. Jones circled around the perimeter and got an edge on Matty Guokas. Guokas saw he was in trouble and tried to knife in and knock the ball out of Jones's hands. When he failed, Jones was all alone, and he banked it home. The Celtics were up by three with the clock ticking away and the 76ers' dream fading fast.

Then Jackson made another mistake as the 76ers hustled back on offense. Larry Siegfried bumped the ball out of Luke's hands. Sam Jones picked it up and started a solo fast break.

Guokas was the only man who could stop Jones, and he did, wrapping his arms around the veteran as they stumbled out-of-bounds underneath the Celtics' basket, heading straight for the support. Jones didn't like it. Guokas had played surprisingly well against Boston, and perhaps Jones had had enough of this rookie for one game. Sam swung his arm out toward Matty and the scuffle was on. Chamberlain arrived first to pull Jones off of Guokas, as big Wayne Embry arrived to counter Wilt. Both benches emptied with the referees right in the middle of the melee. A Boston fan came out of the seats to throw a fist instead of a firecracker, but the police led him away. The substitute ABC announcers called it an intelligent foul. Sam Jones hadn't seen it that way. More important, Sam hit both free throws and the Celtics led 119–114.

The 76ers' last hope came when Matty Guokas was fouled and went to the line. He made the first, then fired a line drive on the second attempt. It hit the backboard, and Jackson grabbed the intentional miss and scored. It had turned into a three-point play, and had narrowed the score to 119–117. Philly was still breathing, but needed some help. Chamberlain fouled Russell after the inbounds pass, and the Celtics player-coach went to the line for two. Russell had made only three of seven free throws earlier, but this time he coolly knocked them both down to ice a 121–117 win.

Russell had played his heart out. He took down 28 rebounds to Chamberlain's 22. On offense, Sam Jones and John Havlicek combined for 63 Boston points to offset Jackson's 29 and Greer's 23. It hadn't been a pretty game, with both teams barely shooting 40 percent. Wilt managed his second triple-double of the series, adding 20 points and 10 assists.

Guokas's heroics had fallen just short.

"It was a pride game for them, a disappointment for us," said Guokas.

Years later he watched a tape of that game from the old Classic Sports cable channel, now part of the ESPN family of networks.

"Watching it again was hard for me," said Guokas. "The way we played you wanted to cover your eyes. Spacing was brutal, but nobody even knew the concept then. We were exhausted for some reason, we weren't moving. Boston was a step quicker."

Boston had also staved off elimination for at least one more night. They were hoping the 76ers would somehow start doubting themselves and begin thinking that they couldn't finish off the Celtics after all.

I certainly refused to think that way, even though I admit that I was worried the Celtics were ready to pull a few more tricks out of their magic hat and make the Sixers squirm.

The Boston backers at school were loaded for bear on Monday morning, boasting that the Celtics had the 76ers right where they wanted them and talking a sweep of the next three games to steal the series in miracle comeback fashion.

"We all were very, very disappointed," said Coach Hannum. "We wanted to establish our superiority over the Boston Celtics. We would have liked to have done it right there in Boston, and we felt very, very sad, but very, very determined about what we had to do when we got that team back down to Philadelphia."

On game night, Hannum paced the 76ers' dressing room before the showdown, walking back and forth in the shadow of a sign hanging on the wall that read: "Welcome 76ers. The 1966–1967 NBA champs." It had been put there on the opening night of the season by Ed Newborn, the head man at Convention Hall.

"We left it up as a spur for our ambitions," said Hannum. Right beside it he had written numbers indicating, in sequences of five, the team's goals at various times during the season.

On this night, the sign was again a reminder of what had to be done to make the words come true.

Another sign hanging from the first tier of Convention Hall proclaimed: "NO. 4 NOW." No 76ers fans wanted this series to go back to Boston.

Tonight was the night.

Even Pennsylvania governor Raymond P. Shafer wanted to see this one along with the manic "snake pit" faithful. He sat at courtside with owner Irv Kosloff and GM Jack Ramsay.

The Celtics spoiled the fun on the opening tap, with Havlicek taking it from Russell. He scooted past Wally Jones with a left-handed dribble, sprinted down the lane, and put it up with the opposite hand for a quick 2–0 Boston lead. In fact, the entire first quarter belonged to Boston, which raced to a 37–26 margin in the opening 12 minutes. The 76ers fought back in the second period, outscoring the Celtics 39–33 and cutting the lead at halftime to 70–65.

No one expected such a high-scoring game, especially after both teams struggled offensively just two nights earlier.

The 76ers came out gunning in the second half, mainly in the person of Wally Jones. He was about to go nuts!

The 76ers trailed 72–71 with just under 10:30 to go in the third quarter when Sam Jones missed a shot from deep outside. Jackson tipped the ball to Chamberlain as it came off the board, and Chamberlain dished to Wally, who was streaking up the sideline with Chet Walker on the other wing and Russell the only Celtic back to protect. Wally sent a perfect bounce pass to Walker, and Russell had to commit as Walker closed in on the hoop. Suddenly, Walker sent it right back to Jones for the layup. The 76ers took the lead, and the crowd latched on to the moment.

"The momentum of the team started to move then, and we knew we had them as soon as we got ahead," recalled Wally. During a nine-minute sequence, the 76ers outscored the Celtics 27–6.

After Jackson got an easy jam, Jones continued his single-handed assault. He hit the familiar jackknife jumper from outside, arms flailing, legs kicking outward. Next time up he got a pick from Jackson and hit the jackknife from the other side. Moments later, he moved crosscourt on the dribble against Sam Jones, pulled up, and knocked it in. Up the sideline, again against Sam, Wally executed a perfect behind-the-back dribble, shedding the rival Jones and nailing the jumper. Wally hit eight of nine in that frantic, critical sequence, living up to his nickname, Wally Wonder.

Wally said Billy Cunningham helped him adjust his shot in that second half. Jones had struggled from the floor from the outset, but Cunningham came to his rescue at halftime. "Billy told me I wasn't following through on my shots," recounted Jones. "He was right. As soon as I hit my first shot, I just felt this streak come on and every time I had the ball I felt so confident that I just continued to shoot."

The 76ers' power and poise finally asserted themselves for good. By the end of third quarter, the 76ers had turned a five-point deficit into a six-point lead. In the final period, the 76ers could do no wrong. Cunningham hit a left-handed driving layup. Greer made a knifelike move past Boston sub Jim Barnett, switched hands in the air, and drained a running jumper. Guokas added an easy layup off a fast break.

The roof had caved in on Boston.

With just over four minutes left, the 76ers led 131–104.

About a minute later, a fan on Convention Hall's 34th Street side stood on his chair, put a giant cigar in his mouth, and lit it. It was fitting, somehow, because that's what Boston coach Red Auerbach always did when his team had whipped its opponent.

The "Boston is Dead" sign was now being paraded around behind the scorer's bench by a few of the Convention Hall faithful, who, along with the 76ers, had waited so long, so anxiously, for this very moment. The chanting had begun. "Boston is dead, Boston is dead."

Dead, after eight straight NBA titles.

Russell looked as the final buzzer—the death knell—sounded.

He was tired and beaten.

His sad eyes darted downcourt to watch Chamberlain and the winning 76ers erupt in a celebration of joy and relief.

He and his Celtics had not experienced this in nine years.

They didn't want to believe it.

"Under ten seconds to play in that last game, Luke got it at half court and was going in for a layup," said Cunningham. "Russell tried to run down and block the shot! I thought, 'He doesn't believe the scoreboard right now. [The Celtics] don't lose in the playoffs.'"

But for Russell and the rest, reality was setting in.

They were not going to win the NBA title this season.

The championship streak was snapped.

The dynasty was done.

At long last, the Philadelphia 76ers had prevailed.

It had actually happened.

Philadelphia had beaten Boston.

In the playoffs.

Decisively.

Four out of five.

"They're playing the same game we've played for the last nine years," said a disappointed K. C. Jones of the Celtics. "In other words, team ball."

The time had finally come for this proud, powerful team.

And in a very small way, my time had come, too.

I found myself running all through the house after the game, jumping up and down, squealing with delight, knowing that, finally, the Boston jinx was up. I was celebrating at their funeral. I was deliriously happy for my 76ers.

Hundreds of 76ers fans were having a ball courtesy of their team. They were beside themselves with a sort of vengeful glee. They stormed the court, laughing and dancing, hanging on the hoops, hugging their heroes, savoring the fact that the 76ers had punished the Celtics particularly hard in the fourth period, outscoring them 40–22, pouring it on for a 140–116 triumph.

Combining the final six minutes of the first half with the full second half, the 76ers scored 97 points to the Celtics' 57.

Overall, Chamberlain averaged 32 rebounds a game to Russell's 23.

Greer led the 76ers in scoring with a 28.2 average, while Havlicek was a one-man offensive gang for Boston, averaging 30.

Alex Hannum was a Celtic-killer again.

"Early in the year I decided to give our team a chance to cool off for just a couple of minutes up in the dressing room before we allowed the press to come in," said Hannum.

"The tremendous feeling you have of coming back to that room with your own group and looking at one another and knowing that you have done it. This moment was truly a moment of tremendous elation and tremendous pride. The really big celebrating, the yelling and screaming, came later with the reporters and the fans. But that moment, walking back to that dressing room, is one I'll never forget.

"This was something that we and the Philadelphia fans had been looking for all of these years, the chance to dethrone that team.

"Wilt and Hal have been chasing these guys for so long, it's especially gratifying to them," Hannum added.

Hannum was met by Greer and Dave Gambee for the first of several champagne dousings.

Governor Shafer avoided the bubbly, but wanted to be pictured with a winner. He made the locker-room rounds congratulating every player, including a happy, but weary, Chamberlain.

"Just very, very tired," said Wilt, who turned in his third triple-double of the series with 29 points, 36 rebounds, and 13 assists. "It's a long, long climb, so to speak, because you never can tell when the Celtics are dead, and it's always good that you know they're finally out of the way. I really feel that this was the greatest Celtics team, so in beating this team, I think it helped to make up a little for the other losses we had over the years."

Chet Walker also summed up the long struggle. "It was something all the 76ers have been looking forward to a long time, and it finally happened."

"We did not only defeat a great basketball team," said Hal Greer, "we destroyed a tradition."

Said Billy Cunningham, "This was the greatest thrill in my life to beat Boston four out of five."

Philly TV play-by-play man Al Meltzer said, "They not only beat them, they took them apart. Philly vented all of its spleen. Tore 'em up one side and down the other. Everybody played superbly."

"We felt we were gonna do it," said GM Jack Ramsay, "and nothing could stand in our way. I think that's what it takes to become a champion, and this team had it. It had the skill and the willingness of the players to blend their talents into a strong, cohesive force, and it had the proper direction at the top from the coach."

The funniest sight in the locker room had to be the usually quiet owner, Irv Kosloff, jubilantly celebrating with his team. For once, "Kos" went out of character, shaking up a bottle of champagne and threatening to spray his players with it. Greer had poured an ample supply on the boss's head just a few minutes earlier.

"Bottles of champagne poured all over my head, all over my suit, all over my clothes, and finally ran down into my shoes," said Kosloff. "I emptied one shoe and actually champagne poured out of the shoe. The suit I put aside when I got home and didn't have it cleaned for about a month. I just enjoyed that wine-fermented odor. It just carried me back to that night many nights thereafter."

And at the end, there was Chamberlain, reaching his long right arm way up high and extending four fingers. It was a not-so-subtle reminder from the man who would be king that there were four more games to win before the NBA title belonged to Wilt and his 76ers.

"It's hard to explain how I feel now," said Wilt. "But I'll really feel it in July or August. That's when people used to look at me as somebody seven-one who couldn't be a winner.

"Now I'll feel like one.

"But just because we beat Boston doesn't mean we're the champions. I know we beat them and they were champs. But they're not the champs anymore."

In that 1996 interview with the NBA, Chamberlain said, "We had been so superior all year long that it was anticlimactic for us to beat them. It just didn't mean very much. By the time we got to playoff time, everyone knew we were by far the best team in basketball."

Asked about the Celtics–76ers matchups of the mid-60s, he added, "My enduring image is that we were unlucky. I look back and I always think about how unlucky we were. But then on the other side, I look at how lucky we were to be able to play against the best, because the best always brought the best out of you. The real piercing of the armor happened gradually. We had to take a whole year to pierce it. By the time we finally got to them, it was about time that they lost just one time. It's kind of a strange feeling. You felt that you did something but you felt like it's way overdue. As great as they were, they weren't running away from the league. They weren't playing your .890 ball or .900 ball. They were playing .630s and .620s and .640s, and the other teams were playing .580s and .590s. It was much closer than people imagined. The Celtics just had the ability to win when it counted.

"I never got to hating them. I always respected their abilities. I hated them only when I was playing against them. There were guys out there who I really didn't like because they did bad things to me and they still won, and they were lucky enough to win those close ones. But I never hated them as a unit. I respected their ability to come to the call when it was needed."

Vince Miller said that Chamberlain was happy after the victory over Boston. "But Wilt always felt that with a drop of the ball that way or a drop of the ball this way, he could have won two or three more other [playoffs versus Boston]."

Of Bill Russell, Wilt told the NBA, "Even though it was a great duel and a great matchup, it was not all together the matchup that you've been hearing about over the years. Basketball is a team game, and when I faced teams, nobody wanted to face me alone. The Celtics used their whole team against me. Where I see him as the tremendous player is as a rebounder. He was the only guy who could rebound along with me, and I sometimes thought he was a better rebounder than I was. He used more things to get to the ball than I had to use. I always had the highest respect for his rebounding and his team defensive concept. He and I were very close."

Columnist Leonard Koppett analyzed the 76ers–Celtics matchup this way, praising the 76ers and honoring the fallen Celtics:

An interregnum, the first in more than a decade, exists in the National Basketball Association today. The Boston Celtics have been dethroned—but the 76ers who dethroned them are not yet entitled to be crowned in their place. To succeed the Celtics, who were champions for the last eight years in a row, the 76ers still have to beat San Francisco. No one is more aware of this than Wilt Chamberlain, who engineered this shift in power. Tuesday night, as soon as the 76ers reached their dressing room after the exhilarating last quarter that had given them a 140–116 victory and semifinal series, four games to one, Wilt made a speech:

"We've got to get four more wins before this season is over. Let's not lose sight of that."

He was forceful, almost solemn. Such an attitude had as much to do with Philadelphia's success as Wilt's unmatched physical endowments. The key word was spoken afterwards by Alex Hannum, the 76er coach:

"He was dedicated out there."

And yet the romance of sports legend refuses to be imprisoned by fact. When and if the 76ers do win the title, memories will always focus on the Boston series as the scene of the true victory. Therefore, various facets should be summed up.

The personal battle between Chamberlain and Bill Russell was something to see. Most of it took place above the level of the bucket. ("The flashiest high-altitude duel since Eddie Rickenbacker vs. Baron von Richtofen," someone observed.) It is easy to overlook how superb Russell was—and that's the real measure of how overwhelming Wilt was: he did it against Russell.

In five games, Wilt took down 160 rebounds (to Russell's 117), scored 108 points (to Russell's 57), and made 50 assists (to Russell's 30). In no sense, however, was there anything wrong with Bill Russell.

Bill simply faced the same problem a 6-5 or a 6-6 man would face playing him. Wilt is that much bigger than Russell, and when Wilt went all out, there was nothing Russell could do to stop him. To put it another way, only Russell's excellence against Wilt made it possible for these games to be so hard fought.

While these two were, literally, the pivot of the action, many others took turns in the spotlight. Luke Jackson rebounded and hit jumpers from deep in the corner. Chet Walker was hot when needed. Wally Jones hustled and hit some indescribable long shots. Hal Greer systematically racked up points like a cash register (and led Philadelphia with 146 points). Billy Cunningham was a lifesaver in two games and a dead weight in two others. Matt Guokas was surprisingly ready for a rookie and of great value in emergencies. These are the men who made the 76ers a history-making team, with Wilt's help—or by helping Wilt.

The final aspect, of course, was age—Boston's age. It told. In each of the 10 halves played, the Celts faded toward the end—the shots just missed, the defense loosened. Ultimately, Boston's defeat merely proved again that nothing lasts forever.

Indeed, the San Francisco Warriors were now the only remaining obstacle to NBA supremacy for the 76ers and Wilton Norman Chamberlain.

The championship journey, which started against Boston in the Penn Palestra after the 76ers were evicted from their regular home arena by those circus animals, would soon end in a place called the Cow Palace.

SECOND ROUND PLAYOFFS
76ers Win Best-of-Seven Series, 4–1

76ers	127	Bost.	113
76ers	107	Bost.	102
76ers	115	Bost.	104
Bost.	121	76ers	117
76ers	140	Bost.	116

76ERS VS. CELTICS—EASTERN FINALS
Game 1, March 31, 1967, at Philadelphia

BOSTON

	FG-FGA	FT-FTA	REB	ASTS	F	PTS
Howell	5-14	3-3	7	0	5	13
Sanders	2-5	0-0	0	0	4	4
Russell	7-14	6-7	15	4	3	20
Jones, Sam	11-25	2-2	3	12	3	24
Jones, K.C.	4-6	2-2	0	3	3	10
Embry	1-4	0-0	4	0	1	2
Havlicek	8-28	6-8	9	3	1	22
Nelson	4-8	0-0	4	0	1	8
Siegfried	4-8	2-2	6	3	2	10
Totals	46-112	21-24	48	25	23	113
	(.411)	(.875)				

PHILADELPHIA

	FG-FGA	FT-FTA	REB	ASTS	F	PTS
Walker	6-13	6-7	5	1	5	18
Jackson	2-11	1-2	15	4	4	5
Chamberlain	9-13	6-10	32	13	3	24
Greer	17-35	5-5	3	6	1	39
Jones	10-19	4-6	3	7	4	24
Cunningham	6-11	1-2	8	2	1	13
Guokas	1-3	0-0	1	1	2	2
Gambee	1-1	0-0	0	0	0	2
Totals	52-106	23-32	72	34	20	127
	(.491)	(.719)				

	1st	2nd	3rd	4th	Final
Boston	26	23	31	33	113
Philadelphia	32	34	28	33	127

Note: Team rebounds included in total rebounds

76ERS VS. CELTICS—EASTERN FINALS
Game 2, April 2, 1967, at Boston

BOSTON

	FG-FGA	FT-FTA	REB	ASTS	F	PTS
Barnett	2-9	0-0	2	1	1	4
Havlicek	9-18	8-9	9	1	4	26
Howell	11-15	0-1	5	0	5	22
Jones, K.C.	1-8	0-0	4	7	5	2
Jones, Sam	3-16	3-3	4	3	3	9
Nelson	3-6	0-0	1	0	1	6
Russell	5-14	4-6	24	5	3	14
Sanders	3-10	0-1	7	1	4	6
Siegfried	5-12	3-4	3	1	5	13
Totals	42-108 (.389)	18-24 (.750)	71	19	31	102

PHILADELPHIA

	FG-FGA	FT-FTA	REB	ASTS	F	PTS
Chamberlain	5-11	5-9	29	5	4	15
Cunningham	5-11	3-6	9	3	2	13
Greer	5-18	7-11	0	5	3	17
Guokas	0-1	2-2	1	0	2	2
Jackson	5-10	5-6	9	2	5	15
Jones	10-26	2-2	2	0	4	22
Walker	9-14	5-8	9	0	2	23
Totals	39-91 (.429)	29-44 (.659)	68	15	22	107

	1st	2nd	3rd	4th	Final
Boston	21	37	17	27	102
Philadelphia	21	34	29	23	107

Note: Team rebounds included in total rebounds
Officials: Earl Strom, John Vanak
Attendance: 13,909

76ERS VS. CELTICS—EASTERN FINALS
Game 3, April 5, 1967, at Philadelphia

BOSTON

	FG-FGA	FT-FTA	REB	ASTS	F	PTS
Howell	8-13	3-4	7	2	2	19
Havlicek	13-33	7-8	8	4	4	33
Russell	3-13	4-5	29	9	2	10
Jones, Sam	10-24	2-3	7	5	5	22
Siegfried	6-18	4-5	6	5	5	16
Jones, K.C.	0-6	0-0	5	2	5	0
Sanders	1-3	0-0	1	1	1	2
Barnett	0-0	0-0	0	0	1	0
Nelson	1-1	0-0	3	1	1	2
Totals	42-111	20-25	66	29	26	104
	(.378)	(.800)				

PHILADELPHIA

	FG-FGA	FT-FTA	REB	ASTS	F	PTS
Walker	8-17	2-2	2	0	2	18
Jackson	4-15	3-3	13	3	3	11
Chamberlain	8-14	4-8	41	9	3	20
Greer	9-24	12-14	6	6	5	30
Jones	9-16	3-3	3	3	5	21
Cunningham	5-17	1-1	2	3	3	11
Guokas	1-5	2-2	1	1	0	4
Totals	44-108	27-33	68	25	21	115
	(.407)	(.818)				

	1st	2nd	3rd	4th	Final
Boston	26	26	29	23	104
Philadelphia	24	35	25	31	115

Officials: Earl Strom, John Vanak
Attendance: 13,007

76ERS VS. CELTICS—EASTERN FINALS
Game 4, April 9, 1967, at Boston

BOSTON

	FG-FGA	FT-FTA	REB	ASTS	F	PTS
Barnett	0-0	0-0	0	0	2	0
Embry	2-6	0-0	1	0	1	4
Havlicek	13-30	5-7	13	4	4	31
Howell	7-14	3-8	7	1	6	17
Jones, K.C.	3-6	0-0	0	3	3	6
Jones, Sam	13-28	6-6	7	1	3	32
Nelson	1-3	0-0	1	0	1	2
Russell	2-7	5-9	28	5	5	9
Sanders	1-4	0-0	2	0	4	2
Siegfried	6-18	6-7	5	11	6	18
Totals	48-116	25-37	64	25	35	121
	(.414)	(.676)				

PHILADELPHIA

	FG-FGA	FT-FTA	REB	ASTS	F	PTS
Chamberlain	8-18	4-11	22	10	2	20
Cunningham	0-8	4-5	4	0	5	4
Greer	10-17	8-11	6	4	4	23
Guokas	4-9	3-4	1	2	2	11
Jackson	12-21	5-5	18	1	3	29
Jones	1-7	5-6	1	0	5	7
Walker	6-16	6-8	6	1	4	18
Totals	41-96	35-50	58	18	25	117
	(.427)	(.700)				

	1st	2nd	3rd	4th	Final
Boston	34	32	25	30	121
Philadelphia	32	28	28	29	117

Officials: Mendy Rudolph, Richie Powers
Attendance: 13,909

76ERS VS. CELTICS—EASTERN FINALS
Game 5, April 11, 1967, at Philadelphia

BOSTON

	FG-FGA	FT-FTA	REB	ASTS	F	PTS
Howell	7-14	1-1	8	0	4	15
Havlicek	16-36	6-8	6	2	5	38
Russell	2-5	0-1	21	7	5	4
Jones, Sam	9-23	1-2	2	3	6	19
Siegfried	8-18	8-9	6	8	4	24
Sanders	0-0	0-0	1	1	2	0
Nelson	3-8	0-0	3	1	3	6
Embry	0-4	0-0	2	1	3	0
Jones, K.C.	2-4	0-0	4	1	6	4
Barnett	2-4	2-2	2	0	0	6
Totals	49-116 (.422)	18-23 (.783)	55	24	38	116

PHILADELPHIA

	FG-FGA	FT-FTA	REB	ASTS	F	PTS
Walker	9-14	8-9	12	4	0	26
Jackson	3-8	1-1	9	1	2	7
Chamberlain	10-16	9-17	36	13	1	29
Greer	12-28	8-11	2	4	2	32
Jones	10-18	3-6	2	6	5	23
Cunningham	5-12	11-12	8	2	4	21
Guokas	1-7	0-0	4	5	5	2
Totals	50-103 (.485)	40-56 (.714)	73	35	20	140

	1st	2nd	3rd	4th	Final
Boston	37	33	24	22	116
Philadelphia	26	39	35	40	140

Officials: Mendy Rudolph, Norm Drucker
Attendance: 13,007

SEVEN

The San Francisco Treat

To hear Rick Barry tell it, he could have turned Wilt Chamberlain into a good foul shooter. And, but for a swollen right ankle, he brags that he would have single-handedly beaten the 76ers in the 1967 NBA championship series.

Throughout his career, Barry was always outspoken.

And rarely outshot.

He brought that confidence, swagger, and the rest of the San Francisco Warriors with him to face the 76ers for the league title.

Barry was the focus of the 76ers' defense. Stop him and you stopped the high-scoring Warriors.

The Warriors averaged the most points of any team against the 76ers in the regular season, 126.2, beating them twice, second only to Boston's five victories. San Francisco had scored more than 140 points against the 76ers in those two wins. The Warriors won 140–127 during Philly's short February losing streak and triumphed 145–131 in the third to last game of the season. That game gave the league and its fans a preview of the probable championship series. The Warriors won the West by five games over the St. Louis Hawks, posting a fair-to-middlin' 44-37 mark (24 games below the 76ers' record) and seemed primed for the playoffs. They also knocked off the Hawks in a six-game Western Conference final series.

Barry won the league scoring title, pumping in more than 35 points per game, and snatching the crown away from the remodeled Chamberlain, who finished third behind Barry and Oscar Robertson.

It was the first time since Chamberlain entered the league in 1959 that anyone but him was the NBA's top scorer.

Barry—never gun shy— had to take lots of shots to win the honor, throwing up 2,240 field goal attempts and making 1,011 of them for a 45 percent shooting mark. He put it up from anywhere, anytime.

"Rick Barry is the toughest forward in the NBA to guard because he is in constant movement," said Billy Cunningham.

Of the scoring title, Barry said, "If [Wilt] wanted it, he could have had it."

Barry was right.

Wilt was scoring less but winning more. He took and made the fewest shots of his career in 1966–67, hitting 785 field goals out of 1,150 tries for 68 percent, his best field goal percentage ever. Just five years earlier—in the season of his 100-point game and 50.4-point scoring average—Wilt had put up 2,000 more shots and made 812 additional baskets.

He certainly was a changed man.

Because while Chamberlain "allowed" Barry to pass him by in baskets, Chamberlain was building his new reputation as the biggest and best offensive assist man ever, racking up 630 of them for third place in the league.

Then there was the little matter of free throw shooting.

Both Barry and Chamberlain used underhand foul shots.

That's where the similarity ended.

Barry rarely missed from the line, shooting 88 percent for the season. Wilt's free throw percentage was pitiably half that.

To this day, Barry says he could have helped the Dipper.

"I used to tease him," Barry recalled. "If I just could have taught him my technique. He had a terrible technique. He didn't hold the ball in the proper position—used way too much wrist. He was cocking it, snapping it," said Barry.

"I would hold the ball in the same spot, take a certain number of bounces, breaths. I would toss it very soft just to get it over the front of the rim," Rick remembered.

Ironically, the free throw professor needed some coaching of his own during the championship series, missing seven free throws in game three against the 76ers in the Cow Palace.

"Missing seven free throws in one game! Unheard of for me, unconscionable," Barry remembered later.

Perhaps Barry should have taken some advice from his coach, Bill Sharman, the best free throw man in playoff history. In more ways than one, Sharman and Barry were cut from the same mold.

Like Barry, Bill Sharman was one of the best free throw makers in the history of the NBA during his years with the Boston Celtics. Lifetime, Sharman shot 88 percent from the line, including a high point of 93 percent in 1958–59. Come playoff time, Sharman was even more deadly. He popped in 91 percent of his post-season foul shots, including a streak of 56 straight.

Like Barry, Sharman was also a player in perpetual motion, always running, always circling, leading his defender into pick after pick or leaving him behind on the floor.

Also like Barry, he was a pure shooter, leading the Celtics in scoring for four straight seasons and finishing with a career shooting mark of 43 percent.

If any coach could understand the talents of a Rick Barry, it was Sharman. He also understood that Philadelphia always fell in the playoffs, usually to Boston. Besides bringing the Celtics' fast-breaking tempo to San Francisco, he also hoped to bring along a little of the Celtics' post-season prowess.

While Philadelphia was a staunch workingman's town, San Francisco was always a trendsetter in the arts, culture, and lifestyles. For several years, it had set a fashion trend of sorts on the basketball court. The hometown gold and blue uniforms of the Warriors were far different from all the rest. They didn't have the words "San Francisco" or "Warriors" emblazoned on the front or back. That was old-fashioned.

Instead, the words were: "The City," with "The" written in script just below the right jersey strap, and "City" written underneath in larger, sleek block letters. Below the words was a large circle, enclosing the player's number and an artist's rendering of the Golden Gate Bridge. The back of the jersey depicted San Francisco's most popular attraction, a cable car, with the player's number right in the center.

Rick Barry thought "The City" logo was ill-conceived because it excluded Warriors fans outside San Francisco proper.

"It alienated people who lived in other areas," said Barry. "It didn't make sense from a marketing standpoint."

Whether the uniform was trendsetting or pretentious, it reflected perfectly the personality of the Warriors' mercurial owner, Franklin Mieuli.

A public relations man with a flair for the dramatic, Mieuli bought the Warriors a year after they moved to San Francisco from Philadelphia.

His first move was hiring Alex Hannum to coach the team and manage Wilt Chamberlain.

Early on, the strategy worked.

The Warriors went to the NBA finals in 1964, but were quickly disposed of by the Boston Celtics, 4–1.

Impatient as he was flamboyant, Mieuli made drastic changes the following year. Early that season, he traded Chamberlain back to the new 76ers franchise in Philadelphia. After two losing seasons he fired Alex Hannum in 1966.

Mieuli told a Philadelphia sportswriter,

> They ought to build a monument to me in this town. I let them have the world's greatest basketball player, and I let one of the world's best coaches go.
>
> We had won with Wilt and lost with Wilt. We were dead last in attendance. It was no fault of Wilt's.
>
> There's nothing normal about Wilt. He's an exceptional athlete, and he's different. He's not an easy guy to love. There's his facial expressions. And he had to bend down to plead with a referee. I'm not God, I can't change people.
>
> But it was a tough decision. We had a half-million dollars involved. It was drastic surgery and I knew it. Listen, I had a hard time peddling him. Wilt is an enigma. He's too good. He's too much. Amazingly, there was no reaction. Wilt had used up all his brownie points in San Francisco.
>
> Alex is something different. He's a likable guy, a good coach. His case is like Ben Franklin. If Franklin's parents hadn't come to the United States, he might have been a great man in England, but he wouldn't have played a tremendous role in their history. He came here at the right time and the right place, and he became a great man.
>
> Okay, I traded Wilt, I let Hannum go. We finished first in our division, and we outdrew Philadelphia money-wise at the gate. How dumb am I?

Chamberlain was unhappy to leave San Francisco. It had become his home. He loved the West Coast and loved San Francisco in partic- ular. Unceremoniously, Mieuli had sent him packing, for the likes of Paul Neumann, Lee Shaffer, Connie Dierking, and cash.

By now, the cash was gone and Shaffer was out of basketball. Dierking played for Cincinnati and Neumann was the only man left with the Warriors, a journeyman starter at best.

"Franklin Mieuli decided to trade Wilt over my objection," said Hannum.

"It took a lot of brass to do what he did," Chamberlain barked.

No love lost between Chamberlain and Mieuli.

Although Mieuli thought himself wise for dumping Wilt, it was Hannum, ironically, who stopped his boss from dumping potential superstar Rick Barry even before he played a game.

The Warriors drafted Barry in 1965 out of the University of Miami, but Mieuli had never seen him play. Some scouts whispered in Mieuli's ear that Barry might not make the grade in the pros. Mieuli was in the market for a starting guard, so he decided to offer Barry to the Los Angeles Lakers for Gail Goodrich. Hannum nixed it, hoping to rebuild the Warriors around the scoring ace. Mieuli went along, and Barry became the top threat to Hannum's dream of champi- onship glory with the 76ers.

Of Barry, Hannum said: "He's just the all-American boy and has everything going for him. And he's only twenty-three years old. If fel- lows like Wilt and Russell go up into one hundred thousand dollars for a salary, I think you have to start thinking about Rick like at one hundred twenty-five thousand dollars."

Of Mieuli, Hannum said: "I can't criticize his moves, because he's proven to be successful. But I was very disappointed when I left there. I worked hard with that team. I feel fortunate I found another job. The field of professional sports is a tough business. It can be very rewarding and very disappointing."

No love lost between Hannum and Mieuli.

Off-court story lines aside, the personnel matchups decidedly favored Philadelphia, even with the high-scoring Barry and 6' 11" center Nate "The Great" Thurmond, one of the only other big men in the league who could successfully work against Wilt and knew firsthand the Dipper's strengths and weaknesses.

For his part, Chamberlain billed Thurmond as a better center than Bill Russell.

The pair played together for Hannum in San Francisco for two plus seasons and forged as formidable a frontline duo as any in the league. Now, Wilt teamed with Luke Jackson, so Thurmond would have his work cut out under the boards.

His up-front help was 6' 8" Fred Hetzel, hot in the playoffs so far and carrying a 15-point scoring average against Philly; Tom Meschery, a 6' 6" jut-jawed strongman who also played a couple of years with Chamberlain on the Warriors; and 6' 10" Clyde Lee, a rookie out of Vanderbilt.

Luke Jackson, Chet Walker, and Billy Cunningham brought too much frontline strength, finesse, and speed for the Warriors to match.

In the backcourt, Duke's Jeff Mullins and Neumann both chipped in 13 points per game, and Jim King added 11. Veteran Al Attles was in reserve, and as a group they were considered one of the best guard quartets in the league.

But they would need their combined best efforts to stop Philly's guards, Greer and Jones, not to mention a quickly maturing Matty Guokas. Wally often had a hot hand against the Warriors, scoring 18 points per game against them in the regular season.

Overall, it was a simple matchup of youth versus strength.

Perhaps the biggest problem faced by the 76ers was the anticlimactic nature of this series. Despite all their efforts to remain clearly focused on the goal of the NBA title, the drubbing of Boston still seemed like the real championship.

Management had broken out the champagne after the deciding game, something usually reserved back then for winning league laurels, not just the conference crown.

That act alone indicated that beating the Warriors was already an afterthought.

"The only thing we have to fear is the lack of fear itself," worried Hannnum.

Chamberlain had raised four fingers to his teammates in the bubbly-soaked locker room as a reminder that their job was not finished. They still had to play the Warriors.

"I've been this far before, and I know we are in for a tough series. Maybe tougher," Wilt declared.

"When we were playing Boston we had to beat tradition and pride and awe for a team that had won eight straight championships. But it was a team with old legs. We just wore them down with strength.

"San Francisco doesn't have any old legs. It's a young team and a very good team. It will run your butt off and it can shoot. Just check the statistics and see how well it scored against us, and we had the second best defensive team in the league," reminded Chamberlain.

The 76ers had put on several scoring shows themselves against San Francisco in the regular season, tallying 140 and 139 in wins over the Warriors. They had netted 131 points per game against Sharman's shooters, their second highest scoring average against regular season opponents (the 76ers averaged 134 points per game against Baltimore).

"I'm sure we'll see much tougher defense in the playoffs," Hannum reasoned.

"They were so far out in front of the rest of their division in the regular season that they played more relaxed on defense. But you notice
how tough they played the 'D' against St. Louis [in the playoffs], and
they will be bearing down that much tougher against us.

"On the other hand, I know we'll play better 'D' in the playoffs. This
is what will win the games, just like it wins most big games. We
played some great defense at times against Boston, and we'll have to
be just as tough against San Francisco," said Hannum.

Philadelphia fans weren't buying it. They didn't see the Warriors as
a legitimate threat to spoil the 76ers' incredible season.

Only 9,200 fans came to the opening game at Convention Hall,
down almost 4,000 from the sellout crowd for the final playoff game
against Boston.

No matter how big the crowd was, Rick Barry wanted to spoil the
evening.

"We felt we had a chance to beat them," recalled Barry. "We were
more than they were bargaining for. We felt we had nothing to lose.
They didn't expect us to win. I went out and played as well as I could
possibly play."

On a bum right ankle at that.

Chamberlain came with a heavy chest cold.

Then the battle began.

It seemed too easy at first for Philadelphia. The 76ers shot a white-
hot 62 percent in the first quarter and raced off to a 19-point second
period lead. Visions of a sweep were already dancing through the
stands.

The 76ers saw the lead drop to eight by halftime, but they built it
back to 14 after three periods, 107–93.

Then the Warriors began the fourth quarter comeback that sent the
76ers reeling and finally brought the quiet crowd to life.

Jim King sparked the comeback with a three-point play, and veteran Tom Meschery nailed three long outside shots to cut the margin to 122–118 late in the game.

Chet Walker got the lead back up to seven with two buckets to give the 76ers a 128–121 margin.

The Warriors then added five points when Wally Jones missed a pair of shots. With the score 128–126 in favor of Philly, Chamberlain was fouled but failed to convert. Moments later, the Warriors' Jeff Mullins tied it with two free throws, and then with 28 seconds left in regulation, the Warriors had possession again.

Barry took the inbounds pass and dribbled around until seven seconds remained. Then Barry scooted toward the right baseline, flipping a backward pass to Thurmond.

Nate lurched inside toward the hoop and went for the layup.

Chamberlain went up with Thurmond and blocked the shot, sending the game into overtime.

Hannum breathed a sigh of relief. Sharman wanted a foul called.

The Warriors had outscored the 76ers 35–21 in the final quarter and out-rebounded them 30–14, as the heavy cold seemed to catch up with Wilt.

But in the extra period, the 76ers regrouped, outscoring the Warriors 13 points to seven and winning 141–135. San Francisco seemed deflated by the controversial "non-call" at the end of regulation.

"What can you say?" Sharman complained. "I can't comment on it; it would cost me five hundred dollars. We set up that last play exactly as I wanted it. We just didn't get the foul."

"He didn't get none of the ball," a dejected Thurmond told reporters. "And you don't miss layups like that."

"It wasn't a perfectly clean block," admitted Chamberlain, "but I got enough of it to keep it away from the basket."

Rick Barry put it this way, and bluntly: "I saw Wilt move to help

Chet Walker guard me, so I flipped it to Nate. The statistics show they won the game, but in my mind, we won it.

"Had we won that game, you don't know what's going on in their heads."

Despite his bad ankle, Barry popped for 37, but was guilty of gunning, putting up 43 shots and hitting just 15, including a horrendous opening quarter of three for 16. A defensive switch in the third period, when Hannum put Jackson on Barry, also limited his impact.

Chamberlain finished with 16 points, but managed 33 rebounds against Thurmond's 31. Most of Thurmond's caroms came in the second half against the wilting Wilt.

Meanwhile, Greer and Jones combined for 62 points for the 76ers, with Wally hitting 12 points out of the gate to give Philly its early lead.

"The difference is Wally Jones," Barry piped up. "But I think he's playing over his head. He's not known to shoot like that. We've got to play him honest now and that gives us trouble. Who do we put our best defensive player on, him or Greer?"

"San Francisco has shown us once more that they've got a great team, a truly great team," reminded Hannum. "I think we will concentrate on our business from here on out," referring to the potential letdown following the Boston blowout.

"We won the game and that's good," said Hal Greer. "But I'm not proud of it. If we had just played our normal game we would have won by twenty. If anybody was taking them lightly, they shouldn't be now. Once we got a big lead we let up. Maybe their catching up will be a good thing for us and make us realize that beating Boston isn't going to help us beat the Warriors."

"We didn't play as well as we should have played," added Cunningham. "They got too many easy shots in the second half and there was no reason for it. We just weren't bearing down like we did against

Boston. There was no tension in this game. We played about twenty minutes of good ball, then scrambled to pull it out."

So the 76ers had a foothold on the title series, but it was Rick Barry's ankle that was drawing most of the talk before game two.

The talk was coming from Barry and his coach.

Sharman didn't like what he saw on the stat sheet from game one.

"Look at this," he pointed out to reporters. "[Barry] made 37 points [with 15 field goals], but he took 43 shots. He's not hitting from the outside like he should. It's because he hasn't been working out. He's only been attending meetings."

Sharman wanted Barry to practice, believing the extra work would increase his overall accuracy. Barry conceded he had been off target, but he insisted that he could only practice if he subjected himself to painkilling injections.

"I got to get a treatment to work out, and I just don't want to take any shots for a workout," pleaded Barry. "Right now, I think rest will do the ankle better than working out. I don't mind the shots for a game, but not for a workout.

"It doesn't hurt me during the game. I take this stuff. I don't know what they're shooting in it. But when it wears off it hurts. I'm not shooting as well as I should from the outside. But I don't want to practice.

"I can't practice. He wants me to practice and I can't," repeated Barry.

Barry and Sharman were not only fighting the powerful 76ers, they were fighting each other before the critical second game. The Warriors had just missed stealing the series opener and had to bounce back after the controversial call and deflating loss. They could not afford to go down two games to Philly.

Sharman was floating flattery, but sounding defensive.

"We'll have to be at our very best to beat them," said Sharman. "Philly is so great. You never know who's going to pop out of nowhere and beat you. It's not like playing Los Angeles or Cincinnati. With them you work on Baylor and West, or Robertson and Lucas. Against Philly, you have to stop 'em all."

Meanwhile, the 76ers, fresh off the first game scare, came out strong, determined to crush the Warriors right away. The Convention Hall crowd was slightly bigger than the first game with more than 9,400 in the stands, but the number was still disappointing.

San Francisco came out of the gate cold, shooting 23 percent on 6-of-26 from the field in the first period. Philly wasn't much better, missing 9 of 11 before parlaying a 9-1 run into a 26–17 lead at the end of one.

Chamberlain embarrassed himself by missing 12 straight free throws, but he dominated the boards, setting a playoff record with 26 rebounds in the first half.

And despite a hard crash to the floor with Nate Thurmond as both battled for a rebound, Billy Cunningham added nine points of "instant offense" to stretch the lead to 57–46 at halftime.

With Thurmond nursing a badly bruised hip after the collision with Cunningham, Sharman teamed him with rookie big man Clyde Lee to start the third quarter. Together, they tried to neutralize Chamberlain underneath. But no matter what the Warriors did on the boards, they could not cure a plague of poor shooting.

They didn't nail a field goal until the 4:38 mark of the third quarter. At the same time, the 76ers' offense kicked in, pushing the lead to 16, 85–69, at the end of three.

With Barry hobbling around and forward Fred Hetzel also nursing his own foot injury, the Warriors could not mount a comeback.

The final was 126–95, marking only the second time all season that

San Francisco was held under 100 points. It was the 76ers' biggest win margin over the Warriors, topping a 29-point spread in a late season contest.

While recognizing the Warriors' physical limitations in this game, Alex Hannum gave the 76ers' defense most of the credit for holding down Barry and company.

"We played our best defense, maybe our best of the year," Hannum said after the game. "We were active out there, and the Warriors had a tough time getting the shots they wanted.

"I'm extremely happy with the way we played. Holding them under one hundred points is really a feat. But, in all fairness, I'd have to say Hetzel and Thurmond were bothered by those injuries, and Barry was nursing his sore ankle. I know the guy, and I know how he plays when he's healthy."

"Weak shooting and rebounding beat us," said Bill Sharman in his post-game comments. "That's the second time this season we failed to hit a hundred, and I'm pretty sure our percentage from the floor is our worst."

He was dead-on.

The Warriors shot 38 of 129 from the field for a paltry 29.5 percent.

Barry's percentage was way off again, too. He fired 28 times but connected on only 10, finishing with 30 to lead his club.

"What were the rebounds?" Sharman asked out loud. Grabbing a score sheet, he said, "See, 101 to 83, that was like giving them 18 more shots. You simply can't do that. Rebounding is like pitching in baseball. 75 to 80 percent of the game. And the 76ers had it today."

Chamberlain had the rebounding locked, corralling 38, but he really could have used that advice from Barry at the free throw line. Wilt was a miserable 2-for-17 from the stripe and netted only 10 points for the game. Greer had 30 and Cunningham 28 to pick up the slack.

"We beat them every way you can beat a team," bragged Greer. "It was kinda brutal, the way we waded through them."

Cunningham chose to put it another way.

"We played *great* defense," said Billy. "We worked hard out there to keep them from getting the shots they wanted to take. We would work hard outside, force them inside, and then Wilt would just smother the play."

The blowout was so bad, even little-used, late-season add Bob Weiss came off the 76ers bench to contribute 4 points late in the game.

Hannum didn't want to hear about blowouts. With the series moving to San Francisco, the 76ers' coach was not about to belittle the Warriors and give them fodder for the locker-room bulletin board.

"When we get out there, with that home crowd, we can expect some fine games," Hannum cautioned.

But down deep, with the 76ers seemingly back on their game and the Warriors struggling with injuries and a coach–superstar controversy, Hannum and his guys seemed ready to ride a cable car in for the kill.

Game three was center stall at the Cow Palace, and Warriors boss Franklin Mieuli took the occasion to rub Philly's nose into the manure just a little bit.

In a pre-game ceremony, he paraded out Philadelphia's very own, now-transplanted basketball guru Eddie Gottlieb to present the "Gottlieb Award" to Rick Barry as the Warriors' Most Valuable Player. The man who moved *Philadelphia's* Warriors west to the Golden Gate in 1962 and took a management position with the team was clearly the enemy now, even though he helped broker the deal to bring basketball back to Philadelphia by way of Syracuse.

The festivities must have made Chamberlain grimace a bit, after

Mieuli's blatant refusal to allow the presentation of Wilt's MVP award at the NBA All-Star Game in San Francisco back in January.

Barry, the trophy in his arms and his foot filled with painkiller, gingerly took the court for the opening tip with the other walking wounded, Thurmond and Hetzel.

But then he bolted like an angry steer from a Cow Palace chute.

He poured in the first seven points for the Warriors and ran up 17 in the first period. But Billy Cunningham scored in a flurry to keep the 76ers in front after one, 35–32. It was going to be a shoot-out.

Both teams scored 10-point runs during the second period, but Barry ended the period with a five-point spurt to spark the Warriors to a 69–63 halftime lead. The Warriors were doing it under the boards, too, running up a 47–30 edge in first-half rebounds.

As the third quarter started, the Warriors picked up the offense where they left off, streaking for eight straight points and pushing San Fran to a 77–63 bulge. Barry kept bombing and rolled up a staggering 55 points by game's end, just five short of Elgin Baylor's playoff scoring record of 61, set five years earlier. His 48 field goal attempts equaled Chamberlain's post-season mark, also set in 1962.

Wilt was second-guessing himself after Barry's performance.

"I tried as hard as I could," pleaded Chamberlain, "but now that I look back there were things I could have done that I didn't. Maybe they wouldn't have worked out any better, but again, maybe they would."

Barry got too many uncontested jumpers when Chamberlain stayed under the basket to protect against Barry's drives, rather than jumping out on the switch when Nate Thurmond picked Barry's prime defender, Chet Walker. Wilt was also a bit unhappy with his statistical effort against the Warriors. His scoring average was down four points from the Boston series, his assists were off two. He was holding his own in rebounds, still averaging 32 rebounds for the two series. Free throw shooting was killing Wilt and the 76ers. In the three games, he had been to the line 35 times, making only eight of them for a 23 percent average.

Meanwhile, Barry was livid over his performance at the foul line in game three. This was the game in which he missed those "unheard of" 7 of 18 attempts.

The 76ers came back to make a game of it, but the final was 130–124 San Francisco, cutting the 76ers' series lead to 2–1.

There would be no sweep. There would be a fifth game back in Philly.

But the question was, would the 76ers come home with the series tied or jump to a 3–1 lead, poised to win it all in front of the home fans?

San Francisco's home fans spilled over from the sold-out Cow Palace (with a record attendance of 15,117) and packed a downtown closed-circuit venue, paying $3.50 per person to watch game four. It was another Mieuli marketing ploy to milk a little more money out of the championship series. But no matter where Warrior fans were watching, they went home unhappy.

Barry came out gunning again but this time Wally Jones was there for the 76ers to match him—shot for shot. Philly jumped to a 34–27 lead after one, riding Jones's hot hand. He scored all of his 14 points in the opening 12 minutes of play, besting Barry's 13.

"I really felt ready to gig, to smoke, out there," Wally offered later in his usual hip, energetic style. "And then I go and twist my ankle and wind up sitting on the bench while Hal and Chet [who popped 14 of his 33 points during a pivotal stretch] get all the glory."

The 76ers engineered an 18-2 run in the second quarter and held on to an 11-point bulge at the half, 60–49. They capitalized on Hal Greer's firepower and rookie Matty Guokas's pinpoint passing and harassing defense against Barry.

Greer took command in the middle section of the game, scoring 29 of his 38 points to keep things out of reach. Greer pumped out 35 shots overall, hitting 15 for 42 percent, comparable to Barry's 17 of 41 for 39 percent and 43 points. The field goal percentage for the rest of the Warriors was equally bad, with Thurmond going 4 of 18, Mullins 6 of 15, Jim King 9 of 20, and Clyde Lee 5 of 14.

The final was 122–108 in favor of the 76ers.

"We knew we had to have this one," Greer declared. "If we had lost it would have been all even, and we didn't want that. So we just went out there and worked our butts off and got ourselves a win."

Despite Greer's heroics, Warriors coach Bill Sharman cited his club's poor shooting and Wilt Chamberlain's play as reasons for the loss.

"I honestly haven't seen Wilt play that well in my life," said Sharman. "There were times there when he wouldn't let us get the ball near the basket. He had to block at least fifteen shots, and goodness only knows how many others he kept out by forcing us to take the shots we didn't want to take."

Chamberlain's numbers were not impressive by Wilt's own standards. He finished with a mere 10 points, taking just six shots from the floor and making only three. He dipped below .500 as usual from the free throw line with a 4-for-9 effort. His rebounds were strong with 27, but his overall presence clogging up the middle made the big difference.

Sharman was chagrined over his team's offense, which clicked for only 35 percent from the floor and an uncharacteristically weak 60 percent from the free throw line.

"Nobody can beat Philly shooting that poorly," whined Sharman. "This is one of the all-time greatest teams, probably the greatest, and you've got to be almost perfect if you hope to beat them."

Barry's shortcomings from the floor caught the attention of *Sports Illustrated*'s Frank DeFord.

DeFord kept a running count of Barry's work from press row, concluding that the shooting star touched the ball 59 times on offense during the game. The sideline scrutiny showed that when Barry had the ball, he either shot it, was fouled, or lost possession on his own. Simply translated, that meant he had passed the ball a grand total of 11 times the entire 48 minutes.

Hannum wasn't taking the bait when asked afterwards about Barry's ball hogging.

Instead, he changed the subject and played it safe again.

"I know San Francisco is going to come back stronger and tougher than ever," said Hannum. "We can expect all we can handle Sunday."

He must have been using a crystal ball.

The two teams boarded the same plane for the journey back to the City of Brotherly Love and a Sunday date in front of a national television audience.

Hannum hoped the next time he saw "The City" would be during an off-season vacation trip.

It turned out to be a whole lot sooner than that.

As the potential championship-clinching fifth game neared, some of Philadelphia's sports pages turned into obituary columns, noting the imminent demise of the weary Warriors.

"Burial arrangements are scheduled for the Philadelphia Convention Hall chapel with Wilt Chamberlain and Hal Greer and a handful of other powerful, talented gentlemen acting as pallbearers," wrote Jack Kiser in the *Daily News*.

"Warrior coach Bill Sharman isn't about to pronounce his team a corpse, not in public anyway, but he knows he'll need more than a few minor miracles to pump plasma back into the tired, wounded body."

The 76ers seemed on target to end it, and the NBA wanted to proclaim this powerful team champion, perhaps even successor to the Celtics dynasty, on ABC-TV's *Game of the Week*.

There was extra incentive for Hannum's heroes to take it in five games. They were scheduled to leave early in the week for a three-day vacation/celebration trip to the Bahamas. A flight back to San Francisco would delay the revelry.

Besides winning his first league title, Chamberlain also wanted it over early for another reason. After the Bahamas, he was headed for Italy that Friday to join his old team, the Harlem Globetrotters, for an exhibition tour.

Even the wounded Larry Costello, who had been riddled all season with injuries, told Hannum he would play if needed.

Whatever it took.

The champagne was on ice in the locker room and at a nearby Walnut Street restaurant.

Everybody wanted to end it then and there.

"We just thought we were gonna do it," remembered Matty Guokas. "Nobody brought clothes to travel."

That was their first mistake.

The Philadelphia faithful responded better for this big game. A total of 10,229 poured into Convention Hall, but again the figure fell significantly below the Boston numbers.

The Warriors showed some defense early and jumped out to a 9–6 lead after the opening tap, but then the 76ers got going. A couple of buckets by Wally Jones put them on top 24–19 midway through the quarter. Barry followed later with a burst, and the 76ers led by only two, 32–30, at quarter's end.

Philly's Chet Walker was the main man in period two.

He kept muscling and maneuvering for good shots, and the Warriors kept fouling him to make sure he didn't get any. What he got was 16 free throws in the quarter, making 13 of them, including five straight to up the 76ers' lead to 49–43. By halftime, however, the Warriors had come back to within three, at 64–61.

In the third quarter, the 76ers took command and all signs pointed to a home court presentation of the Podoloff championship trophy, named after former NBA commissioner Maurice Podoloff.

Luke Jackson pounded the boards for 14 rebounds in the third, and the Warriors stayed cold. Barry scored only one basket after knocking in 25 points in the first half. Sharman even benched his star for several minutes, and the two had words. While the petulant Barry pouted, foul shots by Cunningham and Walker punched the lead to 94–81, the biggest bulge of the ball game for the 76ers.

As the fourth stanza started, the score stood 96–84 for the 76ers. They were 12 minutes away from ending this long, record-shattering season.

But in an instant, the 76ers shut down and a wily Warrior veteran cranked up.

While Philadelphia missed 14 of 17 shots and sloppily threw the ball away nine times in the fourth quarter, Tom Meschery took over, despite playing with five personal fouls.

Six minutes flew by and Meschery hit for 11 big points, bringing the Warriors back into the game. He finally fouled out with four minutes left, and the score tied 102–102 on a Barry 15-foot jumper. The damage had been done.

A five-minute Philly scoring drought ended with a Greer side jumper at the 3:06 mark, giving the 76ers a new lead at 105–103.

Jim King answered for San Francisco to tie it.

Again the 76ers went to Greer, who was shadowed closely by the scrappy King. Hal made his move past King, but referee Mendy Rudolph whistled Greer for charging. Greer went ballistic, and Rudolph was having none of it.

Mendy blew a technical foul on Greer, and it became a turning point.

Free throw deadeye Rick Barry converted the "T," giving San Fran the lead—a lead it would never relinquish.

After Thurmond and Greer exchanged free throws, Jim King popped a jumper that missed, but the Warriors' Thurmond was there for the most critical of his game-high 28 rebounds, and he sent it back out to Barry.

The Warriors ran a clear-out, and Barry drove the lane for a left-handed layup. It went in, and he was fouled in the act. The three-point play put San Fran up 110–106.

With just under two minutes left, the 76ers turned to Greer yet again and the "Bulldog" went right baseline looking for a bucket. He crashed into Clyde Lee, and once again ref Rudolph whistled another charging call on the frustrated Greer.

Eggs started pouring out of the balcony, splattering onto the court and halting play.

But the Warriors kept cooking, and after Greer fouled out and Chamberlain muffed two foul shots, Barry bombed in a long corner jumper.

The matter was decided.

The final was 117–109. The 76ers scored only 13 points in the final period to 33 for the Warriors, and they committed nine turnovers. "The City" boys had pulled a major upset, sending the 3–2 series back across country for game six, to be played in less than 24 hours.

"Meschery was the man who killed us," admitted Hannum. "We weren't working on him, especially after the fifth foul. We were setting up plays for Greer so the Warriors wouldn't have a chance to keep fouling Wilt."

Considering Chamberlain's 2-for-12 performance at the foul line, the strategy was right. Even Wilt grudgingly agreed when asked if he should have gotten the ball inside more during the final quarter.

"I think so," Wilt conceded slightly. "But we were working outside plays, which have been working all year, and you can't second-guess what's going on out there."

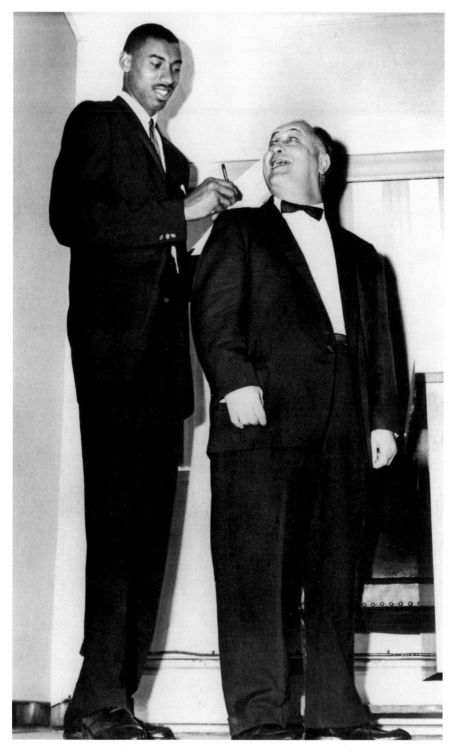

This could be the start of something big! In May 1959, Wilt Chamberlain signs his first NBA contract on the back of Philadelphia Warriors owner Eddie Gottleib. Three years later, Gottleib moved Wilt and the Warriors to San Francisco, paving the way for the new 76ers franchise.

76ers co-owners Ike Richman (*left*) and Irv Kosloff (*right*) flank Walter Stahlberg, the New Jersey man who won a contest to name the team (August 1963).

Fresh from a gold medal–winning performance with the U.S. basketball team in the 1964 Olympics in Tokyo, Luke Jackson signs his first Philadelphia contract with 76ers co-owner Ike Richman.

Dolph Schayes, the great star of the Syracuse Nationals turned first coach of the 76ers, talks with newly acquired Wilt Chamberlain in January 1965. Wilt's close friend Vince Miller called the relationship between Schayes and Chamberlain "rotten." Schayes was fired after losing to the Boston Celtics in the 1966 playoffs.

Wilt gets a breather next to Coach Alex Hannum after suffering a minor eye injury and hurting his right knee in the season opening win over the New York Knicks in October 1966. Rookies Matt Guokas and Bill Melchionni (*right*) hope to see some action.

Wally "Wonder" Jones does his usual aggressive and harassing defensive job against Dick Barnett of the Knicks in January 1967.

Forward Chet Walker in a familiar role, working for a shot one-on-one against Walt Hazzard of the L.A. Lakers, the man who helped his best friend Wally Jones return to basketball with the 76ers.

The greatest rivalry in professional basketball history in full display as Chamberlain stuffs one over Boston's Bill Russell in a 1967 regular season game. By season's end, Wilt would have his first title, finally destroying the Celtics and his longtime adversary in the playoffs.

Matchmakers wanted Wilt to take on the then Cassius Clay for the heavyweight boxing championship of the world. Wilt thought he could beat anybody at anything, but the champ's draft difficulties with Uncle Sam stopped the title fight before the big payday could be arranged. This publicity shot was the closest the two titans got to each other.

Luke Jackson, the NBA's first true power forward, demonstrates his force by pulling down a rebound against Leroy Ellis of the Baltimore Bullets in March 1967.

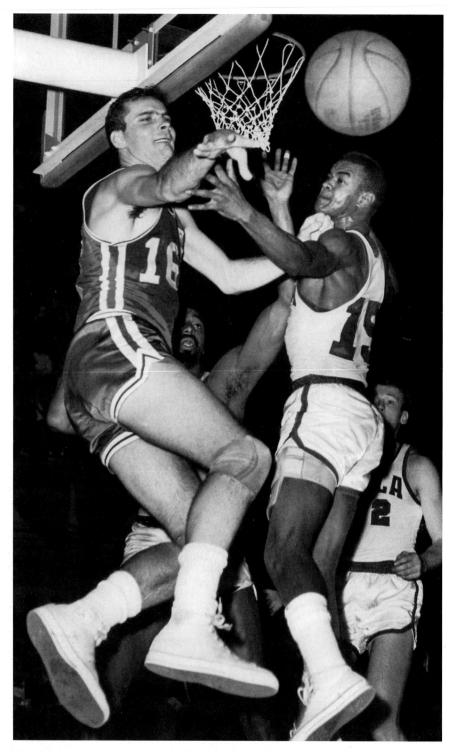

Usually a major force on offense, 76ers star guard Hal Greer takes one on the chin try-ing to defend Cincinnati Royals strongman Jerry Lucas in a March 1967 contest.

"Instant Offense" Billy Cunningham looks for room against Chicago's McCoy McLemore in a 14–point win for the 76ers in December 1966.

The fiery "Sarge," Alex Hannum, barks orders to his team as they go on to crush the Celtics in their Eastern playoff finale, 140–116, on April 11, 1967.

With a victory over the Celtics well in hand, Hannum and Wilt share a quiet moment just before the 76ers clinch the playoff series against Boston and move on to meet the San Francisco Warriors.

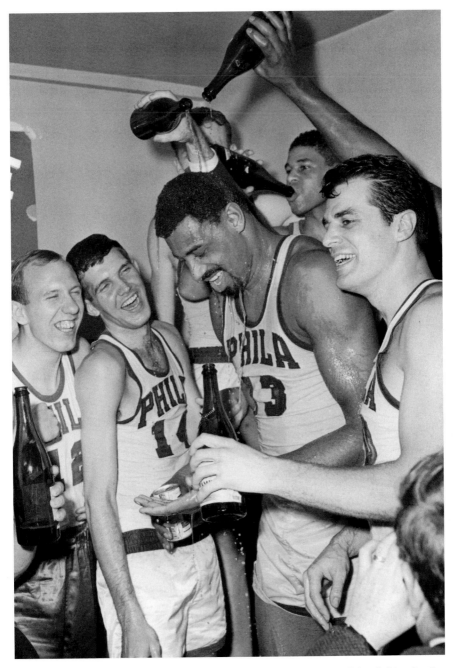

The champagne flowed in the 76ers locker room after they defeated the Celtics for the Eastern Conference championship, but Wilt warned everyone that there were four more wins to get against Rick Barry and the dangerous San Francisco Warriors before they could be called world champions. *Photo courtesy of AP Wide World*

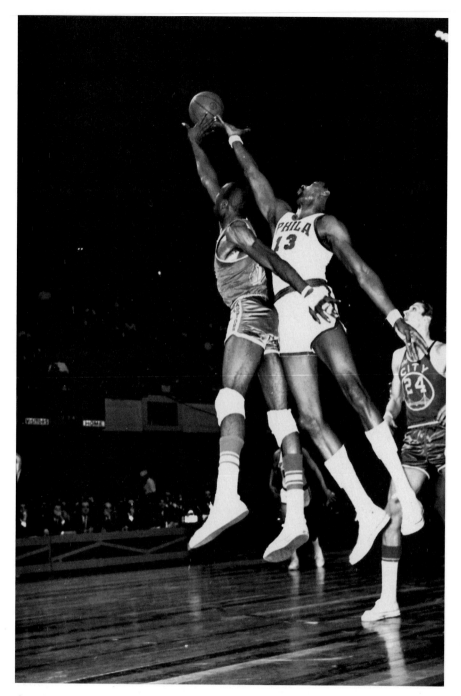

One-time teammates Chamberlain and the Warriors' Nate "The Great" Thurmond battle for a rebound in the opening game of the NBA championship series in April 1967. The 76ers won 141–135 in overtime at Convention Hall.

It was a constant battle between Billy Cunningham of the 76ers and the Warriors' Rick Barry during the championship series. Billy called Barry the toughest forward to guard in the league because he was in perpetual motion. Barry complained that an injured ankle kept him off his game and prevented the Warriors from upsetting the 76ers in the finals.

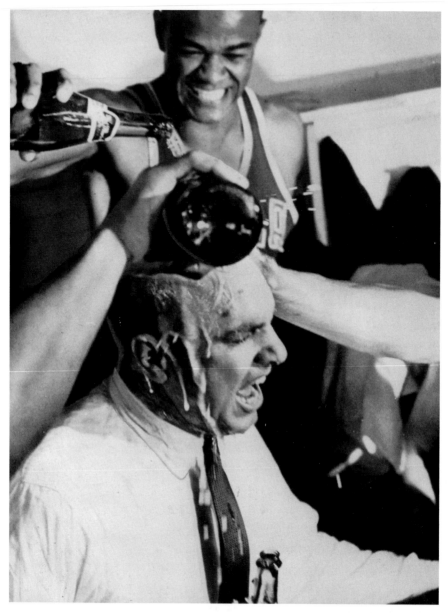

Hal Greer douses Alex Hannum with the bubbly in San Francisco after the 76ers slipped by the Warriors 125–122 in game six of the finals to win their first NBA title. *Photo courtesy of AP Wide World*

Everyone is all smiles in October 1967, when Wilt Chamberlain finally signs a new contract with the 76ers. But after another playoff loss to the Celtics, the 76ers' short reign was over. Hannum resigned to pursue opportunities in the American Basketball Association and return to the West Coast. Wilt initially made noises to Ramsay about being player-coach but later told Ramsay he wanted to be traded. Ramsay dealt Wilt to the Lakers, and took the coaching reins himself. Owner Irv Kosloff was glad to get the high-priced Chamberlain off the payroll.

Wilt, wearing a warmup jacket from his alma mater, Philadelphia's Overbrook High School, greets his old boyhood teammates at the Spectrum in 1980, when the NBA honored the 1967 76ers as its best team ever. Vince Miller, Chamberlain's closest friend over the years and also an Overbrook alum, is to Wilt's left.

The official team photo of the 1966–67 World Champion Philadelphia 76ers. *Photo courtesy of the Philadelphia 76ers*

Wally Jones had a particularly tough fourth quarter, missing six shots and opening the door for the Warriors' comeback.

"Our 12-point lead [after three quarters] was a good one," Hannum recounted, "but not commanding. You have to give the Warriors credit. They played good defense in the last period.

"Some of our key players got tired. We lost our drive. We lost the defensive rebounding that forms the fast break. We got a little cautious.

"The thing I remember most is the series of calls involving Rudolph and Greer. Whether Hal was at fault for chipping away, or the official at fault for listening, I can't say.

"The two maddest men on the court were Greer and Rudolph. A technical makes me mad, because I hate to see funny, outside things decide the outcome of a game."

"The technical was the turning point of the game," said Greer. "Sometimes you have to think of what you're doing. Other times it just comes out of your mouth. I just blew my top. All I said was, 'We're not playing Boston, Mendy.' "

Wally Jones was way down and Chamberlain saw it. The next day he went to Hannum about it.

"I don't care what happened . . . Don't let that Wally Jones get down on himself. We need him too much," Wilt exhorted Alex.

Alex told Wally, "Forget last night. Out here I want you to shoot every time you've got the shot. Don't even think about it. Just shoot."

The champagne would have to wait. The 76ers had blown their chance to win it all at home, and *Daily News* sports columnist Stan Hochman let them have it:

> The world's greatest basketball team blitzed into the final
> quarter leading by 12 points. Then the world's greatest basket-
> ball team scored three field goals in 12 minutes. Mainly

because TWGBT plodded up and down the court like five kids carrying buckets of sand to a schoolhouse fire.

The Warriors beat TWGBT and afterwards somebody covered the champagne like a corpse. The players trudged through the locker-room litter, getting ready for another long plane ride. They did it mechanically, with empty-eyed sloth. They had packed for long plane rides before. They had never celebrated an NBA championship before.

In fact, that whole idea of packing caused real headaches for the 76ers.

"We had to scramble to catch a six o'clock flight," said Matty Guokas. "We barely talked to the media. We drove home and got some clothes and just made the flight."

"I vividly remember making an announcement at the shoot-around before game five," recalled trainer Al Domenico. "'Make sure you bring your luggage to the game!'

"I caught so much stuff. The players yelled, 'They have no chance.' Only one brought a suitcase, me!"

"I went down to Convention Hall without a suitcase," remembered Andy Musser, then 76ers radio play-by-play man. "Called my wife, had her pack something quickly, and bring it down. I didn't have a ticket, so I bought my own for about three hundred dollars, and I've never been reimbursed," Musser chuckled.

Greer forgot his overcoat, Hannum failed to pack a belt but got an extra from Billy Cunningham, and even traveling guru Al Domenico left his sneakers behind in the frenzy, borrowing a pair later at the arena from the San Francisco trainer.

When the unexpected and unwelcome flight touched down in San Francisco, the players deplaned, weary and still stunned by Sunday's surreal turn of events in Philadelphia.

They were quickly jolted back into reality when a few of the players picked up copies of a San Francisco morning newspaper.

"And then they choked," blared the words written by a local columnist, referring to the 76ers' fade in Sunday's fourth period.

Now the players weren't just tired and cranky. Those words made them angry.

They jumped into rental cars and headed for a downtown hotel to try to get some rest before the Monday night game.

It was bad enough that the 76ers had to return to "The City" for a sixth contest. Even worse was the fact that there would be no day off to recuperate from the coast-to-coast flight. It was something the NBA would never allow now. There has to be time to promote and market a critical game in today's media world. But back then, the teams plugged ahead as scheduled.

Hal Greer echoed the sentiments of all the players as he stood in front of the hotel entrance looking around at the San Fran skyline and the mountains beyond.

"Ain't this a kick in the head. What in the hell are we doing here?"

Hours later, when they arrived at the Cow Palace, they made sure to remind themselves that they were there to finish the Warriors off, once and for all.

Once in the locker room, those four little words were written on the blackboard:

AND THEN THEY CHOKED.

If the 76ers needed motivation, they had found it.

The Cow Palace was crammed with 15,612 screamers, with another 4,500 watching again from the closed-circuit venue downtown. A late-night television audience in Philly watched on WPHL, Channel 17, with Al Meltzer and Charlie Swift at the microphones, even though Meltzer wasn't so sure there was enough interest in the series for the fans to justify missing sleep.

"People didn't follow it, know about it, or care about it," recalled Meltzer in a 1999 interview on the 76ers–Warriors title series.

If both teams were tired from the long journey and quick turn-around, it didn't show in the opening 12 minutes. Perhaps operating on adrenaline and excitement, the teams set a playoff record for scoring in a quarter—84. The 76ers led 43–41 after one.

Chamberlain tried to take the scoring burden on his shoulders from the outset, but Nate Thurmond was pushing him hard defensively, frustrating Wilt by forcing him away from the basket for fade-aways.

In the second period, Warrior Jeff Mullins got untracked after a so-so series and pumped in 11 points to propel San Francisco to a 72–68 halftime lead.

Meanwhile, Chamberlain, not to be outdone, used his power and force of will to manage 17 first-half points against his old teammate Thurmond. In the locker room later, Wilt said, "I felt much better being four down at the half than being four up. We play better coming from behind than from in front."

But when the third period opened, the Warriors got an early jump. Guard Jim King, who hit on two key baskets in the late stages of the first half, popped in another two-pointer right away. After a Thurmond free throw, the Warriors extended the lead to 75–68, their biggest margin of the game.

Then the two teams traded baskets for several minutes, before the Warriors got a quick run. Al Attles fed Fred Hetzel for a bucket, and Thurmond tipped in a Barry shot.

Then, when Chamberlain got nailed for a charging violation while taking a fadeaway jumper, Hannum hit the ceiling and the 76ers seemed in trouble.

Free throws were actually keeping the 76ers in the game. With over six minutes gone in the third quarter, the 76ers had been to the line 41 times, making 26. Conversely, the Warriors had made only 14 trips, canning 12.

But San Francisco was pumping in field goals. Barry hit a pair, pushing the lead to 90–80.

Chet Walker retaliated for the 76ers, but a Jim King steal led to a Mullins stuff, and King himself knocked one in off a rebound to up the lead to 94–82.

Just when it seemed like the 76ers were weakening, they got hot as the Warriors went cold. Philly went on an 11-2 spurt to quickly drive back into the game. Cunningham ended the period with two more free throws, and the 76ers had cut the lead to a manageable distance, 102–97.

But the 76ers still seemed to be struggling, and needed a spark to carry them through the pivotal fourth period. Just as he had ignited a major rally for the 76ers in game four at Boston, rookie Matty Guokas again answered the call.

With about 10 minutes left, the Warriors up by four, and Barry on the bench, Gook got offensive-minded.

First, he launched a long jumper that hit nothing but net. Seconds later, he flew by Thurmond for a high-speed layup that sent the ball through the hoop and Matty into the padded support. He hit with such impact that he had to be helped back to the bench. But he had done his job. His back-to-back baskets had tied the game.

"Once Gook got those two baskets I knew we were ready to take it all," Chamberlain said later.

And ready they were. The "momentum" had shifted.

Chamberlain got charged up under the boards, and the offense got going again.

Chet Walker left Clyde Lee in the dust for a bucket to put the 76ers up 108–106. Then Cunningham caught fire, adding six points to build the 76ers' bulge to 114–109 with just over six minutes to go.

The Warriors wouldn't fold.

Baskets by Barry and Mullins cut the lead to one, and Barry had the ball again.

Luke Jackson chased him but got caught up in traffic as Barry dribbled away. Chamberlain, who was out on top guarding Thurmond in the high post, switched with Jackson, as Thurmond took Jackson down inside. That left Chamberlain between the foul line and the outer foul circle, eyeing Barry, who bounced the ball and looked for daylight.

Suddenly, Barry broke to his left, as forward Tom Meschery angled out to set a pick on Wilt.

It worked.

Barry got a split-second of daylight as Chet Walker came off the switch and tried to get to Rick.

Too late, as Barry poured in a 17-footer and the Warriors were back on top 115–114.

Chamberlain was fouled on the next play, but just when everyone thought Wilt would botch the free throws, he came through, swishing them both to ease the 76ers ahead again, 116–115.

Moments later, another foul was called, this one on Tom Meschery. Luke Jackson strode to the line.

Jackson missed, but Chamberlain was right there for the critical carom. He stuffed it down with a patented "Dipper Dunk." The 76ers were up by three, 118–115.

The lead moved to 122–116 with 2:16 to play, and the 76ers seemed in control. But Jim King nailed a jumper, and Barry parlayed a Thurmond-blocked shot into a fast-break layup.

It was 122–120.

Cunningham converted a free throw, but Barry added two of his own, making it 123–122 with just 46 seconds on the clock.

Then the 76ers got too cautious and made a critical mistake. Trying to guard the one-point lead and run as much time as possible, they failed to get a good shot or even get to the line.

The 24-second clock expired.

The Warriors had the ball back with 15 seconds.

San Francisco decided to go to the well once more, drawing up the play that almost won the first contest in regulation.

It would be a two-man game: Barry the Brash teaming with Nate the Great.

Mullins took the ball out at mid-court and got it into Barry, who worked against Walker at the right sideline.

Thurmond immediately moved out to lay a pick on Walker, and Wilt moved out with him to help.

Instantly, Barry changed direction, using a left-handed dribble and heading toward the right lane line.

Wilt and Chet approached him as Barry spotted Thurmond open, floating back from the pick toward the basket.

Barry went up at the right foul line extended, prepared to pass to Nate. But Wilt closed the gap quickly, and Barry had to change his mind in midair, forcing up a shot from his right hip that missed.

"I got a lotta help from Chamberlain," Walker said later, "and between the both of us, we were able to stop him, and we managed to force him into a bad shot."

Barry saw it as all Chamberlain's doing.

"Wilt took the biggest step I ever saw a human being take and closed off the passing lane," remembered Barry.

Jackson went up for the rebound and fell to the floor fighting for it with Jim King.

Referee Earl Strom called a jump ball and the two lined up in the Warriors' offensive circle, the 6' 9" Jackson against the 6' 2" King. There was no doubt who had the height advantage on the critical jump.

Hannum called time.

Sharman pulled a trick.

He ordered 6' 6" Tom Meschery into the game, and the tough forward nonchalantly walked into the circle to face Jackson. The 76ers screamed at the change, but the referees apparently weren't listening.

They mistakenly let Meschery replace King, and the Warriors picked up four vital inches on the sneaky switch.

Jackson's job would be much tougher now against the rugged veteran Meschery, who had been a thorn in the 76ers' side in the game five upset.

Luke leaped as high as his legs could take him, winning the tip by batting it backward toward Chet Walker.

With just four ticks on the clock, Thurmond wrapped up Walker immediately. Fouled in the backcourt, Walker got two free throws.

In his usual free and easy style, Chet chucked them both up and in. The 76ers had made 41 of an amazing 64 attempts to San Francisco's 22 of 29. It turned out to be the difference in the game.

Before the Warriors could react, the buzzer went off, and the 76ers had won it all.

They took the Warriors 125–122, winning the series in six games.

The 76ers were world champions.

Billy and Chet were the first to hug. Wilt ran in from under the basket to join them. Trainer Al Domenico and sub Dave Gambee led the bench contingent onto the floor. Wally Jones tried to jump on top.

"We choked, huh?" the usually quiet Walker shouted at the San Francisco sportswriters in the jubilant locker room after clinching the game with his free throws in a 20-point effort. "Well, we came three thousand miles to show the world that we don't choke. We're champions, baby, and champions don't choke."

At that moment, a member of the 76ers' traveling party congratulated the writer for inspiring the team with the phrase in the morning newspaper. The writer protested that the line was changed to "And then they died" for later editions. But that was too late to stop the fire it started in the 76ers.

After the series was over—and to this day—Rick Barry insists that the results would have been different if he had been healthy.

"It was discouraging not to be one hundred percent, not to be able to play my best basketball," Barry lamented. He scored 44 in the final game and averaged 40.8 per game for the series.

"The Sunday flight [and Monday game] was to their advantage. I had less time to rest and get the ankle treated. I hit 16 of 38 in the final game. Twenty of 38 is more like where I should have been."

"Gook, Gook," Chamberlain screamed, pointing to the rookie Guokas. He had guarded Barry fiercely in the final game and helped with nine points, including the two big, consecutive baskets to tie it late.

"The rook showed us how. He showed us he has the championship guts when he hit that bomb from outside, then drove past Nate for that layup. We just couldn't let that kind of thing go to waste."

Billy Cunningham, who scored 11 of his 17 points in the crucial final period, went from swigging celebratory champagne to throwing it back up.

"All of a sudden I got sick," said Billy. "The emotion was just too much. It just hit me that this was it, the championship. And all of a sudden my stomach started turning over."

"We finally did it, we *all* did it," bellowed Luke Jackson, nursing a battle scar above his eyebrow suffered in a skirmish under the boards. "And I couldn't feel better."

Ditto from a quiet Hal Greer, who chipped in 15 points.

"I couldn't feel better."

"Never in doubt," bragged Wally Jones, who once again proved Rick Barry right when he said earlier in the series that Jones was a big difference for the 76ers.

"We had them all the way," Jones said triumphantly, after leading the 76ers in scoring with 27 clutch, final game points. Hannum's encouragement to keep shooting despite a bad stretch in game five had paid off.

"The whole season was just magical, something where a team played almost perfect basketball," said Jones.

"We did it the hard way. We did it on the road," added Chet Walker. "It's a great thing to be world champs because you're not only the best basketball team in the United States, you're the best basketball team in the whole world, and that includes Russia and China and every place. It's a great feeling. Nothing could compare with it."

"It's not easily done," added GM Jack Ramsay. "It's a rigorous schedule. The playoffs are hard fought, and the best team does win this. We were the best team, and we won."

And what about Chamberlain, his loser label finally shed.

"How does it feel after all these years of being tagged a loser?" Wilt wondered out loud. "A little bit of joy tomorrow, a little bit the next day, and so on. It's plenty enough to last me the whole summer," Wilt said. The Dipper had scored 24 in the final game and pulled down 23 rebounds.

Years later, Wilt had this to say about his world champion 76ers: "I know that nobody could beat that team. Just nobody. We played as a team, we had all the qualifications of a basketball team in the way of size, ability, and thinking. There have been smarter teams. The New York Knicks of the early seventies I think was one of the smartest teams that I've run across. The Boston Celtics were smart and good, but sometimes you need a little bit more than just being smart, and we had all of that."

"I honestly don't know when I've been more happy," crowed the joyous Alex Hannum. Later, he added, "It's something you can't put into words. We knew we could do it. We knew we wanted to do it. We felt that this was the year we were going to do it. This is the greatest team ever assembled."

The party lasted all night long, moving from the locker room to the hotel bar, shifting to Nate Thurmond's downtown nightclub and an all-night restaurant.

Jones and Cunningham left together.

"After we won it, Wally and I got into a rental car to head back to the hotel," remembered Cunningham. "There was heavy traffic and we were sitting in the car, and I guess it was such a relief, we started talking about religion. Wally was at that time thinking of the Muslim religion and I was a Roman Catholic and we were discussing our beliefs!"

"We were talking about religion and people," added Jones. "Talking about the gifts the Creator gave us."

When Hannum arrived at the hotel, he circled the room, individually congratulating his men.

"We made it, baby, we made it," he yelled, stopping once to plant a kiss on the head of an ecstatic Hal Greer.

Ramsay and Guokas were firmly ensconced at the bar. They toasted and talked about how the Warriors had sneaked Meschery in for the jump ball at the end.

"That's the old Villanova trick," laughed Ramsay and Guokas, both St. Joe's guys. They made sure 'Nova's Wally Jones couldn't hear.

Cries went up from players and onlookers alike for a few words from the coach.

"Here is my one and only speech," said Hannum, brandishing a basketball.

"This is the ball that won us the world championship tonight. Everybody has signed it, and now I'm going to present it to a guy who has given of himself all year so we all could get to this moment. Take it, Wilt."

Wilt took it, but he had other plans for it.

"Without a doubt, I definitely consider this a great honor," said the happy Chamberlain. "But I'm going to present the ball to Mrs. Ike Richman, in honor of the late Ike Richman, who is somebody I think you'll all agree deserves this."

His teammates applauded.

"If it weren't for Ike Richman, Wilt never would have signed," said Hannum.

The celebration lasted until it was just about time to board the plane back home at 8:30 A.M.

Wilt walked proudly through San Francisco International Airport, coat in one hand, game ball in the other.

"He's got to be the happiest guy in the world right now," said Hannum.

Then, 35,000 feet high, the 76ers did a little business.

The treasure chest was filled to the brim with the spoils from finishing first in the Eastern Division ($17,500), having the best winning percentage in either division ($5,000), beating Cincinnati in the playoff first round ($10,000), topping Boston in round two ($20,000), and besting the Warriors ($35,000).

The team sat down in the sky lounge of United Airlines Flight 60, somewhere over the Nevada desert, to divvy it up. The total was $87,500, and 12 full shares of $7,186.66 each were voted to Hannum, 10 players, and trainer Al Domenico.

Late season sub Bob Weiss was given $480, and smaller stipends were doled out to the equipment manager and locker-room assistant. The guys set aside $240 to buy gifts for GM Ramsay and owner Irv Kosloff.

When the plane taxied in at Philadelphia International late that afternoon, 76ers public-address announcer Dave Zinkoff leaped up the stairway to greet each player as they got off the plane, hugging and high-fiving them.

Greer was first off, still wearing the sweater he flew out with three days earlier, wearing shades and a short-brimmed black hat. Through the sunglasses he could see a brass band and a crowd of 500 people to welcome the champs home.

Jackson was right behind him, with Alex next (wearing a coat and tie!), then Chamberlain and the others.

Signs sprang up reading: "Boston Bled, Now the Warriors are Dead" and "Hail Champs."

Fans crowded around Hannum, Chamberlain, and all the players for nonstop hugging, handshakes, and pats on the back.

"I don't remember a parade," said Billy Cunningham decades later when asked if the city formally honored the team with a major downtown event.

"Basketball just wasn't at the level then that it is now," said Cunningham, who coached the 1983 76ers to the NBA crown and rode in a Broad Street parade that drew two million people.

Next stop was the three-day jaunt to the Bahamas.

"This was not a reward from the 76ers management as such," asserted Hannum, concerned about NBA rules prohibiting team rewards.

"This is a close group, it has been all year. After the team won the Eastern Division championship back in March, they decided to form a trip for after the season and after the playoffs—win, lose, or draw.

"Management said that, in lieu of the accomplishments of this team—even up to that point—they would pick up the check. This trip was not contingent on winning or losing a title, and that's not putting a premium on winning anything. So, I don't think it would carry a fine from the league."

Ironically, when Warriors owner Mieuli heard about the 76ers' trip, he promised his players a Hawaiian vacation if they won the title.

They never went.

Chamberlain was also looking ahead to a second trip later in the week. He had booked an 11-game tour of Italy with the Harlem Globetrotters and possibly a few games in England.

"One reason I am going to Italy is because I promised a friend of mine there, about four years ago, that I'd come over and play again someday," recalled Wilt. "So I may as well go now."

Even Pennsylvania governor Raymond P. Shafer, who was very visible during the locker-room celebration following the series win over Boston, had something extra to celebrate. After sending a telegram to the 76ers reading, "You have proved you are the real champions. All Pennsylvania is proud," he sent out another message, this one across country.

Prior to the start of the series with San Francisco, he wagered a bushel of Pennsylvania apples against a crate of Governor Ronald Reagan's California oranges that the 76ers would win it all.

"The greatest thirst quencher in the world—victory and oranges," wrote Shafer in a telegram to the man who would be one day become President of the United States.

"Want to try again next year?"

NBA FINALS
76ers Win Best-of-Seven Series, 4–2

76ers	141	S.F	135 [ot]
76ers	126	S.F.	95
S.F.	130	76ers	124
76ers	122	S.F.	108
S.F.	117	76ers	109
76ers	125	S.F.	122

76ERS VS. WARRIORS—NBA FINALS
Game 1, April 14, 1967, at Philadelphia

SAN FRANCISCO

	FG-FGA	FT-FTA	REB	ASTS	F	PTS
Barry	15-43	7-8	8	7	3	37
Hetzel	4-12	4-4	5	1	4	12
Thurmond	10-20	4-5	31	3	3	24
Neumann	2-9	3-4	2	1	2	7
Mullins	7-18	2-2	7	6	6	16
Meschery	9-22	2-4	12	0	6	20
Attles	2-5	0-1	7	4	3	4
King	6-11	3-4	5	3	2	15
Olsen	0-0	0-2	3	0	2	0
Totals	55-140 (.392)	25-34 (.735)	80	25	31	135

PHILADELPHIA

	FG-FGA	FT-FTA	REB	ASTS	F	PTS
Walker	8-18	7-12	8	4	5	23
Jackson	3-9	2-3	10	3	6	8
Chamberlain	6-8	4-9	33	10	2	16
Greer	13-29	6-9	10	6	5	32
Jones	13-26	4-5	10	8	3	30
Cunningham	11-22	4-8	5	3	4	26
Guokas	3-4	0-0	3	1	2	6
Totals	57-116 (.491)	27-46 (.586)	79	35	27	141

	1st	2nd	3rd	4th	OT	Final
San Fran	30	35	28	35	7	135
Philadelphia	43	30	34	21	13	141

Officials: Earl Strom, Richie Powers
Attendance: 9,283

76ERS VS. WARRIORS—NBA FINALS
Game 2, April 16, 1967, at Philadelphia

SAN FRANCISCO

	FG-FGA	FT-FTA	REB	ASTS	F	PTS
Barry	10-28	10-12	10	1	4	30
Hetzel	1-4	1-1	2	0	1	3
Thurmond	3-14	1-3	29	2	0	7
Neumann	2-7	1-2	1	2	3	5
Mullins	6-16	0-1	3	3	2	12
King	4-15	3-5	10	6	1	11
Meschery	4-13	2-2	7	1	5	10
Attles	1-4	0-0	0	2	2	2
Lee	4-17	1-3	8	1	4	9
Ellis	1-4	0-0	1	2	2	2
Warlick	0-0	0-0	0	0	0	0
Olsen	2-7	0-0	5	0	0	4
Totals	38-129	19-29	76	20	24	95
	(.295)	(.655)				

PHILADELPHIA

	FG-FGA	FT-FTA	REB	ASTS	F	PTS
Walker	7-17	4-4	8	3	4	18
Jackson	2-10	2-4	15	1	3	6
Chamberlain	4-10	2-17	38	10	2	10
Greer	13-30	4-4	12	9	4	30
Jones	8-16	0-1	5	3	5	16
Cunningham	13-24	2-4	6	2	4	28
Guokas	4-5	0-0	5	3	2	8
Gambee	2-3	2-2	2	1	1	6
Weiss	2-3	0-0	2	2	1	4
Totals	55-118	16-36	93	34	26	126
	(.466)	(.444)				

	1st	2nd	3rd	4th	Final
San Fran	17	29	23	26	95
Philadelphia	26	31	28	41	126

Officials: Norm Drucker, Mendy Rudolph
Attendance: 9,426

76ERS VS. WARRIORS—NBA FINALS
Game 3, April 18, 1967, at San Francisco

SAN FRANCISCO

	FG-FGA	FT-FTA	REB	ASTS	F	PTS
Attles	2-4	0-0	5	1	5	4
Barry	22-48	11-19	12	5	4	55
King	11-19	6-6	9	6	4	28
Lee	4-9	0-1	8	1	4	8
Meschery	5-13	0-0	7	2	5	10
Mullins	3-8	0-0	4	5	4	6
Neumann	0-3	2-2	2	3	3	2
Thurmond	6-13	5-6	25	4	5	17
Totals	53-117	24-34	71	27	34	130
	[.452]	[.705]				

PHILADELPHIA

	FG-FGA	FT-FTA	REB	ASTS	F	PTS
Chamberlain	12-23	2-9	26	5	3	26
Cunningham	7-14	5-10	5	3	6	19
Gambee	2-4	4-4	3	0	3	8
Greer	6-19	9-10	7	4	3	21
Guokas	1-4	0-0	0	1	4	2
Jackson	4-11	1-2	11	2	4	9
Jones	8-18	2-3	1	7	4	18
Walker	7-16	7-7	6	6	3	21
Totals	47-109	30-45	59	28	30	124
	[.431]	[.666]				

	1st	2nd	3rd	4th	Final
San Fran	32	37	29	32	130
Philadelphia	35	28	29	32	124

Officials: Earl Strom, John Vanak
Attendance: 14,773

76ERS VS. WARRIORS—NBA FINALS
Game 4, April 20, 1967, at San Francisco

SAN FRANCISCO

	FG-FGA	FT-FTA	REB	ASTS	F	PTS
Attles	1-5	1-3	7	4	5	3
Barry	17-41	9-12	7	3	5	43
King	9-20	5-7	6	3	2	23
Lee	5-14	1-4	18	3	1	11
Meschery	1-7	0-0	5	0	6	2
Mullins	6-15	2-2	6	2	6	14
Neumann	1-5	2-3	1	0	1	4
Thurmond	4-18	0-2	25	5	2	8
Totals	44-125	20-33	75	20	28	108
	(.352)	(.606)				

PHILADELPHIA

	FG-FGA	FT-FTA	REB	ASTS	F	PTS
Chamberlain	3-6	4-9	27	8	2	10
Cunningham	7-21	1-1	9	3	5	15
Greer	15-35	8-9	9	4	3	38
Guokas	1-5	2-4	5	3	4	4
Jackson	3-5	2-2	4	3	4	8
Jones	6-10	2-2	3	2	4	14
Walker	10-18	13-18	11	2	1	33
Totals	45-100	32-45	68	25	23	122
	(.450)	(.711)				

	1st	2nd	3rd	4th	Final
San Fran	27	22	29	30	108
Philadelphia	34	26	31	31	122

Officials: Mendy Rudolph, Joe Gushue
Attendance: 15,117

76ERS VS. WARRIORS—NBA FINALS
Game 5, April 23, 1967, at Philadelphia

SAN FRANCISCO

	FG-FGA	FT-FTA	REB	ASTS	F	PTS
Barry	14-37	8-8	10	2	4	36
Hetzel	6-13	2-3	6	0	3	14
Thurmond	7-21	3-7	28	1	4	17
Attles	2-3	0-0	9	6	4	4
Neumann	0-1	0-0	1	3	1	0
King	6-16	2-3	5	2	4	14
Mullins	4-12	5-6	3	5	3	13
Lee	1-2	0-0	0	1	0	2
Meschery	7-14	3-4	7	2	6	17
Totals	47-119	23-31	69	22	29	117
	(.394)	(.741)				

PHILADELPHIA

	FG-FGA	FT-FTA	REB	ASTS	F	PTS
Walker	6-16	13-16	13	3	5	25
Jackson	4-9	3-4	14	0	4	11
Chamberlain	9-15	2-12	24	4	4	20
Greer	7-19	6-7	5	7	6	20
Jones	7-22	2-2	1	6	2	16
Cunningham	6-13	1-5	7	4	3	13
Guokas	1-3	0-0	1	1	0	2
Gambee	1-1	0-0	1	1	1	2
Totals	41-98	27-46	66	26	25	109
	(.418)	(.586)				

	1st	2nd	3rd	4th	Final
San Fran	31	30	23	33	117
Philadelphia	32	32	32	13	109

Officials: Mendy Rudolph, Norm Drucker
Attendance: 10,229

76ERS VS. WARRIORS—NBA FINALS
Game 6, April 24, 1967, at San Francisco

SAN FRANCISCO

	FG-FGA	FT-FTA	REB	ASTS	F	PTS
Attles	3-4	0-0	5	3	5	6
Barry	16-38	12-13	6	2	5	44
Hetzel	4-11	0-0	3	1	3	8
King	9-16	1-1	14	7	3	19
Meschery	3-9	0-0	5	2	5	6
Lee	1-2	0-0	2	1	4	2
Mullins	9-19	5-7	7	3	3	23
Neumann	1-1	0-0	0	4	2	2
Thurmond	4-13	4-8	22	5	6	12
Totals	50-113	22-29	64	28	36	122
	(.442)	(.758)				

PHILADELPHIA

	FG-FGA	FT-FTA	REB	ASTS	F	PTS
Chamberlain	8-13	8-16	23	4	3	24
Cunningham	4-13	9-13	2	3	5	17
Gambee	0-2	0-0	0	0	1	0
Greer	5-16	5-7	5	7	2	15
Guokas	4-6	1-2	1	1	1	9
Jackson	5-13	3-6	21	2	4	13
Jones	8-18	11-15	1	6	4	27
Walker	8-17	4-5	7	2	5	20
Totals	42-98	41-64	60	25	25	125
	(.428)	(.640)				

	1st	2nd	3rd	4th	Final
San Fran	41	31	30	20	122
Philadelphia	43	25	29	28	125

Officials: Earl Strom, John Vanak
Attendance: 15,612

EIGHT
One-Year Wonders

♪ *"You'll love the spirit of the 76ers,*
Watch them fast break down the floor.
Crashin' the boards and movin' the ball,
Now they're driving for another score.
Join in the spirit of the 76ers,
Rooting for the team to come through.

"There's Hal and Larry, Matt and Bill
and Wally Jones to pass it,
Luke and Billy, Chet and Dave
and Wilt to guard the basket." ♪

The lyrics and music of the first verse were original but the words
of the last verse were set to the music of "Yankee Doodle Dandy,"
replacing these lyrics:

"Yankee Doodle went to London
just to ride the ponies,
stuck a feather in his hat
and called it macaroni."

That next year began with a song, celebrating the spirit of a new champion and a new season. The 76ers had become marketable in Philadelphia, and public relations became a priority.

Not only did the team get its own jingle, it got its own 30-minute season highlight film, which opened and closed with the 76ers' fight song. The film, produced by a Philadelphia company called TelRa Productions, featured color highlights of all the playoff rounds, individual player profiles, footage of the airport celebration after the 76ers won the championship, a behind-the-scenes look at the team's front office people, and a quick plug for the Spectrum, the 76ers' brand-new arena.

"The Spectrum in Philadelphia will put the Philadelphia sports fan on a par with anyone in the country," said Alex Hannum on the film, voicing over shots of the new complex. "We at the 76ers are really looking forward to have a truly home court advantage where the building is perfect and where every fan can see every bit of action."

The film was distributed to schools and organizations around the Delaware Valley to take advantage of Philly's status as championship favorite in 1967–68 and to fuel ticket sales in the new arena. Compared to Convention Hall, the best seats increased a buck, from $5 to $6, and the cheapest reserved seats jumped from $1.50 to $2.

The front office published a team yearbook chock-full of player photos and bios, a day-by-day, game-by-game recap of the championship season and team/player statistics of every type, compiled by Harvey Pollack, the numbers wizard of the 76ers.

WCAU Radio decided it wanted to join the bandwagon, too. The CBS O&O got the rights to be the voice of the champion 76ers for all home and away games, following up on the success of airing the previous year's playoffs. Andy Musser teamed with longtime local basketball authority Sonny Hill to provide the play-by-play and color commentary.

"WCAU was never interested in carrying a full schedule of games," remembered Musser. "In 1965–66 we carried less than half the games and never went west of St. Louis." In addition, a schedule of 27 television games were set for WPHL-TV, Channel 17, with Al Meltzer handling the play-by-play.

The 76ers were going to be showcased by the local broadcast media like never before.

Expectations were staggeringly high for the 76ers after their 68-win season and march through the playoffs. In a sense, their incredible regular season mark made it almost impossible for the 76ers to top themselves, but a 60-plus win season seemed a certainty.

First, the team had to overcome several contract disputes. As usual, Chamberlain was in the middle of one of them.

Prior to the championship season, because of the lingering dispute between Wilt and Irv Kosloff over Ike Richman's impossible promise to cut Wilt an ownership slice of the 76ers, Kosloff and Jack Ramsay gave him a one-year deal to end his holdout and get him into training camp (despite his protestations that the San Francisco house fire kept him away).

According to Wilt, the key to that deal was that it released the team from any Richman-era commitments it either had or didn't have, and, in return, there were no strings binding Wilt to Broad Street after the season was over.

Word surfaced that the deal actually freed Chamberlain from the controversial reserve clause, which bound a player to one club from the moment he signed his first contract until such time as the club chose to release him or trade him.

From Chamberlain's lofty vantage point, he was free and clear to negotiate with the ABA.

"I was released from all obligations," said Wilt. "I'm able to do whatever I want to do this particular year, with the possible exception of going to another NBA team."

"I can't confirm or deny any of Wilt's statements," said a harried Kosloff. "We're hopeful of initiating and completing negotiations for a new agreement with Wilt."

Ramsay put it this way: "We agree that Wilt has the right to renegotiate a contract with us, but we also feel he has an obligation to play with the 76ers."

Ramsay asserted that the one-year contract Chamberlain signed to play the previous season bound him to Philadelphia for that year and the following one. Ramsay said one of the concessions granted Wilt was that he would have a new opportunity to bargain.

Wilt contended he had no deal and could go anywhere, claiming the 76ers were trying to make a liar out of him by saying he was still bound by the reserve clause.

"They haven't gotten to the complete, frank, honest truth of the matter yet," said Chamberlain.

"Knowing Wilt," added Ramsay, "I think he wants to play in the NBA. I think he wants to play for the team that won the championship, a team that is well coached, has good personnel. I mean it. I think those things are important to Wilt."

"You know the NBA is a major league," offered Hannum. "If there's another league in operation, it will be a minor league. I think Wilt wants to play with the best."

Lots of talk, but very little action until just weeks before the start of the season.

After considerable haggling, Chamberlain finally signed a new $250,000 deal in October 1967, posing for a happy picture with Kosloff, Ramsay, and Hannum at the Sheraton Hotel.

He had given up his demand to become a free agent, but managed to miss the entire training camp, once again joining the team for an exhibition game in Allentown Pennsylvania, against the Knicks. It was a replay of last pre-season.

"I got satisfaction, respect," said Wilt. "The free agent factor was resolved in the bargaining, after all, everything leads to a monetary end. I got enough. The IRS will be getting most of it, maybe all of it."

Hal Greer wanted a better deal, too.

"Jack [Ramsay] told me what he wanted to give me, and I think I'm worth more than that," Greer told reporters. "We had a helluva year last year, we all did, you've got to get it when you can."

Greer, who worked for Atlantic Richfield Company in the off-season coordinating basketball clinics in Philadelphia, made $25,000 with the 76ers during the championship year. Reporters asked if he was aiming for a $10,000 raise.

"No, you're way off, low. When you do the job, you're supposed to get paid. We have the best owner in the league in Irv Kosloff. You'd hate to have trouble with a man like that, but this is a business."

Greer ultimately signed for somewhere between $37,500 and $40,000.

Hannum was in the final year of his two-year deal, and while seemingly loving life, he faced some unsettling job issues with the 76ers.

He started a basketball school at St. John's Preparatory School in Danvers, Massachusetts, going head-to-head with schools operated by Red Auerbach, Bob Cousy, and Sam Jones.

"This wouldn't have been possible without a world championship team who were about beating the Celtics," said Hannum. "It is the sheer pleasure of coaching a great basketball team. I've been bouncing around these stinking basketballs since I was thirteen or fourteen. To be part of what might be the greatest team ever is a source of tremendous pride and personal satisfaction.

"A year ago I'd walk down the street in Philadelphia and people didn't know me, except for a few knowledgeable basketball fans who knew me as the old hatchet man that used to come into the Arena. Now I feel I am a part of Philadelphia. If I just walk three or four blocks in Center City, there's gonna be several people stop me and say hello and say they hope we have a good season."

Hannum was saying all of the right things.

What he wasn't saying was that he apparently declined a contract extension with the 76ers. It was offered in the summer after he coached them to the title and would have increased his existing two-year deal in years and in dollars.

"I asked him if we wanted to extend his contract, and he said no, he did not," claimed GM Ramsay in an interview with George Kiseda of the *Bulletin*, which was published in mid-season.

"Alex has indicated in the past that he does not want a long-term contract," added Ramsay. ". . . I'm sure he feels he doesn't want to tie himself down for an extended period in this capacity or in this area, but you'll have to talk to him about that."

Kiseda asked if Hannum had permission from the 76ers to talk with expansion teams like Phoenix and Milwaukee, or if those organizations sought permission to speak with him.

"Well," Ramsay said, "I'm gonna hedge on that if you don't mind because I don't want to get into a discussion on what his plans are for the future. After this year, he's able to examine the possibilities for the future for himself."

Ramsay said Hannum did not want to be "obligated," but the GM refused to draw the conclusion that Hannum would not ultimately stay with 76ers.

When the story broke in February, Hannum did more than hedge. He initially dodged questions from reporters.

"For the rest of the season, I think I'm gonna have to take the position that I've got no comment to make about other employment."

But when pressed, he said this:

"I would like to win a world title again and bargain for a new contract. If the jobs [with new franchises] are not filled at the time I'm ready to talk turkey with the 76ers, it's conceivable my bargaining position would be better.

"I want to be in a position to make the best deal I can for myself. I would guess that the best deal I can make for myself would be with the 76ers."

And, despite Hannum's public comments during the Chamberlain contract talks that the ABA would be a minor league, he confirmed that he had talked to a lot of ABA people, but insisted he received no offers to bolt.

"If I become interested in the future, they would like to talk to me," Hannum declared.

So, the inside story was that neither Chamberlain nor Hannum was completely satisfied with their contractual status quo, and hindsight would prove that these pre-season difficulties were tip-offs of trouble ahead.

Intrigue aside, the 76ers were finally ready to play ball and defend their crown.

Their personnel were pretty much back intact. Although Larry Costello was now a combination player/assistant coach and Dave Gambee was sacrificed in the expansion draft to the new San Diego franchise, the Philly front-liners were set to go.

Little did they know they would be stopped from winning it all once again by two events in the latter stages of the season and an aging enemy that just wouldn't go away. And their long-term success would be set back by the two key people who really wanted to move on.

Overall, the season went smoothly for the 76ers.

They jumped out to an early lead on the Eastern Division competition and never looked back.

They finished 62-20, eight games better than the Celtics, but six and a half games below the standard they set in the title season.

Chamberlain finished third in scoring for the second consecutive season, averaging 24.3 points per game, almost exactly matching his mark from the previous year.

But Chamberlain was far prouder of another statistic.

After reconstructing his game prior to the 1966–67 season and finishing an amazing third in assists, Wilt bettered himself in the 1967–68 season, leading the league in assists with 702 (8.6 per game), up from 630. He bested such playmaking luminaries as Lenny Wilkens of St. Louis and even Cincinnati's brilliant Oscar Robertson.

To top that, Wilt also won the league rebounding title again—averaging 23.8 a game—and, by doing so, he became the first and only player ever to lead the NBA in both assists and rebounds in a single season.

One game during the season showcased Wilt in all three of his favorite categories. It was another of his history-making triumphs.

On February 2, Chamberlain scored an incredible double-triple-double in a 131–121 home court victory over the Detroit Pistons.

Wilt scored 22 points, grabbed 25 rebounds, and handed out 21 assists.

The assist mark was a 76ers record and put Wilt in fourth place all-time for single game assists, behind only Bob Cousy (28), former teammate Guy Rodgers (28), Jerry West (23), and Oscar Robertson (22).

The 76ers were playing their game, running the offense through Chamberlain.

Super statistician Vince Miller posted the numbers on the locker-room blackboard at halftime.

Fourteen points off of 12 passes into the pivot in the first quarter, and 22 points off 19 passes in the second stanza.

"I always pass up shots," said Wilt after the game, disingenuously downplaying his efforts. "Every time I get the ball, I'm passing up shots. Unless I'm triple-teamed and there's no space to go, I'm passing up shots."

Wilt, who always loved his numbers, loved this one.

"It's the thrill of doing something new and different. Anytime you do something new, it's exciting."

Pistons coach Donnie Butcher marveled at Chamberlain's assist performance and how the 76ers used the pivot.

"If they play this type of game, I'll tell ya, they'll repeat as world champions."

On the scoring front, Wilt wound up working both extremes during the season.

In November, in a game against San Francisco, Chamberlain did not take a single shot.

Not a one.

0 for 0.

Late in the fourth quarter, he did attempt a dunk shot, but Nate Thurmond blocked it before it left Wilt's hand and no shot attempt was credited. He finished with one point, but the 76ers won, 117–110.

"You'll have to ask Wilt," said Hannum. "All I can say is this was not my instructions."

"The important thing is still to win, isn't it?" queried the *non*-Dipper. "And we did win, didn't we? I didn't plan on having no shots. You call it zero percent, I call it one hundred percent."

Then three months later, Chamberlain found himself at the other extreme. He scored his 25,000th point in a 138–117 win over Detroit in the Spectrum, an altogether completely expected feat, but amazing nonetheless. Oddly enough, Chamberlain hit the new mark from, of all places, the foul line. The free throw that did it banked high off the glass, hit the rim, and fell in.

"Another masterpiece from the foul line," Wilt joked later.

Owner Irv Kosloff asked the Dipper how it felt to set the record.

"It feels like it's worth a whole lot of money," said Wilt. That may not have been what "Kos" wanted to hear from his perennial contract malcontent.

Chamberlain heard and saw a standing ovation from the Spectrum crowd.

"A lot of girls stood up," cracked Wilt. "That's because I'm getting better as I get older."

To no one's surprise, the assist-minded Chamberlain was still rewriting the record books in scoring.

The 76ers clinched their third straight Eastern title in mid-March, beating the Knicks 119–108 in New York, while Cincinnati beat the Celtics 137–111 in the Boston Garden.

"Congratulate us. Three in a row," yelled Chet Walker.

Luke Jackson had a slightly different opinion.

"This doesn't mean anything, this Eastern Division championship," said the big guy. "Remember the year we won the Eastern Division title and blew the playoffs [1965–66]. We're not overly excited because we know we've got a lot of work to do."

"It's like we backed into it," chimed in Wally Jones. "It was more fun beating Boston last year."

"All it comes down to is a home court edge [in the playoffs]," said Chamberlain. "If you want me to jump up and touch a ceiling because we got a home court edge . . . But it's nice."

"It wasn't even on my mind, cinching the thing," said Coach Hannum. "I wanted to win a ball game. I knew it was coming. I thought this coming week sometime, but not today. I don't expect Boston to lose at home."

The champagne finally arrived and Chamberlain did the toasting. He poured his thirst-quencher into a Dixie cup and offered the following poem:

"I'm gonna make this short and sweet. Another championship we shall repeat."

"Norman the orator," laughed Wally. "You were deep."

"Remember, I was an English major in college," Wilt shot back.

The celebration was short-lived, and there was even a little grumbling that neither owner Kosloff nor GM Ramsay was on hand to congratulate the three-time East champs.

Besides that accomplishment, the 76ers had lots more to make them proud.

As a team, the 76ers had set a two-year record of total dominance on the basketball court.

Their overall record over the two campaigns was 130-33, for a record-setting winning percentage of .798.

Even the Boston Celtics in their era of dominance couldn't match that. Their best was .756 with 121 wins and 39 losses in 1963–64 and 1964–65.

So, it was playoff time, and the guys who hadn't bragged too much about regular season success turned out to be prophetic.

The 76ers drew the steadily improving New York Knicks. The first round, five-game mini-series format had been eliminated, so this would be a seven-game war. For the 76ers, there would be heavy losses.

The teams split the first two of the best of seven, with Philadelphia winning the opener, 118–100, but losing the second game 128–117.

Game three would be the telling battle.

It was a rugged, tightly played affair at the Palestra.

After one quarter, the 76ers led 27–26, then Billy Cunningham went on a tear. He made the first three baskets for the 76ers to open the second period. Then, when the Knicks threw up a zone press, Billy broke it time and time again with passes down low to Wilt for easy dunks. Near the end of the quarter, Billy added three more field goals and moved the 76ers to a 57–49 lead at the half, a half in which Cunningham chalked up 12 points, five rebounds, and four assists.

He was still smokin' at the start of the third period, pouring in eight points in three minutes to bounce the 76ers' lead to 10.

Late in the game, Chet Walker took over, making several key baskets down the stretch as the game tightened. With six seconds left in regulation and the 76ers down by 113–111 after a bucket by the Knicks' Cazzie Russell, Walker took the inbounds pass from Chamberlain and got unexpectedly matched up against New York's Walt Frazier. Chet took the smaller guard baseline and popped a short jumper to tie it and send the game into overtime.

Then just six seconds into the extra period, disaster struck the 76ers.

Cunningham drove toward the basket and collided with the Knicks' long, lanky, and bony rookie Phil Jackson. Referee Mendy Rudolph whistled a charging foul on Cunningham, fouling him out of the game. But it was more than too many fouls that would bench Billy. Cunningham had broken his wrist. His best career playoff game ended in disappointment, frustration, and pain.

"I saw the opening and I drove," said Billy. "I got by, I think . . . Cazzie and I ran into Phil Jackson. The first thing I thought about was the call. I thought I was going to the line."

The right wrist was broken in three places, and even though Cunningham shot with his left hand, this injury would put him out for the rest of the playoffs.

"I think we can do it as long as our forwards don't get into foul trouble," said Cunningham, trying to be encouraging.

The 76ers won game three 138–132 in double overtime to take a 2–1 series edge, but as Alex Hannum glumly said afterwards:

"We won the battle, but it was very costly."

Even with their "instant offense" gone, the 76ers managed to finish off the Knicks, winning two of the next three for a 4–2 series win.

The stage was set for yet another clash between the archenemies. Boston also needed six games to knock off the Detroit Pistons, and the series between the Celtics and 76ers was set to tip off at the Spectrum on April 5th.

But just before it did, something terrible happened. Something very terrible.

On April 4th, the Reverend Dr. Martin Luther King was gunned down on the balcony outside his room at the Lorraine Hotel in Memphis.

America was stunned. Its urban centers erupted in flames, and Philadelphia was no exception.

The playoffs were set to open the next night, and the 76ers weren't sure they wanted to play.

The Celtics had made a firm decision after meeting with Auerbach and Russell. They agreed to take the court.

In his autobiography, Chet Walker recounted the doubts about playing that swirled around the 76ers.

"Before the game, Wilt closed the dressing room door so we could have a ballot. But now it was too late to have our say. To vote against playing, with the fans already in the Spectrum, would have triggered a riot. I didn't think this game would get our minds off the tragedy of Dr. King's death, but I didn't want to take a chance on contributing to more rioting by not playing.

"When the 76ers took their vote, Wilt and Wally Jones voted against playing. Greer said he didn't want to play either, but he felt it was too late to call the game off. I abstained. I couldn't bring myself to participate in this dreary charade. Everyone knew where I stood. We voted 7–2 to play, but I'm convinced if we'd met earlier in the day and voted then, the results might have been reversed. At about two-thirty, Wilt had told General Manager Jack Ramsay that he didn't want to play, and Ramsay had invoked contracts, fan safety, the city's volatile mood. As far as I was concerned, it was a done deal."

"If it would have happened today, you would have done something different," said Ramsay in a 1999 interview. "But there were difficulties in rescheduling and we decided to go with the game."

The mood was glum in the locker room, and things got no better during the game. The 76ers' indecision about playing followed them onto the basketball court. The Celtics took game one, 127–118.

"It would have been a great thing if we had not played, but we all agreed to play," recalled Hal Greer. "The Celtics beat us that game, and after that it just seemed to go downhill."

Well, not exactly.

The 76ers somehow righted themselves and took the next three games, by scores of 115–106, 122–114, and 110–105.

But then things did, indeed, turn sour.

Perhaps the 76ers were still torn by King's death, the subsequent national mourning, and civil strife in their own city.

Perhaps Cunningham's loss was finally taking effect.

Perhaps it was Wilt pouting.

Perhaps it was simply poor shooting down the stretch.

Perhaps it was just the old Celtics refusing to quit, vowing to make one last vengeful stand against the team that crushed them a year earlier.

The Celtics came back strong, winning the next two 122–104 and 114–106, setting up game seven at the Spectrum.

No team liked to tangle with the Celtics in a game seven. They had never, ever lost one.

This seventh game would be no exception.

It was played somewhat in slow motion, with both teams tentative and mistake-prone. The 76ers managed only 40 points in the first half, and in the second half Chamberlain took just two shots (shades of the November game), kicking the ball back outside repeatedly to shooters who seemed tired and off target.

The Celtics were up 97–95 with a minute to play when Chet Walker, still operating under the cloud of the King assassination, drove on Boston's Don Nelson with a chance to tie it. He tossed up an off-balance five-footer that bounced around on the rim for what seemed forever, before it finally fell into the hands of a waiting Bill Russell.

The Celtics won it 100–96. It was unheard of to come back from a 3–1 playoff series deficit, but the Celtics had done it.

They had won another seventh game. Another seventh game over the 76ers.

That night, Chamberlain, defending his style of play in such a pivotal game, said Hannum did not tell him to shoot. Years later, in an interview conducted by the NBA when the league celebrated its 50th anniversary, Wilt put it this way:

"They blamed me for not shooting the ball because I only took two shots in the second half. Well, during those years, I was passing off a lot. I won the assist title. The Celtics were smart, they put all four guys on me and let the rest of the guys shoot. Billy Cunningham, Hal Greer, Chet Walker, and Wally Jones—all fantastic shots—had a bad, bad day: 8 for 24, 8 for 25, and 8 for 22, and I'm giving them the ball. So when the game is over people say, 'Why didn't you shoot, Wilt?' Well, I got four guys on me and here are the best shooters in NBA history, but they were missing that night. I was accused of not doing my job, not putting the ball in the basket, even though I had 38 rebounds, 15 blocked shots, and scored twenty-something points in the first half. But because I only took two shots in the second half, I get blamed. I think that sometimes that's a little unfair."

Hannum would only say that Wilt was "magnificent" in that game seven and took some of the blame on himself. He thought the best team had lost. The players were abjectly disappointed. There would not be back-to-back titles. The 76ers were not the new NBA dynasty.

Change was coming and coming fast.

Just 10 days after their playoff loss, Alex Hannum said good-bye.

Hannum, Kosloff, and Ramsay made the joint announcement at a Spectrum news conference that Hannum had fulfilled the two-year contract and wanted to move on despite Kosloff's attempts to convince him otherwise.

Alex would only say that he was considering "several opportunities in basketball on the West Coast."

Basketball insiders liked the ABA's Oakland and Los Angeles franchises as the best bets to lure Alex back to courtside.

Hannum had indicated he didn't intend to make Philadelphia a permanent stop when he signed on. But he also had something to prove to himself and the league after getting dumped in San Francisco after a pair of losing seasons.

"I don't think Alex really wanted to come to Philadelphia in the first place," noted Kosloff. "It was clear to me he wanted to go back [to California] after the first year. It's hard to change Alex's opinion. He's very strong-willed."

"I wanted a one-year contract [but signed for two]," said Hannum. "I came here to get back in a winning way. I don't think I came here with the idea of staying. What I'm searching for now is a chance to build something. I don't know whether it's going to be a house or a basketball team. I want to build something."

Again, Hannum said all the right things at the farewell press conference on April 29, 1968.

"It is with a great deal of regret that I leave Wilt and the rest of the 76ers," Hannum emphasized. "I hate to leave Wilt. Coaching Wilt is one of the most pleasant experiences I've had in sports."

He called his time in Philly "completely satisfying . . . a pleasant experience." He insisted that reports of friction between him and Ramsay were "erroneous," and called his boss "one of the great men in basketball."

The Ramsay stories were linked to Hannum's unhappiness over not being consulted before the St. Joe's coach was hired.

"Nobody crosses Alex Hannum twice," Hannum reportedly told a friend later. "Not even Irv Kosloff."

Hannum clarified the situation for reporters, saying, "I was concerned that we have the right man for the job. I fully concur that we—the 76ers—do have the right man for the job." Before he was hired, Hannum himself had made noises about doing both jobs, but Kosloff said he had to pick one job or the other, and Alex picked the bench slot over the front office. But when Kosloff and Ramsay offered him a coaching contract extension, Alex declined.

Again, Hannum insisted everyone was parting ways on the friendliest of terms.

And while Hannum was always getting credit as the one coach who could manage Chamberlain, was the relationship all that rosy? Was there tension all along, more tension than met the eye?

The *Bulletin*'s George Kiseda recounted one episode that he witnessed, which had them at odds during a flight home from Boston after a December loss to the Celtics:

"Hannum was talking in parables about the importance of winning and Chamberlain listened for a while, a smirk lurking behind his goatee.

" 'I think there are more important things than winning,' barked Wilt. 'I think you have to learn how to lose, too.' "

"Then Chamberlain got something off his chest that obviously had been itching there for some time.

"He said he did not like Hannum's habit of going around the dressing room shaking hands after every victory but never after a defeat. He said he did not expect a handshake when he played badly in a victory.

" 'It makes me feel like a hypocrite,' said Chamberlain. 'I think you're a hypocrite when you do it.'

" 'I have to place a premium on winning,' Hannum said as the compartment iced up. He said he was sorry to learn that Chamberlain found it difficult to shake hands with him. He said he would continue to offer his hand to Wilt to take it or leave it. From that moment it was hard to imagine that the relationship between Hannum and Chamberlain would ever be the same."

After Hannum's announcement, Chamberlain told Kiseda: "I'm not going to lose my friendship with Alex because it was based on dealing squarely with him. I wouldn't back down from him no more than he would from me, but I think Alex has talked out of both sides of his mouth. I remember when he used to cry a blue streak to the refs [when he coached against Wilt] about all the things I was doing wrong and he never made the same type of gestures toward other superstars. He used to laud them. I never understood this. I asked him about it and his answers never made sense. He never lambasted [Bill] Russell and yet the Celtics were the team to beat while he was lambasting me."

But, in the "NBA at 50" interview, a much more mellow Chamberlain said of Hannum:

"He's the best professional coach in any league as far as I'm concerned. He did what he had to do, and he did it better than anybody. On the press, on referees, on players, the whole deal.

"Alex Hannum was a master at being sort of a psychologist, but he was a big rough tough player himself, an ex-Marine, and a very, very bright man. He got each of us to do our job in the manner that he wanted to see it done."

So, even before Boston had clinched yet another title by beating the Lakers in six games, the 76ers were shopping for a new coach.

Ramsay took himself out of the running immediately.

Chamberlain put himself *in* the running.

Ramsay insisted he wanted a bench coach.

Wilt said, ". . . no one knows player Wilt better than Wilt."

Wilt's teammates added their opinions.

Hal Greer: "I don't think it would be a good move. I don't think a guy can coach and play effectively at the same time. But if anybody could do it, maybe Wilt could."

Luke Jackson: "It would be just another coach to me, except he'd be playing."

Wally Jones: "You never know how you're going to react to a new coach, but I think he's capable of doing the job. I'm sure he wouldn't have the same personality as a coach that he has as a player."

Billy Cunningham: "You never know how anyone's going to do."

Matty Guokas: "It would be very difficult for Wilt to do it, because it's been very difficult in the past. He knows us so well it would be even more difficult, but Wilt has always accepted challenges. I think it might have a good effect on him as a player. He might demand a little more from himself."

Bill Melchionni: "I think he could possibly do a good job, but it's a hard thing to say. I've never seen him coach. I think it would give him added incentive."

Trainer Al Domenico: "I think if he's the coach it's got to be a tremendous beneficial aid to the team. Wilt knows every second of the ball game what's going on on the court, not only with our team but with the other guys. He comes back to the huddle and makes suggestions and they usually work out."

Besides himself, Wilt was also warming to the idea of his old mentor Frank McGuire as new coach of the 76ers. McGuire had coached Wilt and the Philadelphia Warriors to a winning record during the 1961–62 season. Wilt painted McGuire as one of the only coaches he could play for. Bill Sharman was the other.

In the end, all the speculation made little difference.

Wilt wasn't long for the 76ers.

Jack Ramsay remembered it this way:

"Wilt came to us after the season, we were looking for a new coach. Wilt asked, 'How are you doing, who are you talking to? What would you think if I was player-coach and you helped with the Xs and Os?'

"[Other coaches] were reluctant to say yes or no because they didn't know whether [Wilt] was going to stay.

"Wilt's attitude was very good. He said if we couldn't get the kind of guy we wanted, he would coach, if I would help him.

"I thought that Wilt would play hard to match Russell. He was going to the West Coast for a week, and I said we would talk when he got back. We got together, I said, 'Wilt, I think you've got a good idea.'

"He said, 'I changed my mind. I want out. I am not going to play here again. If you don't trade me, I will jump to the ABA.'

"I was surprised. He was holding all the cards, really. If he didn't want to be here, I don't want him."

That was only half of the story.

Chamberlain wanted a much bigger financial deal from the 76ers—a big salary increase, a three-year contract, and a piece of the team. Kosloff and Ramsay were not dealing.

On July 7, 1968, Chamberlain was part of another blockbuster trade, just like the one that sent him to Philadelphia three years earlier.

The 76ers shipped him to the Los Angeles Lakers for Darrell Imhoff, Archie Clark, and Jerry Chambers.

Al Domenico called the Wilson Sporting Goods Co. and canceled an order for four basketball jerseys, size XXL, and four pairs of pants, size 35.

Somehow, that made it official.

Less than three months after their final game of the season, the 76ers had lost their head and their backbone. Alex and Wilt were gone.

"I was sorry to see it happen," said 76ers broadcaster Andy

Musser. "Hannum was not a Philadelphian. Wilt was, but was out of town so much and wanted to make more money."

His new boss, Lakers owner Jack Kent Cooke, explained why he was able to sign Wilt when the 76ers couldn't.

"I think Wilt had persuaded himself that he wanted to play on the West Coast and particularly in Los Angeles," said the millionaire owner with an ego equal to Chamberlain's.

"I'm very pleased with the man. I'm enormously attracted to him personally. I like him. I'm hopeful that Wilt plays out his playing days in a Laker uniform."

The 76ers knew their run was over. It was the end of a very short era that, years later, they all remembered painfully.

"If that team had stayed together for so many years, we would have won quite a few more championships," said Hal Greer.

"Because of what Wilt was promised and never given, they got rid of him, and that was one of the worst things that ever happened to that team," Wally Jones said sadly. "That was a tragic thing."

"Breaking up that team was such a shame, a shame of a situation," recalled Billy Cunningham. "The team should have won several titles. Looking back it was a shame it happened so fast."

"He's a personal friend and probably I'm the closest friend he has, but I know it's a business, and it has to be a business to me," said Vince Miller. "Because he's going, I can't pull up stakes and go also. I gotta go with the 76ers."

Years later Miller said, "I think Jack Ramsay wanted Wilt gone. It was his fault."

As it turned out, Ramsay wound up with the controls again, with or without Chamberlain. He took over the coaching reins the next season. His Wilt-less teams posted three consecutive winning seasons, but Ramsay's club could manage only a 30-52 mark in the 1971–72 campaign.

Ironically, that same season, Wilt won his second NBA title with the Lakers, a team that bested the 76ers' 68-13 season with a 69-13 mark.

Ramsay knew it was time to go and college coach Roy Rubin was named head man of the 76ers for the 1972–73 campaign.

The once-powerful 76ers were abysmal.

Rubin's record was 4-47 (almost the exact opposite of the 76ers' record at one point during the title season) before he was fired in favor of Kevin Loughery, who went 5-26 for the remainder of the year.

In just five seasons, the Philadelphia 76ers had gone from the NBA's greatest team ever to the worst, 9-73.

How far the mighty had fallen.

The Philadelphia 76ers, a team that for one year was wondrous, had become a one-year wonder.

It would take a full 10 years before the 76ers would return to full championship glory.

Appropriately, a member of those great 76ers would make them great again.

Billy Cunningham had watched the 1977 Portland Trailblazers steal the NBA title away from the heavily favored 76ers and Dr. J, Julius Erving. Billy's old boss Jack Ramsay was the Blazers' coach.

The humbled 76ers told their fans, "We owe you one."

But the memories were bitter and the 76ers needed a new start.

Coach Gene Shue was canned just six games (2-4) into the next season, when it became quickly apparent that the 76ers would not pay that debt under the existing administration.

Cunningham was hired to make things right.

After only one season, he took the 76ers to the 1980 NBA title series, losing to the L.A. Lakers. The infamous sixth and deciding game saw Magic Johnson fill in at center for the injured Kareem Abdul-Jabbar and lead the Lakers to the championship with a stunning and memorable 42-point performance.

In 1982, the Cunningham-led 76ers broke the Celtics' playoff hex. For the first time in club history, the 76ers beat the Celtics in a seventh game in the Boston Garden—one of the sweetest victories in the history of the 76ers.

Once again the 76ers matched up with the Los Angeles Lakers in the NBA finals.

Once again the Lakers were just a bit too much for the spent 76ers. L.A. took the series 4–2.

Then in 1982–83, with Moses Malone at center and the incomparable Dr. J alongside him, the 76ers avenged themselves, sweeping L.A. in the finals and putting together a torrid 12-1 playoff run.

Billy liked to light up cigars after winning the big games.

It was a habit he probably picked up in the 60s from a guy who coached Boston.

NINE
Best Ever

Were the Philadelphia 76ers truly the best NBA team ever?

Were they truly the most powerful club ever put together for a single season?

How do they compare with the other great NBA teams that came just before them and long after them?

Just to review, the 1966–67 Philadelphia 76ers destroyed the NBA record books by winning 68 games and losing only 13 in the regular season (.840). At one point, they were 46-4, unheard of at the time. In the playoffs, they slipped just slightly to 11-4 for an overall mark of 79-17, but still good enough for a winning percentage of .822.

No other team in NBA history had come even close to that. The great Boston Celtics championship club of 1964–65 was the closest, with an overall mark of 70-22 or .760.

Many thought the record set by the 76ers would last a long, long time. But it came under pressure just four seasons later as the Hannum-tutored Larry Costello coached Lew Alcindor, Oscar Robertson, and the Milwaukee Bucks to a 66-16 record. The Bucks shot a record 50.9 percent from the field and posted an .805 winning percentage. They dominated in the playoffs, going 12-2, with a 13.2 point differential. Their final winning percentage was .812.

The very next year another team challenged and surpassed the 76ers' record, and wouldn't you know it, Wilt Chamberlain was involved. When it came to numbers of any kind, Wilt always liked to top himself, and with the Lakers, he did. L.A. compiled a season record of 69-13, one win better than the 76ers and one percentage point better, .841 to .840. L.A. had an unprecedented 33-game winning streak during the season. The 76ers' best was 11 straight, which they accomplished twice. But the 76ers won 37 of their first 40 games, a feat comparable to the Lakers', though not a streak of consecutive wins.

The Lakers also racked up the most road wins (38, two shy of the 76ers' record 40). And they scored 100 or more points in 81 of their 82 games (one better than the 76ers' mark of 80 of 81). They also went 12-3 in the playoffs en route to the NBA title, pushing their overall record to 81-16, a new best-ever winning percentage of .835.

The very next season, Boston went wild under coach Tom Heinsohn, veteran players like John Havlicek, and new stars Dave Cowens and Jo Jo White, amassing a 68-14 record or .829. Their record of 12-6 in the playoffs brought them to an 80-20 title season, but dropped their percentage to .800.

In 1982–83, Moses Malone and Julius Erving brought the 76ers back to prominence with a 65-17 record and a near sweep of the playoffs. The 76ers went 12-1 (for a then best-ever .923 winning percentage) in the post-season. It brought their overall mark to 77-18, good for a percentage of .811.

It was two seasons later that the Celtics put together another powerhouse. Boston's 1985–86 team, led by the imposing front line of 6' 9" Larry Bird, 6' 10" Kevin McHale, and 7' 1" Robert Parish, posted a 67-15 mark for .817. Adding a 15-3 playoff record, the Celtics won the

NBA crown and finished 82-18 for an .820 percentage. The Celts were 40-1 at home in the regular season and 10-0 at home in the playoffs.

That stellar season was chronicled in a book by Peter May called *The Last Banner: The Story of the 1985–86 Boston Celtics, the NBA's Greatest Team of All Time.*

May wrote: "The 1985–86 Celtics could beat a team inside. It could beat a team outside. It could beat a team with defense. It had the greatest front line in NBA history, and most importantly, had an almost perfect record at Boston Garden."

The 1991–92 Michael Jordan–led Chicago Bulls matched the '86 Celtics' regular season mark of 67-15. They went 15-7 in the post-season to finish 82-22, a percentage of .788, taking their second of three straight NBA titles.

Then there were the Chicago Bulls of 1995–96, the first season that Michael Jordan came back from retirement after a flirtation with professional baseball. The Bulls went 72-10 for the best regular season winning percentage in NBA history, .878. During one stretch, they went 41-3, slightly bettering the pace of the 76ers. The 76ers were 40-4 after 44 contests, a game off the Bulls' pace. Looking at the overall record, when their playoff record of 15-3 is added in, the Bulls finished 87-13 or .870—again a best-ever mark.

Amazingly, the Bulls lost the same number of games in 100 tries as the great 76ers did in their regular season run of 81 contests, 13.

In essence, looking at the number of wins and overall winning percentage, these are statistically the best eight teams in the history of the National Basketball Association, offered in chronological order.

It should be noted that in 1980 the NBA voted the 1966–67 76ers the best team in the then 35-year history of the league.

In fact, on Wednesday, December 10, 1980, they were honored as such in formal ceremonies at the Spectrum. Up until that time, only the 69-13 Lakers were considered to be in the 76ers' class.

The players returned for the event, and it was a gala night.

It was after that celebration that the other teams already mentioned rolled up winning records to challenge the supremacy of the 76ers.

In the 50th anniversary year of the NBA (1996–97), a panel of media members who regularly covered the league were asked to select the top 10 teams in NBA history, without ranking them.

All of the teams previously noted made that list, with the surprise exception of the '70-71 Bucks. Three other teams were added:

The 1969–70 New York Knicks of Coach Red Holtzman, Willis Reed, and Walt Frazier beat the Lakers in the famous game in which a badly injured Reed hobbled out to inspire his teammates and fans at Madison Square Garden.

The 1986–87 "Showtime" edition of the L.A. Lakers roared to a 65-17 regular season record under the leadership of Coach Pat Riley and the play of Earvin "Magic" Johnson and Kareem Abdul-Jabbar. They finally defeated their old nemesis Boston in the NBA finals, 4–2.

The 1988–89 Detroit Pistons went 63-19 in the regular season and swept the Lakers four straight in the championship series. Led by Coach Chuck Daly, guard Isiah Thomas, and rebounder Dennis Rodman, the "bad boys" went 15-2 in the playoffs.

In my judgment, of all of these teams, only two are really worth holding up against the 76ers, the '71–72 Lakers and the '95–96 Bulls. That's based on sheer numbers. Both had better winning percentages than the 76ers and both won more games.

But because Chamberlain was the Lakers center *and* the 76ers center at the peak of both team's powers, it is hard to truly match L.A. with Philly because Wilt cancels himself out.

However, a comparison of the Wilt-led 76ers to the Michael Jordan–led Bulls is a far more interesting one.

Consider the fact that each team featured the premiere offensive player of their respective eras, one a center, the other a guard.

Nobody could dominate a basketball court like Wilt Chamberlain.

And nobody could dominate a basketball court like Michael Jordan.

Two of the greatest all-time NBA superstars, the very identities of their teams, playing different positions, offering unmatched skills.

Now we've got ourselves a debate.

In fact, Dr. Jack Ramsay—now a popular ESPN TV and Radio NBA basketball analyst—says the 76ers' offense was very similar to the triangle style perfected by the Bulls.

"It was basically a low post offense, had a lot of ball movement, not unlike what the Bulls did," explained Dr. Jack.

"Set up the triangle with your post player high or low," Ramsay explained. "So you have a post player, a wing player, and a perimeter player in the triangle on one side and the other two players on the weak side.

"The ball gets moved to the reverse side, and a new triangle is set over there. Ball goes to the post, gets action as the two perimeter players work off the post man.

"Larry Costello used it in Milwaukee with Alcindor and Oscar."

When asked if the 76ers were the best ever, Ramsay said this:

"It is hard to compare from different eras, but it was a very, very complete team. Could beat anybody today, one of the greatest teams of all time."

Hannum put it much more strongly:

"I think this team would have dominated the league today, too, as long as [the refs] would respect the rule book. If they've got rules, enforce them. Too much physical contact. I get disgusted that they don't play the game the way we used to play it. We were just as physical, if not more so, but it was different. We played according to the rules. You couldn't and wouldn't whine and protest every call.

"Only two other teams compare, Boston and the Knicks under Holtzman, Bradley, and DeBusschere."

"Such a dominant physical team, truly special," said Billy Cunningham of the 1985–86 Celts. "McHale, Parish, and Bird were very gifted, but there's never been a front line as physical as [the 76ers]."

"I hate to compare generations," said Hal Greer. "Different times, different athletes, different conditions. [The] Sixers are right on top, when you talk about the greatest teams of all time."

Billy Melchionni concurred: "This team has to be up there when you talk about the greatest in history."

Matty Guokas said of his 76ers, "Hard to compare eras, but definitely one of the ten best ever. Would crush a lot of teams today. Would still be a dominant team."

But how about against the 72-10 Bulls?

From a coaching standpoint, the matchup seems even. Phil Jackson has proven himself to be one of the outstanding coaches in NBA history, winning eight world titles with two different teams and running off two streaks of three championships in a row.

For his part, Hannum did something no other coach could do in his era—he twice beat the Boston Celtics for the NBA crown.

The Boston Celtics *were* basketball back then. But Hannum knocked them off in 1958 at the Hawks' helm and did it again nine years later with the 76ers. That put him in a very elite coaching group of one.

As for player personnel, the Bulls were, for all intents and purposes, a three-man team: Jordan, Scottie Pippen, and Dennis Rodman. The rest of the players were basically journeymen role players. Frankly, Jordan made them all look better than they were.

There was no doubt scorers could score against Philly. Rick Barry proved that in the championship series by averaging 41 points a game and hitting 55 in game three.

So it follows that Michael Jordan could easily pile up points against the 76ers, even fighting off the Oscar Robertson–like harassment that Wally Jones would have applied. Jordan would have had to work for his shots against Wally Wonder. No other guard would push him harder.

Conversely, who on the Bulls could stop Wilt from doing anything he wanted? Luc Longley?

I think not.

Jordan would get his points and steals all right, and Chamberlain would get his points, his rebounds, and his assists.

Of course, in the great tradition of "Hack-a-Shaq," the Bulls might have tried "Whack-a-Wilt." But Wilt had a way of hitting the free throws when the most pressure was on, so the strategy might have backfired.

And ask yourself this question.

Would Michael Jordan drive the lane with his usual reckless abandon if he knew Wilt was lurking there? Knowing Jordan, he would have tried, but he probably would have been slammed to the deck a few times in the process, by either Wilt or Luke Jackson.

Wilt had never fouled out of a game, but he made his presence known in the middle. He was among the most powerful, dangerous men ever to play the game. He used that power, but never misused it. The Bulls and Jordan would have most certainly felt it.

In a May 1999 newspaper interview, Chamberlain scoffed at the contention that Jordan is the greatest pro player ever:

"And then you have to listen that Jordan is the greatest, as a guard or whatever. I don't see how you would form your mouth to do that.

And can you remember, in the fourteen years of Michael Jordan driving to the basket with his tongue hanging out, ever seeing him laying on the floor with his tongue out?" said Wilt.

The thuggery of the NBA (disguised as tough defense), which seemed to blossom with the "bad boy" Pistons and evolve into an overall bruising style of basketball in the '90s, would not have impeded or threatened the 76ers one iota. Not with Wilt Chamberlain and Luke Jackson around. They would have given as good as they got, or even better.

Specifically, the Philly front line would have caused big problems for the Bulls. The talented Pippen would have had a strong impact for Chicago, but the 6' 7" 228-pounder would have taken a beating from the 6' 9", 250-pound Jackson. And 6' 8", 220-pound rebounding whiz Dennis Rodman would have had to cope with Chamberlain, Jackson, Chet Walker, and Billy Cunningham at one time or another. Rodman gave what Bulls general manager Jerry Krause called "the nasty factor." But that's because no one else in the league could contend with him.

He'd have been a matchstick for Chamberlain or Jackson. Can any fan imagine Rodman playing games with either guy like he did with Karl Malone? Rodman wouldn't have pulled one of his psyche jobs on Wilt or Luke. They were too smart, too confident, and too damn strong for that. They could get just as nasty.

Rodman led the league in rebounding in '95–96 with 14.9 per game. His best number ever was 18.7 rebounds per game with the 1991–92 Detroit Pistons.

Chump change for Wilt Chamberlain.

Having Luke Jackson next to him would have just been icing on the cake against someone like Rodman.

In the backcourt, Jordan would likely have guarded Hal Greer. In all of his playoff confrontations, Jordan never defended a middle-distance deadeye the likes of Hal. Sure, at 6' 6" he would have slowed the 6' 2" Greer down considerably, but Greer would have gotten his share off of powerful picks set by Wilt, Luke, Chet Walker, or Billy Cunningham. Jordan vs. Greer would have allowed Wally to get streaky on offense against the plodding Steve Kerr.

In terms of a sixth man, the Bulls could offer only Toni Kukoc to match up with Billy Cunningham for a spark off the bench. Kukoc could score in spurts, but he could not equal the "instant offense" of the Kangaroo Kid.

And add this in.

The 76ers were part of a 10-team league, where each club had nine games against every rival, including their toughest ones.

The Bulls certainly didn't play New York, San Antonio, Utah, Seattle, and the Lakers as frequently as Philly played Boston, San Francisco, Los Angeles, Cincinnati, and St. Louis. And, don't forget that the 76ers had only 30 "official" home games, playing 17 other contests on the so-called neutral courts. They were still road games, no matter what they were called. The 76ers won 14 of 17.

The Bulls were part of a talent-diluted, 29-team league, and too many teams spread rivalries very thin, making key matchups a rarity.

Simply put, the Bulls' 72 wins were a lot easier to come by than the 68 victories for the 76ers. The 76ers were far more battle-tested than the Windy City five.

Even Tom Heinsohn said that the Bulls' success was linked to a thinned-out talent pool after NBA expansion into Toronto.

"I think you have to see how expansion has played a part in all of the big records—even with the team I coached in '72–73," argued the Celtics Hall-of-Famer.

"The Lakers went 69-13 in '72 and we were 68-14 the year after. But a couple of years before that, [Cleveland, Buffalo, and Portland entered the league in 1970–71]."

Let's review.

At center, the biggest advantage of them all with Wilt and the 76ers over Longley and the Bulls.

At forward, advantage 76ers with Jackson and Walker over Pippen and Rodman.

At guard, Jordan with the obvious singular advantage, but in tandem, Greer and Jones made it more than competitive against MJ and whoever his partner was.

Off the bench, Cunningham had the advantage of energy and consistency over Kukoc.

On the bench, a dead heat with Hannum and Jackson, the ex-Marine against the Zen master.

NFL Films and ESPN once did a fantasy Super Bowl matchup between the Pittsburgh Steelers, team of the '70s, and the San Francisco 49ers, team of the '90s.

It didn't necessarily prove anything, with the game highlights constructed from various Steelers–49ers games.

But it was fun to watch and to speculate on what really might have been.

It would be just as much fun to see a concocted confrontation between the champion 76ers and the champion Bulls. With Chamberlain and Jordan center stage, we can only imagine the media hype had it ever been real.

As for me, I know which team I would pick to win a best-of-seven between these two titans.

The Philadelphia 76ers would win it all—in six games, just like they disposed of the Warriors.

Now, there is one other matter.

Because of their amazing 15-1 playoff run in the 2000–2001 post-season—the best record ever in the NBA playoffs—I am sure there are some basketball fans who think the champion Los Angeles Lakers should be up there with the greatest teams of all time.

I'm not one of them.

In the final analysis, champions must be judged on season-long prowess and performance. When you look at the Lakers from that vantage point, the perspective changes.

The Lakers went 56-26 during the regular season, finishing 31-10 at home and a mediocre 25-16 on the road. Playoffs included, their overall win-loss mark was 71-27.

The '67 Sixers finished 79-17, with eight more wins and 10 fewer losses.

Case closed.

But wait, you say.

What about Shaquille O'Neal and Kobe Bryant?

OK, what about them?

Shaq has never, ever, ever played against the likes of a Wilt Chamberlain. He can push Philly's Dikembe Motumbo around and play his psychological word games. It would cut no ice against Wilt. Yes, Shaq is plenty strong, but Wilt never fully exhibited his strength. He would have overpowered the man on offense and defense.

Kobe Bryant was never tested by the 76ers on defense during the final series. But consider how Wally Wonder might have played Kobe, wearing him out, pestering him to no end.

And who would you take? Lakers starters Horace Grant, Rick Fox, and Derek Fisher or Philly's Luke Jackson, Chet Walker, and Hal Greer?

Want to bring Robert Horry off the bench or Billy Cunningham?

Thinking that the Lakers had a big advantage on three-pointers? Well, there was no three-point shot when the 76ers reigned, but Greer, Walker, Jones, and Cunningham would have matched or beaten them in a head-to-head modern-day shoot-out. Without the three-point shot, the Lakers (and Bulls) would not have been nearly as formidable.

So, Lakers fans, don't go there!

The Lakers—Phil Jackson or no Phil Jackson—were not in the same class as Hannum's men.

Face it and get over it.

The title of Chapter 4 said it all about the 1966–67 NBA champion Philadelphia 76ers.

One Year Wondrous.

The best NBA team of all time.

T E N

Final Stats

I remember sitting in my office at Washington's 24-hour local cable news channel late that Tuesday afternoon in October 1999. It had been an uneventful news day, and as it approached time for me to wrap up my work, my mind wandered to more research that I needed to do on this book I was writing about the 1966–67 Philadelphia 76ers. I had been slowly making progress over the first six months of the project and considered myself lucky to have obtained interviews early on with Alex Hannum, Jack Ramsay, Wali (his Muslim first name) Jones, Matty Guokas, and others.

I had also begun my quest to get a one-on-one interview with Wilt Chamberlain. After all, there could be no book without Wilt's first-hand recollections of his first professional title. Bob Vetrone, the former 76ers beat writer, and later their publicity man, was kind enough to slip me Wilt's California home address and phone number while I visited with him in his athletic department office at LaSalle University.

I had felt it would be a dream come true to actually speak to the man himself. For that reason, I suppose I was nervous about even approaching him, but I knew I had to make a run at it.

I decided to write a letter of introduction to Wilt, hoping that when I called, he would at least know who I was and what I was trying to do. Later, I phoned him several times and left messages. There was never a response. I chalked it up to the inherent difficulty of reaching Wilt Chamberlain and getting him to agree to any kind of an interview. I knew his interviews were rare, and I was a total outsider, completely unknown to him. Why would he be interested in talking to me? The likelihood of ever getting to him seemed remote, but I was persistent, hoping that my recent association with Wali Jones might lead to him putting in a good word for me with Chamberlain. Wali had told me that he was going to visit Wilt in Los Angeles in late September and that Wilt would probably come to Miami in December for a charity basketball tournament. It would be a chance for me to get a few precious minutes with him.

Suddenly, I heard the news on my own television station.

Wilt Chamberlain had died.

My jaw dropped. I said to myself, *No, this can't be. Not Wilt.*

I raced downstairs to the sports department to get more information, and my staff confirmed that he was found in his palatial Bel-Air mansion, dead from an apparent heart attack at the age of 63.

Still stunned, I decided to head home. As soon as I got inside, I flipped on ESPN to get the very latest. The news remained slow to sink in. But another thought began to emerge.

With Wilt gone, I knew that my book could truly be the chronicle of his first championship, dedicated to his achievements and his memory. I started taping every television show about his death. I went online and started downloading every article I could find. I remembered that just a few months earlier, Wilt had been named Philadelphia's greatest sports figure by fans voting in a *Daily News* contest. He had nosed out Julius Erving by 96 votes. I immediately thought how lucky he was to win that honor before he passed away.

I found his own words, from a few years earlier, as he tried to answer the question, "What should your legacy be?" They revealed so much of the man:

> I think my legacy should be that I gave credence that you could be big, bigger than most, and still have athletic ability. Even though George Mikan had done a great deal before me, I think I embodied what a big man was able to do. I think I helped bring some good notoriety to being big. I notice that when I walk on the streets now, I'm not stared at so much because people envision basketball players as being big and tall, and they've now become a big part of society. People no longer look at them as freaks. They really have now zoned in on the fact when they see a tall young kid. They don't really chastise him. They say, "Oh man, you're going to be a great basketball player." I believe I proved that you could be seven-foot and still be very, very functional in sports, where it wasn't believed to be during my time.

A few days later, I watched spellbound as the greats of the NBA, friends and foes alike, came to pay their respects to Wilt in L.A.

"I feel unspeakably injured," said Bill Russell. "I've lost a dear and exceptional friend and an important part of my life. Our relationship was intensely personal. Many have called our competition the greatest rivalry in the history of sports. We didn't have a rivalry, we had genuinely fierce competition that was based on friendship and respect. We just loved playing against each other. The fierceness of the competition bonded us for eternity. We loved competition. Wilt loved competition.

"Wilt was the greatest offensive player I have ever seen. I've seen none better. Because his talents and skills were so superhuman, his play forced me to play at my highest level. If I didn't, I'd risk embarrassment, and our team would likely lose.

"He sent me through hell on so many nights. As far as I'm concerned, he and I will be friends through eternity."

"In Dippy's life there were no sad songs," said his longtime friend and former Harlem Globetrotters teammate Meadowlark Lemon. "He lived life to the fullest."

Lemon reminded everyone that on the court, Wilt "was so good, he could do anything he wanted."

His attorney and confidant Seymour Goldberg declared that he was more than just a basketball player. "He wanted to be a man for all seasons," said Goldberg, "and I think he was."

Several days later, there was a second service in Wilt's first hometown, Philadelphia. The mourners came to Mount Carmel Baptist Church on Race Street, site of Wilt's old Sunday school, and just a Chamberlain giant step away from his boyhood home at 401 North Salford.

On that day, the basketball heroes paying respects were Philly's heroes. Billy Cunningham, John Chaney, Tom Gola, and Paul Arizin. Many who were there knew of the special friendship Wilt had shared with Arizin's terminally ill granddaughter, Stephanie.

Cunningham said, "I had to be here to show how I felt about the man, not just the player." Billy recalled rides to and from New York in the big guy's Bentley, when the veteran spoke volumes to the rookie about life in pro ball.

But it was the people from Wilt's neighborhood that made the service special. Some were the guys from the "Brook." They had grown up in Wilt's giant shadow, but were closer to him than anyone. People like Vince Miller.

"It's so hard to put into words," said Miller. "Wilt has been my best friend for over fifty years. How many people can say that?"

"It had me down for quite a bit," said Wali Jones in an interview just a few weeks after Wilt's passing. "He was more than just a teammate. I had seen him two years before where he was great. All he was talking about was his hip replacement, then I found out later he needed a pacemaker. But when I saw him he looked big, strong, and alive . . . and here one year later."

Wali's words were another inspiration to my work. I was going to tell the story of this team, Wilt's team, Wilt's first championship team. My work continued with renewed dedication, building a tribute to this superb and unique collection of athletes. Though Wilt is gone, the other 76ers live on.

Wali Jones works as community relations liaison for the NBA's Miami Heat. He does his best work with kids, and he's done it for almost 15 years in South Florida. Jones's desire to teach and educate young people has always been strong. He heads the Heat's Stay in School, Team Up, and Excellence in Academics programs. He has taught in middle schools and high schools in 10 states, making the most of his degree in educational psychology from Norfolk State. He used to regularly run basketball clinics in South Philadelphia and worked with the city's gangs. He conducts those same clinics today in Miami and around the country, visiting more than 250 sites each year.

I can attest firsthand to the power of his message. In the fall of 1999, I traveled to Hanover County, Virginia, just outside Richmond, where Jones spent two days reaching out to troubled boys, most of them African-American, at a juvenile correction center.

Recalling his own experiences with neighborhood gangs, and the troubles he endured as a young adult, Jones used basketball and inspiration to encourage a commitment to studying and learning. He tried to prepare the youngsters for Virginia's important Standards of

Learning test. Jones's basic message is: "You gotta lotta life to live, so get outta here."

He began forming that message just two years after he and the 76ers won their title.

"In 1969, we established 'Shoot for the Stars Institute' under the name of 'African American Athletes for Action.' Then we changed the name to 'Concerned Athletes in Action.' Then later, after I worked for the federal government in human development training, we changed it to 'Shoot for the Stars,' (Students Training and Teaming Around Responsibility).

"So, we have different trainers who travel around the country, training in school systems and in corrections and doing some work with the justice department."

In 1972, he and fellow Villanova alumnus Jim Washington, who also played with Jones for two and a half years on the 76ers, decided to write their own book, a historical account of long-forgotten black athletes, dating back to the 1870s.

"A lot of kids don't know anything about their heritage," Jones said. "They know nothing about how great these men, these women, were. We had [the book] at the game, advertising it, but it was too militant for Milwaukee."

The book was called *Black Champions Challenge American Sports*, published by the David McKay Company in New York.

In it, the two authors broke down every decade from the 1870s to the early 1970s, telling the stories of black athletes who had been at the tops of their respective sports, but who never received the accolades they should have received because they were black. The story began in the decade of the 1870s because it was two years earlier that Congress had passed the 14th Amendment to the Constitution, guaranteeing equality for all under the law. The book showed that black athletes were far from equal then, and well into the next century.

The preface of the book is stirring:

A beautiful Black child in ugly ghetto New York writes about his experiences in school:

> They send notes to
> My mother
> Like tickets
> To a animal
> Show.
> I'M NO ANIMAL
> I'M NO ANIMAL
> I'M NO ANIMAL

The child is father to the man. If radical changes are not made, this beautiful Black youngster may grow up and enter "that greatest of democratic arenas," i.e., organized sports, only to have to cry out again, "I'M NO ANIMAL."

On the day I visited, Jones had gathered 50 or so young inmates in the correction center's gymnasium to shoot jumpers and run layup lines. But he also read to them from his book.

Those words, "I'm no animal, I'm no animal, I'm no animal," echoed around the gym as he read them out loud. He asked the young men to repeat the phrase. They did it quietly, almost seeming uncomfortable with the words.

Then he asserted, "We are not animals. We are human beings." The youngsters repeated it with him.

"If you respect yourself, others are gonna respect you," Jones said.

"These drills and all the things we've been doing are really things that apply to everything you do in life. That's why I watch whether guys are cheering for each other. I watch whether guys are focused to win, support their team. I'm watchin' guys that are slammin' around, don't particularly care about it. But that's all right, some guys aren't interested in basketball. But these drills are not just for the game per se, but for me to see behavior."

He worked the court and the kids that day with his friend Kenny Hamilton, former coach at Philly's Ben Franklin High School and one of the most successful high school coaches in the city's history.

"We don't want to see you in here no more," said Hamilton. "We want you to learn the behavior skills so that when you get outta here you do things that won't get you back in here. The things that we're doing here are helping you develop self-discipline, group discipline. The more successful you are, the better your chances are of leaving this place."

Jones and Hamilton continually mixed the academic and reading motivation with the basketball competition. They handed out a "Shoot for the Stars" goals study sheet to each student.

On it, the young men would have to list the subjects they were studying in class, and then write two goals next to each subject, for example:

Goal A—I will get a "B"
Goal B—I will study 20 minutes

Jones follows up with the students and makes repeat visits. There is little financial gain in it. His rewards are kids who get out and live productive lives.

"The Creator gave me a gift to communicate with kids. Working with kids is the most you can do."

Afterwards, we shot baskets together in the detention center gym. He can still knock them down from outside. In fact, in 1996 he won a gold medal at the Master's International Senior Games.

He always likes to let the youngsters and older fans alike see his championship ring from the 76ers. He lost it in 1969 while jamming on some conga drums. (Jones always had a thing for music. In fact, he once cut a Top 40 record and appeared on *American Bandstand*, under the tutelage of one of his old Overbrook High basketball teammates, Len Borisoff. Borisoff was better known as Len Barry, lead singer of the 60s Philly rock group The Dovells and solo artist with the 1965 mega-hit "1-2-3.")

Ever creative, Jones melted down his high school ring and refashioned a new title ring with the words "NBA's Greatest Team" engraved on it.

He also makes it a point to tell the kids about the friendship, teamwork, and success of the 76ers, and how those values apply to everyday life.

"That team is with me every day."

He still fondly remembers his teammates through his belief in astrology. "I think it goes to studying people. You look at their mannerisms, their behaviors, their temperaments. When you attack players, certain guys respond differently. I use it for temperament, moods, trying to understand people from where they are coming from. Makes you understand people better. I don't judge."

Chamberlain was Leo to Jones's Aquarius.

"Direct opposite," Jones said. "He knew my spirit was free, and I laughed and had fun. Greatest player ever to put on a pair of sneaks. Believed that he was the best. I really look at him as an example of a man showing how you can achieve. An entrepreneur. Very intelligent, very knowledgeable. People don't know how brilliant he was."

Luke Jackson is a Scorpio.

"Very intense," remembered Jones. "But he knew how to have fun. A warrior. Hardest worker and battler. Prototype power forward. He was the enforcer. He came to play. He did the dirty work. We became Batman and Robin, doing silly things to break the monotony in airports."

Hal Greer's sign is Cancer.

"Consummate pro. I looked up to him. I watched him and stuck by him. He appreciated me 'cause I was not like the other younger guys. I would beat him but he would never say anything. He ignored me. Would just love to shove my arm away. Hal taught me how to be prepared. He made me a professional."

Billy Cunningham is a Gemini.

"Aquarius and Gemini. We always clicked. A great human being. During the summer we played in the Baker League [a Philadelphia playground league, in which Jones would wear a white doctor's coat to the games to show that he was going to operate. A precursor of Dr. J?]. We became best friends. He helped my brother Bill get a scholarship to Denver University. A guy from Denver saw Bill. Billy said, 'You got anything to help this kid?' My brother is now a coach and counselor in Denver. He helped my son get a scholarship, too."

Matty Guokas is a Pisces.

"A guy I really had fun with . . . the Gook and I had fun. He knew the game. Came into his own with our team. Another guy who kept me communicating with that side of our team, the young players from Philly. He could always relate back to that pride of Philly."

Chet Walker is also a Pisces.

"Creative, imaginative," said Jones. "Very, very quiet type of player but it always showed up in the statistics, all the little things he did, all the intangibles. Class."

It was Chet Walker who nicknamed him Wally Wonder.

Even today, he's still working wonders.

Hal Greer and his wife, Mayme, live in Arizona and run a business that helps people and companies build golf courses. Mayme does most of the administrative work while Hal does a lot of schmoozing. He plays charity golf tournaments all over the country. He loves that little white ball.

I sat down with him at the Lansdowne Country Club in Virginia, just outside of Washington, in the summer of 2000. Greer, still tight and wiry, had played a great round on the final day, winning one of the tournament trophies in the event run by Washington Redskins Hall-of-Famer Bobby Mitchell. He had signed enough autographs to wear out his golf grip.

Although Greer had to overcome some personal difficulties after his basketball career ended, the successes of his life are many—like his daughter Cherie. She's considered by many to be America's greatest female lacrosse player.

"Amazing," Greer said of Cherie. "We had a Ping-Pong table in the basement of the house, and she was so small she could barely see over the table," he remembered. "We just hit the ball back and forth, and she was a great athlete then. It was very, very competitive. We play now and she beats me regularly. I'm proud of her. What I like about her most is that she's down-to-earth, no big head, just a great person."

After graduating from the University of Virginia and representing her country in the 2000 Olympic Games, Cherie has a professional career in sports management. She's got the genes to make it work.

Hal Greer went on to be named one of the 50 greatest players in NBA history, as selected by the league in 1996.

And Marshall University's hometown, Huntington, West Virginia, even named a street in his honor of their most distinguished sports alumnus—Hal Greer Boulevard.

Note: *Two Celtics were also at that charity golf event, Bill Russell and Sam Jones. I caught up with Jones before the awards banquet but he declined my request for an interview about the 76ers' championship team.*

"I don't want to talk about that," Jones said. "We lost." We spoke by phone a half dozen times after that, as I continued to pursue an interview, but Sam said he just couldn't fit it into his schedule.

Bill Russell also wasn't talking. An associate of mine had slipped Russell my business card at the tournament, and I approached the basketball legend as he was departing for the airport. He promised to call me the next day, but didn't. Russell's agent never returned any of my calls.

I also tried to get to Red Auerbach, who still lives in Washington, D.C., and attends basketball games at his alma mater, George Washington University. Through intermediaries at the university, I requested an interview with Red on two occasions. He declined.

I guess the memories of that fateful season are still too much for those old Celtics to bear.

Matt Guokas is still very much a part of the NBA scene, more than three decades after winning it all with the 76ers.

Guokas is color analyst on game telecasts of the Cleveland Cavaliers on Sports Channel Ohio and has also done online NBA game analysis on the Web for NBC.

"The biggest memory of that team was that we had the attitude that we could not go out and coast," said Guokas. "We played the same way, game in and game out.

"When Wilt secured the ball [on a rebound], he made the guard come back, and it was walked up and the play would go through him. If someone else got the rebound, then the team would run."

He learned well from Alex Hannum and the veteran 76ers. He later became the team's assistant coach under Billy Cunningham, then took over for Billy C. as head man after the 1984–85 season. He spent two and a half years at the helm, finishing with a 128-88 record before getting the ax following a 20-23 start in 1987–88. His next stop was the expansion Orlando Magic. He was the team's first coach, starting with the 1989–90 campaign. He finished 111-217 in four seasons, but brought the Magic to 41-41 before giving way the following season to Brian Hill.

In the summer of 1999, I asked Guokas to use his coach's eye and analytical skills to size up the 1966–67 76ers.

On Alex Hannum: "Came in with a lot of enthusiasm.[Dolph] Schayes was fired not because of Wilt, but because of management's frustration with losing to Boston again. Alex had been successful with the Syracuse franchise a few years before. [He] had a good influence on Wilt, but they were not very friendly. Wilt was gregarious with everybody on the team, but they were not very friendly."

On Wilt: "Clearly the most dominant player in the history of the game. He realized the talent around him and changed his game. He seemed to get every rebound. Was expected to get 23, 25, or 28 a night. Decided to be the ringmaster, that everything would go through him. He played almost every minute. Wilt was into every game, no matter who he was playing, but his innermost feelings harbored a certain bitterness toward the Celtics."

On Luke Jackson: "Charles Oakley, Dale Davis type player. Played as hard as he could. Enthusiastic, emotional, talked it and walked it. Upbeat guy, not a comedian, but kept the guys loose."

On Hal Greer: "Fierce competitor, one of the great middle-distance jump shooters. Never wanted to sit out. A good one-on-one player who did a great job moving without the ball."

On Chet Walker: "Skilled one-on-one player. Had a great ability to rebound. Could have scored 25 a night but took what came to him because of being surrounded by people like Wilt and Greer."

On Billy Cunningham: "Would have been a starter on any other team in the league. But Boston had made the sixth man very valuable back then, and that made it easier for Billy to accept that role, surrounded by the players we had. Great one-on-one player off the dribble. Great instincts."

On Wali Jones: "Stepped in after Costello was hurt. Battled defensively. Dangerous but streaky shooter."

On Larry Costello: "Started the year as the other guard with Greer. Alex asked him to come out of retirement. He saw that it was going to be a good team. He would either drive the ball to the basket or go with the set shot. Didn't have an in-between game. He would battle you every day at practice . . . tough . . . physical."

On Dave Gambee: "Wilt played every minute and with Chet and Billy and Luke as the three forwards, Dave didn't have much of a chance to play. Was my roommate. Learned a lot about the league from him. He was a garbage man, no great leaping ability, was a good position player, and had the underhand free throw."

On Bill Melchionni: "Excellent jump shooter from the perimeter. Didn't get the chance to play that much, but would usually get four to five minutes in the first half, then often produced down the stretch."

Guokas on Guokas (modestly): "Didn't have much of a role unless the guards got into foul trouble. When Costy got hurt, got more playing time."

His playing time against the Warriors in game six of the championship series paved the way for the 76ers' ultimate victory.

Luke Jackson is retired after 25 years as Recreation Commissioner of Beaumont, Texas.

Despite the presence of Wilt Chamberlain, several of the 76ers named Luke as the team's Most Valuable Player in the title season.

"Luke was always my key player," said Greer. "He was my roommate all those years we played. We ran together and did the whole thing. In my opinion, he was the greatest power forward of all time."

"The key player to me was Luke Jackson," said Billy Cunningham. "No one sacrificed his talents like Luke did for the betterment of the team. He would have been an all-star center. The 76ers would have been outstanding with him at center. He did the dirty work. He sacrificed his offensive skills for the team. An emotional leader, always came to play. When he stepped into the locker room he didn't want to hear about anything but winning. I gained more and more respect for what he did after coaching. He just realized what he had to do."

"We knew anytime we took the court we could win," said Jackson of the '67 team. "We knew Boston was not gonna win that year. We put it to 'em pretty good. But they were a tough team to beat.

"Don't know if we suffered a letdown [in the championship series against San Francisco] or if it was just fatigue. Got in gear after the first game. We wanted to win it at home and may have been pressing. Let it slip away a little. Our fans deserved to see it at home."

Of his teammates, Jackson said: "Overall, all good guys. When you see them today, they are the same people."

The quiet man, Chet Walker, elected not to share his memories for this book. But Walker's career after basketball is out there for anyone and everyone to see.

For one thing, he had a magnificent career with the Chicago Bulls after being traded by the 76ers just two years after they won the title. During Walker's six seasons with the Bulls, they made the playoffs every time, and to this day many 76ers fans think sending Walker away at the peak of his powers was the worst trade the team ever made. Walker himself was stunned by the deal and considered retiring. But he made a new home with the Bulls.

In fact, Walker's scoring numbers were more impressive with Chicago than Philly, perhaps because he didn't have to share his shooting time with the likes of Chamberlain, Greer, and Cunningham. Chet averaged more than 20 points per game during his first three years in the Windy City, hitting a 22-point mark in back-to-back seasons. Even in his final year, 1974–75, Walker racked up a 19.2 scoring average.

Walker left the NBA in a bitter salary dispute with the Bulls. It was a battle that went to court, as Chet sued his team and the league for federal antitrust violations. Walker lost his case and ended his career. He finally had to trade his basketball suit for a business suit. And he didn't pick just any business. He picked show business.

Walker went west to team up with a movie producer friend from Beverly Hills. Although he was anything but an overnight success, Walker stayed with it, producing for televison and the big screen. Among his projects were *Freedom Road*, a 1980 network mini-series starring Kris Kristofferson, and *The Fiendish Plot of Dr. Fu Manchu*, which was the final movie made by the late comic actor Peter Sellers.

But Walker's greatest off-court triumph came in 1989, when he won an Emmy Award for Outstanding Children's Program, Prime Time. He produced *A Mother's Courage: The Mary Thomas Story*. It aired on NBC as a "Magical World of Disney" special. It chronicled the life of the mother of NBA star Isiah Thomas, who grew up on the mean streets of Chicago's West Side. The real-life story was much like his own, growing up in Benton Harbor, Michigan, with his mother holding the family together in the face of poverty and violence.

Walker also penned an autobiography entitled *Long Time Coming*. He lives in Southern California.

•   •   •

There's a great picture of *Coach* Billy Cunningham in the Thursday, June 2, 1983, edition of *The Philadelphia Inquirer*.

In it, he's wearing big sunglasses and holding a celebratory stogie in that talented left hand of his. He'd just gotten back to town after his team won the 1983 NBA championship, sweeping away the Los Angeles Lakers in four straight.

The first time Billy C. won the title with the '67 Sixers, the catch phrase was "Boston is Dead." But this was the "Fo, Fo, Fo" team, a phrase coined by the exuberant Philly big man Moses Malone, whose prediction of an undefeated playoff season with three four-game sweeps almost came true. The Sixers went 12-1 in the post-season.

This was the championship that Julius Erving said the 76ers owed the fans of Philadelphia after the 76ers blew a two-game advantage in the 1977 NBA final series against the Portland Trailblazers, who, ironically, were coached by ex-76ers GM Dr. Jack Ramsay and featured the hippie-type, long-haired version of Bill Walton.

"We owe you one," said Dr. J at the time, knowing full well the 76ers lost to a lesser, lucky team. But it took six more seasons with two more defeats in the playoff finals before the debt was paid, and it was Cunningham who finally led Doc, Moses, Andrew Toney, Mo Cheeks, Bobby Jones, and the rest of the 76ers to the long-awaited crown.

"This team has proved something," rejoiced Billy C. "These are men who failed and then were able to pick themselves up and go over the mountain."

"We really got this for Doc," added Malone. "And once we had it for Doc, we went out and got it for the city, too."

For Cunningham, it ended more than five seasons of coaching frustration, after he took over the team in early 1977. He had been a spectacular success by any standard. He had posted five straight winning seasons and taken Philly to the NBA finals twice against the Los Angeles Lakers.

In 1981, Billy led the 76ers to the Eastern Conference finals against a longtime foe he had vanquished the previous playoff year, Boston. It was a dramatic, tightly fought, down-to-the wire series, which most basketball fans saw only on late-night tape-delayed CBS network broadcasts. This was the NBA's down cycle, fueled by rampant reports of player drug use. The league finals were not ready for prime time. The Sixers lost in seven games to their archrivals, including a heartbreaking 91–90 loss in the final contest at the Boston Garden.

As difficult as that defeat was to swallow, it set the stage for perhaps one of the single most anticipated triumphs in the history of 76ers basketball.

The following season, it came down to the 76ers and the Celtics once again in the Eastern finals. Again, it came down to a seventh game, and again it came in the 76ers' personal playoff House of Horrors—the Boston Garden. The Celtics had never lost a seventh game final in their building, and they were ready for an easy kill.

But Billy's boys battled Boston like never before, posting a three-point lead at halftime, extending it to 12 by the end of the third period, and winning it 120–108.

The monkey was off their back. The ghosts of the Garden were silenced. It was a life-saving win, a franchise-saving win.

"If we'd have lost, this entire franchise would have been very, very shaky. We would have lost the confidence of an entire city," said then-owner Harold Katz.

"We've been living with the ignominy of what happened last spring, living with it the whole year, being reminded of it day after day," added general manager Pat Williams.

Cunningham was vindicated after the local media made the 76ers a beaten foe before the game.

"It hurt, it hurt a lot," he said.

"I hope you like this," Cunningham shouted to a sportswriter. "I hope you like this, and everybody else, too."

Everybody did.

The Lakers spoiled things by beating the 76ers in the 1982 NBA finals, but Cunningham and his crew more than evened the score with their 1983 final series sweep over L.A.

Cunningham stayed at the helm one more season before ceding control to assistant coach Matt Guokas. He did some NBA broadcasting after that, then got back into the management biz by helping to launch the Miami Heat expansion franchise. Billy made quite a financial killing when he sold his interest in the team. Now he just chooses to describe himself as self-employed (he owns a restaurant in Philly and maintains homes there and in Jupiter, Florida) and says he's involved in "a variety of business ventures."

In 1996, he also was named one of the 50 best players in NBA history.

Billy Cunningham wrote the foreword for this book. No one could have done it any better, or more fondly. He embodies everything that links the word *champion* to the Philadelphia 76ers.

Larry Costello not only made his mark as an NBA player, he took it a notch higher as an NBA coach, learning lessons from watching Alex Hannum and turning them into a world title. He led the 1970–71 Milwaukee Bucks to the NBA crown, posting a 66-16 record with another superstar big man, Lew Alcindor, and his old backcourt adversary, Oscar Robertson. He later took his team to the finals a second time, losing to Boston in seven games in the 1974 playoffs. He was boss of the Bucks for eight years, finishing with a record of 410-254 (.617).

Like Hannum, he was a demanding coach. He was meticulous in preparation and developed thick playbooks for his men to memorize. He was one of the first NBA coaches to use a full-time bench assistant, obviously seeing the value of his own service to Hannum during the championship season of the 76ers when he was forced to the bench by recurring leg injuries. But Hannum helped Costy achieve his two biggest goals: a playoff win over Boston and an NBA title.

In recent years, Costello, who lives with his wife in the Fort Myers, Florida area, has been battling illness.

Bill Melchionni also took the management route. After serving his military stint, he averaged 4.6 points per game in the 1967–68 season with the 76ers. He opted out of the expansion draft in 1968, sat out a year, and then signed on with the New York Nets of the American Basketball Association in 1969 when coach Lou Carnesecca came calling. It turned out to be a great move for Melchionni. He became a first team All-ABA guard in 1971–72 and played on both of the Nets' ABA title teams in 1973–74 and 1975–76, the league's final season.

Then he stepped off the floor and into the Nets' front office, serving as the team's general manager for a year and a half.

But the business background Billy built in college sent him in search of greener pastures in the marble canyons. He moved to Wall Street in 1978, and today is a managing director of Credit Suisse First Boston Investment Bank in New York City.

Nicknamed "Cyclops" back then by teammate Jones for his deadeye shooting on the basketball floor, Melchionni turned out to be even more of a deadeye in his third career on the floor of the New York Stock Exchange.

Basketball fans can still find that role player of role players, Dave Gambee, in his beloved Pacific Northwest. The Oregon State alum still lives in Eugene, Oregon, operating his lumber company. In fact, it's a family affair. His three sons work right there with him. After the 76ers' title season, Gambee went on to San Diego in the expansion draft.

"I went from the team that won the most games in the NBA to the team that won the fewest," he joked. He was right. The 76ers had gone 68-13. San Diego finished 15-67.

Further expansion in the 1968–69 season sent him to Milwaukee, where he was reunited for a short time with his Syracuse and 76ers buddy Larry Costello, the Bucks' first head coach. But before that season ended, Gambee was moved to Detroit. Then, in 1969–70, he played his final season with San Francisco.

He actually admitted to me that he doesn't think all that much anymore about his time with the championship 76ers, but said that when he does, the memories are all good.

It wasn't too long between titles for Alex Hannum. Though the Celtics short-circuited his dream of back-to-back NBA crowns with their comeback playoff triumph over the 76ers in 1968, Hannum wasted no time getting another crown, and he did it in his favorite part of the country—the Bay Area. Hannum jumped to the American Basketball Association in the league's second season, taking over as head man of the Oakland Oaks.

This time around Hannum didn't have to figure out how to stop the great Rick Barry. Barry was on Sarge's side for a change. After sitting out his option year with the Warriors following the '67 finals loss to Philly, Barry joined the Oaks. His veteran talent combined with hot rookie of the year Warren Armstrong and Hannum's fiery leadership forged a 60-21 record, good for first place in the ABA West. The Oaks knocked off the Indiana Pacers in the ABA championship series, and Hannum had himself another title in another league, the first man ever to achieve that feat.

Hannum coached for another five years in the ABA. Then he returned to the construction business he started in 1957 to pay the bills he couldn't pay with his paltry pro basketball salary. He never earned more than $8,700 as a player.

"Hamburger players are fined more than eighty–seven hundred dollars for pushing someone now," he told the Basketball Hall of Fame. He was inducted in 1998.

"I'm so thrilled," he said, "because it takes me back to that era, when I played and coached. I'd thought they'd forgotten about us old-timers.

"When I decided it was time to leave basketball, I had several reasons, among them my health. I may have left basketball physically, but I never left it in spirit."

Hannum, now in his late 70s, still holds forth in Coronado, California, near San Diego, where he has lived for the past seven years. He owns a boat called *Second Time Out*. He told me he previously owned a vessel called *Time Out*. He quickly added, "I don't want to get to *Last Time Out*."

As this team celebrates the 35th anniversary of its championship season, almost all of the 76ers are still going strong. Their achievements, their power, their dominance are all assured. Not just in the record books, but in the memories of fans like me, who got so much pleasure from the games they played and the title they won.

Today, I can still very much hear the echoes of their season. That old white radio I used to listen to, resting on its side atop the red Formica counter in the kitchen of my home back in Pittsburgh and bringing me the play-by-play images of my favorite team, is long since gone.

But not the story of that special *Season of the 76ers*.

ELEVEN

Postscript

Philadelphia is not only the City of Brotherly Love. It is perhaps the capital city of murals. They are painted on large walls of the sides of buildings in all neighborhoods of the city. The murals, 1900 of them, are part of a public arts program sponsored by the Philadelphia Department of Recreation. The goal is to create murals of enduring value that reflect the aspirations and experience of the city's diverse communities. The program began in 1984 and is the largest in the country.

On Thursday, April 18, 2001, another in this long line of murals was unveiled. The place was 13th and Vine in Philadelphia. The man in the mural was Wilt Chamberlain. Among those attending the ceremony were Jerrel Green, a teammate of Wilt's from the 1953 YMCA National Championship team, Pat Croce, then president of the Philadelphia 76ers, and Selina Chamberlain Gross, Wilt's sister.

Wilt was pictured, larger than life as usual, in both his old Philadelphia Warriors uniform and his Los Angeles Lakers attire, complete with the gold-colored headband, as well as in close-up, ready to shoot the ball at the basket as he did successfully so many times in his career.

The words next to his pictures were written by another of his sisters, Barbara Clark Lewis. They seem the most fitting way to end this book.

What comes to mind the most for me is when we were walking down the aisle at our high school graduation in June 1955 at Overbrook High School. He was on the left side of the aisle and I was on the right.

As we reached the door to walk, we gave each other the OK sign with our thumbs. Luckily, my name was called first and my family cheered, because when they called Wilt's name, the audience cheered and gave him a standing ovation. I was so proud of him and pretended they were cheering for me as I cried with such tears of joy, realizing that my brother, Dippy, was on his way to becoming a very special and unique person, not only in my eyes, but the whole world.

Appendix A

Most points scored in one game—100 (3/2/62)

Average minutes per game, one season—48.5 (1961–62)

Average minutes per game, career—45.8

Most points by rookie, one game—58 (1/25/60)

Games of 60 or more points—32 (all other NBA players have 19 games of
60 points combined)

Highest field goal percentage—72.7 (1972–73)

Most career rebounds—23,924

Highest career rebounds per game average—22.9

Most rebounds, one game—55 (11/24/60)

Most rebounds by rookie, one game—45 (2/6/60)

League-leading assist average—8.6 (1967–68, only non-guard ever to
lead league in assists)

Most career free throws attempted—11,862

Most free throws made, one game—28 (3/2/62)

Number of games fouled out during career—0 (1,045 games)

Scoring 50 or more points in a game—118 times

Single-season 50 or more point games—45 (1962)

Consecutive complete games played—47

Highest points per game average, one season—50.4 (1962)

Most points by a rookie—2,707 (1960)

Most consecutive field goals—35 (2/17/67 to 2/28/67)

Most Valuable Player, 1960, 1966, 1967, 1968

PLAYOFFS

Most points by a rookie, one game—53 (3/14/60)

Most rebounds, one game—41 (4/5/67)

Highest rebound per game average, one series—32 (1967)

Most rebounds in a half in NBA finals—26 (4/16/67)

CHAMBERLAIN VS. RUSSELL

	Games	Pts	Avg	Reb	Avg	Wins
Chamberlain	142	4,077	28.7	4,072	28.7	57
Russell	142	2,060	14.5	3,373	23.7	85

Appendix B

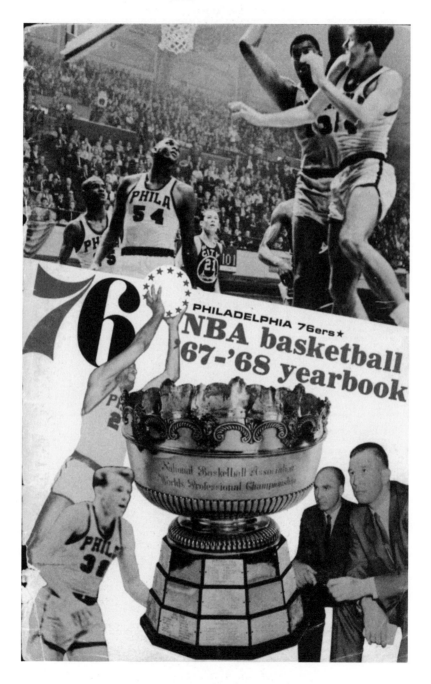

PHILADELPHIA 76ers ★
**NBA basketball
'67-'68 yearbook**

Alex Hannum

Birth Date—July 19, 1923, Height—6-7
Weight—220 Residence—Philadelphia, Pa.

Second year skipper of the 76ers who piloted team to an unprecedented 68-13 record last season en route to the NBA championship . . . Considered one of the most astute coaches in the league with his knowledge of the game and of the rules . . . Known for ability to get the most out of his personnel and for his skill in maneuvering his players . . . Has 8½ years of NBA coaching experience, including two Western Division titles at St. Louis and another at San Francisco . . . Guided St. Louis to NBA title in 1957–58 for last non-Boston title until 76ers won last year . . . Played at University of Southern California and then turned pro with Oshkosh in National League . . . Eventually played for six NBA clubs before retiring after 1956–57 campaign.

HANNUM'S COACHING RECORD

		Won	Lost	Pct.	Finish	Playoffs
1956–57	St. Louis	15	16	.484	1st	6-4
1957–58	St. Louis	41	31	.569	1st	8-3
1960–61	Syracuse	38	41	.481	3rd	4-4
1961–62	Syracuse	41	39	.513	3rd	2-3
1962–63	Syracuse	48	32	.600	2nd	2-3
1963–64	San Francisco	48	32	.600	1st	5-7
1964–65	San Francisco	17	63	.213	5th	
1965–66	San Francisco	35	45	.437	4th	
1966–67	76ers	68	13	.840	1st	11-4
	TOTALS	351	312	.529		38-28

HANNUM'S PLAYING RECORD

	Team	Games	Points
1948–49	Oshkosh	62	365
1949–50	Syracuse	64	482
1950–51	Syracuse	63	471
1951–52	Balt.-Roch.	66	438
1952–53	Rochester	68	346
1953–54	Rochester	72	452
1954–55	Milwaukee	53	313
1955–56	St. Louis	71	385
1956–57	Ft. Wayne-St. Louis	59	191
	TOTALS	578	3443

Wilt Chamberlain

Birth Date—August 21, 1936   Height—7-1/16
Weight—250   Residence—San Francisco, Calif.

Playing ninth year in the NBA in a historic career . . . Finished third in scoring race last year after winning title seven previous years . . . Tallied 1956 points for a 24.1 average to lead team to NBA title . . . Paced league in rebounds with 1957 to win title again . . . His 630 assists set club record and also league mark for center . . . Picked on All-League and on All-Star team for eighth time . . . Raised his career total to over 23,000 points and should hit 25,000 point mark this year . . . Had many sensational shooting streaks last season including a 35 for 35 performance en route to an unparalleled 68.3 shooting percentage . . . Played college basketball at Kansas and one year with Globetrotters before joining NBA.

WILT CHAMBERLAIN'S 1966–67 SCORING VS. EACH NBA RIVAL

	G.	Min.	FG	FGA	FG %	FT	FTA	FT %	R	A	PF	D	Pts.	Ave.
Baltimore	9	399	113	151	74.8	52	96	54.2	206	60	18	0	278	30.9
Cincinnati	9	424	105	151	69.5	47	106	44.3	214	85	19	0	257	28.6
Los Angeles	9	394	101	133	75.9	36	82	43.9	216	87	11	0	238	26.4
Chicago	9	400	94	118	79.7	42	107	39.3	202	51	8	0	230	25.6
New York	9	418	83	117	70.9	38	94	40.4	231	57	25	0	204	22.7
St. Louis	9	414	80	117	68.4	39	98	39.8	213	58	18	0	199	22.1
San Francisco	9	411	73	130	56.2	40	98	40.8	233	79	16	0	186	20.7
Boston	9	423	67	122	54.9	49	107	45.8	240	59	16	0	183	20.3
Detroit	9	339	69	111	62.2	43	87	49.4	202	94	12	0	181	20.1
TOTALS	81	3682	785	1150	68.3	386	875	44.1	1957	630	143	0	1956	24.1

NBA RECORD

	G.	Min.	FG	FGA	FG %	FT	FTA	FT %	R	A	PF	D	Pts.	Ave.
1959–60 Phila.	72	3338*	1065*	2311*	46.1	577	991*	58.2	1941*	168	150	0	2707*	37.6*
1960–61 Phila.	79	3773*	1251*	2479*	50.5*	531	1054*	44.3	2149*	148	127	0	3033*	38.4*
1961–62 Phila.	80	3882*	1597*	3159*	50.5	835*	1363*	61.3	2052*	192	123	0	4029*	50.4*
1962–63 SF	80	3808*	1463*	2770*	52.8*	660	1109*	59.5	1946*	275	136	0	3586*	44.8*
1963–64 SF	80	3689*	1204*	2298*	52.4	540	1016*	53.1	1687	403	182	0	2948*	36.9*
1964–65 SF-Phil.	73	3301	1063*	2083*	51.0*	408	880*	46.4	1673	250	146	0	2534*	34.7*
1965–66 Phila.	79	3737*	1074*	1990*	54.0*	501	976	51.3	1943*	414	171	0	2649	33.5*
1966–67 Phila.	81	3682*	785	1150	68.3*	386	875*	44.1	1957*	630	143	0	1956	24.1
TOTALS	624	29210	9502	18240	52.1	4438	8264	53.7	15348	2480	1178	0	23442	37.6

*Led League

PLAYOFF RECORD

	G.	Min.	FG	FGA	FG %	FT	FTA	FT %	R	A	PF	D	Pts.	Ave.
1959–60 Phila.	9	415	125	252	49.6	49	110	44.5	232	19	17	0	299	33.2
1960–61 Phila.	3	144	45	96	46.9	21	38	55.3	69	6	10	0	111	37.0
1961–62 Phila.	12	576	162	347	46.7	96	151	63.6	319	37	27	0	420	35.0
1963–64 SF	12	558	175	322	54.3	66	139	47.5	302	39	27	0	416	34.7
1964–65 Phila.	11	536	123	232	53.0	76	136	55.9	299	48	29	0	322	29.3
1965–66 Phila.	5	240	56	110	50.9	28	68	41.2	151	15	10	0	140	28.0
1966–67 Phila.	15	718	132	228	57.9	62	160	38.8	437	135	37	0	326	21.7
TOTALS	67	3187	818	1587	51.5	398	802	49.6	1809	299	157	0	2034	30.4

APPENDIX B

Hal Greer

Birth Date—June 16, 1936   Height—6-3
Weight—176   Residence—Philadelphia, Pa.

A real veteran now in his tenth year in the league . . . Has cleared the 13,000 mark in points and could hit the 15,000 mark this season . . . Tallied 1,765 points last year for a 22.1 average, topped only by Chamberlain . . . Also did well in rebounds and assists and was a fine all-around performer . . . Ranks as one of the best middle-distance shooters in league history . . . Picked on Eastern All-Star team for seventh straight year and made All-League second team for the fifth time . . . Is one of circuit's swiftest men and can go all the way through or stop for a jumper on the fast break . . . His one-hand jumper on free throws is distinctive . . . Attended Marshall College before being drafted in 1958 by Syracuse.

HAL GREER'S 1966–67 SCORING VS. EACH NBA RIVAL

	G.	Min.	FG	FGA	FG %	FT	FTA	FT %	R	A	PF	D	Pts.	Ave.
Los Angeles	9	365	89	189	47.1	51	58	87.9	53	40	38	1	229	25.4
Chicago	9	342	79	158	50.0	58	68	85.3	36	44	34	1	216	24.0
Cincinnati	9	329	83	164	50.6	42	52	80.8	44	24	39	1	208	23.1
New York	9	353	89	176	50.6	28	35	80.0	48	27	37	0	206	22.9
St. Louis	9	350	77	183	42.1	50	57	87.7	48	33	30	0	204	22.7
San Francisco	9	363	79	175	45.1	42	52	80.8	49	40	32	0	200	22.2
Baltimore	8	292	74	155	47.7	19	34	55.9	45	33	25	1	167	20.9
Boston	9	387	63	166	38.0	52	72	72.2	44	29	36	1	178	19.8
Detroit	9	305	66	158	41.8	25	38	65.8	55	33	31	0	157	17.4
TOTALS	80	3086	699	1524	45.9	367	466	78.8	422	303	302	5	1765	22.1

NBA RECORD

	G.	Min.	FG	FGA	FG %	FT	FTA	FT %	R	A	PF	D	Pts.	Ave.
1958–59 Syr.	68	1625	308	679	45.4	137	176	77.8	196	101	189	1	753	11.1
1959–60 Syr.	70	1969	388	815	47.6	148	189	79.1	303	188	209	4	924	13.2
1960–61 Syr.	79	2763	623	1381	45.1	305	394	77.4	455	292	242	0	1551	19.6
1961–62 Syr.	71	2676	644	1452	44.3	331	404	81.9	526	313	252	4	1619	22.8
1962–63 Syr.	80	2619	600	1290	46.5	359	434	83.1	460	274	278	4	1559	19.5
1963–64 Phila.	80	3167	715	1621	44.1	435	525	82.9	484	376	291	6	1865	23.3
1964–65 Phila.	70	2600	539	1245	43.3	335	413	81.1	355	313	254	7	1413	20.2
1965–66 Phila.	80	3326	703	1580	44.5	413	514	80.4	473	384	315	6	1819	22.7
1966–67 Phila.	80	3086	699	1524	45.9	367	466	78.8	422	303	302	5	1765	22.1
TOTALS	678	23831	5219	11587	45.0	2830	3515	80.6	3674	2544	2332	37	13268	19.6

PLAYOFF RECORD

	G.	Min.	FG	FGA	FG %	FT	FTA	FT %	R	A	PF	D	Pts.	Ave.
1958–59 Syr.	9	277	39	93	41.9	26	32	81.3	47	20	35	2	104	11.6
1959–60 Syr.	3	84	22	43	51.2	3	4	75.0	14	10	5	0	47	15.7
1960–61 Syr.	8	232	41	106	38.7	33	40	82.5	33	19	32	1	115	14.4
1961–62 Syr.	1	5	0	0	0.0	0	0	0.0	0	0	1	0	0	0.0
1962–63 Syr.	5	214	44	87	50.6	29	35	82.9	27	21	21	1	117	23.4
1963–64 Phila.	5	211	37	95	38.9	33	39	84.6	28	30	19	1	107	21.4
1964–65 Phila.	11	505	101	222	45.5	69	87	79.3	81	55	45	2	271	24ab
1965–66 Phila.	5	226	32	91	35.2	18	23	78.3	36	21	21	0	82	16.4
1966–67 Phila.	15	688	161	375	42.9	94	118	79.7	88	79	55	1	416	27.7
TOTALS	62	2442	477	1112	42.9	305	378	80.7	354	255	234	8	1259	20.3

Billy Cunningham

Birth Date—June 3, 1943   Height—6-7
Weight—215   Residence—Narberth, Pa.

Playing his third year in the league . . . Proved a tremendous asset in ascent to world title last year with his ability to come off the bench and spark team . . . Registered 1,495 points in this reserve role to rank as team's No. 4 point maker . . . Posted 18.5 scoring average . . . A southpaw shooter whose colorful leaping tactics around the basket captivated fans and made the reason apparent for his "Kangaroo Kid" nickname . . . One of best traits is his second effort . . . Played college basketball at University of North Carolina . . . Spent past summer touring city playgrounds giving basketball clinics with Wally Jones.

BILLY CUNNINGHAM'S 1966–67 SCORING VS. EACH NBA RIVAL

	G.	Min.	FG	FGA	FG %	FT	FTA	FT %	R	A	PF	D	Pts.	Ave.
Detroit	9	254	79	144	54.9	55	70	78.6	75	22	25	0	213	23.7
Los Angeles	9	255	63	128	49.2	61	91	67.0	70	24	31	0	187	20.8
New York	9	221	73	166	44.0	26	37	70.3	64	24	30	0	172	19.1
Chicago	9	252	63	129	48.8	43	61	70.5	63	22	27	1	169	18.8
San Francisco	9	241	64	156	41.0	34	57	59.6	65	21	30	0	162	18.0
Boston	9	248	62	138	44.9	35	56	62.5	62	21	33	1	159	17.7
Cincinnati	9	240	60	128	46.9	39	62	62.9	73	27	23	0	159	17.7
Baltimore	9	243	50	126	39.7	47	67	70.1	61	29	37	0	147	16.3
St. Louis	9	214	42	96	43.8	43	57	75.4	56	15	24	0	127	14.1
TOTALS	81	2168	556	1211	45.9	383	558	68.6	589	205	260	2	1495	18.5

NBA RECORD

	G.	Min.	FG	FGA	FG %	FT	FTA	FT %	R	A	PF	D	Pts.	Ave.
1965–66 Phila.	80	2134	431	1011	42.6	281	443	63.4	599	207	301	2	1143	14.3
1966–67 Phila.	81	2168	556	1211	45.9	383	558	68.6	589	205	260	2	1495	18.5
TOTALS	161	4302	987	2222	44.4	664	1001	66.3	1188	412	561	4	2638	16.4

PLAYOFF RECORD

	G.	Min.	FG	FGA	FG %	FT	FTA	FT %	R	A	PF	D	Pts.	Ave.
1965–66 Phila.	4	69	5	31	16.1	11	13	84.6	18	10	11	0	21	5.3
1966–67 Phila.	15	339	83	221	37.6	59	90	65.6	93	33	53	1	225	15.0
TOTALS	19	408	88	252	34.9	70	103	67.9	111	43	64	1	246	12.9

Lucious Jackson

Birth Date—October 31, 1941   Height—6-9
Weight—238   Residence—Philadelphia, Pa.

Set for his fourth season in NBA . . . Averaged 12 points a game last year, just missing the thousand point mark . . . Also snared 724 rebounds to trail only Chamberlain in his best all-around season . . . Considered one of the premier defensive performers in the league among big men . . . Can play center as well as forward . . . One of best assets in his fiery competitive spirit which delights fans . . . Hero of America's 1964 Olympic victory over Russia and won players' vote as NBA rookie of the year in 1965 . . . Played his collegiate ball at Pan American . . . Considered one of the most powerful men in game around boards.

LUKE JACKSON'S 1966–67 SCORING VS. EACH NBA RIVAL

	G.	Min.	FG	FGA	FG%	FT	FTA	FT%	R	A	PF	D	Pts.	Ave.
Baltimore	9	295	52	108	48.1	28	37	75.7	97	16	31	0	132	14.4
Detroit	9	239	45	97	46.4	32	35	91.4	71	8	31	0	122	13.6
Los Angeles	9	284	53	111	47.7	14	28	50.0	85	13	23	0	120	13.3
San Francisco	9	262	44	101	43.6	27	35	77.1	100	15	35	2	115	12.8
Cincinnati	9	299	42	110	38.2	22	30	73.3	93	21	35	1	106	11.8
Boston	9	274	41	102	40.2	23	25	92.0	76	12	20	0	105	11.7
St. Louis	9	234	42	79	53.2	20	26	76.9	68	7	34	1	104	11.6
New York	9	273	39	116	33.6	14	20	70.0	77	18	34	1	92	10.2
Chicago	9	217	28	58	48.3	18	25	72.0	57	4	33	1	74	8.2
TOTALS	81	2377	386	882	43.8	198	261	75.9	724	114	276	6	970	12.0

NBA RECORD

	G.	Min.	FG	FGA	FG%	FT	FTA	FT%	R	A	PF	D	Pts.	Ave.
1964–65 Phila.	76	2590	419	1013	41.4	288	404	71.3	980	93	251	4	1126	14.8
1965–66 Phila.	79	1966	246	614	40.1	158	214	73.8	676	132	216	2	650	8.2
1966–67 Phila.	81	2377	386	882	43.8	198	261	75.9	724	114	276	6	970	12.0
TOTALS	236	6933	1051	2509	41.9	644	879	73.3	2380	339	743	12	2746	11.7

PLAYOFF RECORD

	G.	Min.	FG	FGA	FG%	FT	FTA	FT%	R	A	PF	D	Pts.	Ave.
1964–65 Phila.	11	321	44	130	33.8	25	32	78.1	79	24	31	0	113	10.3
1965–66 Phila.	5	163	21	49	42.9	18	22	81.8	44	8	21	2	60	12.0
1966–67 Phila.	15	543	64	161	39.8	37	51	72.5	176	30	47	1	165	11.0
TOTALS	31	1027	129	340	37.9	80	105	76.2	299	62	99	3	338	10.9

Chet Walker

Birth Date—February 22, 1940   Height—6-6½
Weight—200   Residence—Benton Harbor, Michigan

Embarking on his sixth year in NBA . . . Enjoyed his best professional season last year with 1,567 points and a 19.3 average . . . Played regular forward spot all season long and was deemed Mr. Steady because of his consistent performances . . . His 48.8 shooting percentage topped only by Chamberlain . . . Never has failed to average less than double figures and was picked on East All-Star team for the third time . . . is league's best exponent of the one-on-one play and virtually dares the opposition to set up such a situation . . . Shoots well either with push shot from corners or on drive-ins to the basket . . . Played at Bradley U.

CHET WALKER'S 1966–67 SCORING VS. EACH NBA RIVAL

	G.	Min.	FG	FGA	FG%	FT	FTA	FT%	R	A	PF	D	Pts.	Ave.
San Francisco	9	290	75	151	49.7	49	65	75.4	61	20	27	1	199	22.1
St. Louis	9	324	73	130	56.2	53	65	81.5	92	19	21	1	199	22.1
Los Angeles	9	320	58	112	51.8	76	98	77.6	72	22	28	0	192	21.3
New York	9	316	69	141	48.9	44	57	77.2	94	23	29	1	182	20.2
Chicago	9	295	59	114	51.8	51	61	83.6	70	20	29	1	169	18.8
Detroit	9	287	58	119	48.7	53	64	82.8	67	18	22	0	169	18.8
Cincinnati	9	301	57	131	43.5	46	67	68.7	69	24	30	0	160	17.8
Baltimore	9	270	57	126	45.2	36	46	78.3	71	30	25	0	150	16.7
Boston	9	288	55	126	43.7	37	58	63.8	64	12	21	0	147	16.3
TOTALS	81	2691	561	1150	48.8	445	581	76.6	660	188	232	4	1567	19.3

NBA RECORD

	G.	Min.	FG	FGA	FG%	FT	FTA	FT%	R	A	PF	D	Pts.	Ave.
1962–61 Syr.	78	1993	352	751	46.9	253	362	69.9	571	82	221	3	957	12.3
1963–64 Phila.	76	2775	492	1118	44.0	330	464	71.1	784	124	232	3	1314	17.3
1964–65 Phila.	79	2187	377	936	40.3	288	388	74.2	528	132	200	2	1042	13.2
1965–66 Phila.	80	2603	443	982	45.1	335	468	71.6	636	201	238	3	1221	15.3
1966–67 Phila.	81	2691	561	1150	48.8	445	581	76.6	660	188	232	4	1567	19.3
TOTALS	394	12249	2225	4937	45.1	1651	2263	73.0	3179	727	1123	15	6101	15.5

PLAYOFF RECORD

	G.	Min.	FG	FGA	FG%	FT	FTA	FT%	R	A	PF	D	Pts.	Ave.
1962–63 Syr.	5	130	27	53	50.9	22	30	73.3	47	9	8	0	76	15.2
1963–64 Phila.	5	190	30	77	39.0	34	46	73.9	52	13	15	0	94	18.8
1964–65 Phila.	11	469	83	173	48.0	57	75	76.0	79	18	38	0	223	20.3
1965–66 Phila.	5	181	24	64	37.5	25	31	80.6	37	15	18	0	73	14.6
1966–67 Phila.	15	551	115	246	46.7	96	119	80.7	114	32	44	0	326	21.7
TOTALS	41	1521	279	613	45.5	234	301	77.7	329	87	123	0	792	19.3

Wally Jones

Birth Date—February 14, 1952 Height—6-2
Weight—180 Residence—Philadelphia, Pa.

Playing his fourth year in the league and his third with the 76ers . . . Experienced his greatest campaign last winter when he tallied 1,069 points for a 13.2 average . . . His 303 assists tied him for second spot on the team with Greer . . . Wally was one of the top foul shooters with 83.8 average . . . known as Wally Wonder and the sensational plays he pulled brought him acclaim from the fans . . . His colorful play includes windmill tactics on defense, flapping his hands after foul shots, and shoots with a kicking motion from the field . . . Originally was drafted by Detroit but was sold to Baltimore in a big deal . . . Then came to 76ers in a trade for Johnny Kerr . . . Played at Villanova and at Overbrook High School where Chamberlain, Walt Hazzard, and Wayne Hightower also performed.

WALLY JONES' 1966–67 SCORING VS. EACH NBA RIVAL

	G.	Min.	FG	FGA	FG%	FT	FTA	FT%	R	A	PF	D	Pts.	Ave.
San Francisco	9	289	61	125	48.8	42	47	89.8	34	47	36	1	164	18.2
Baltimore	9	233	56	101	55.4	31	38	81.6	22	38	24	1	143	15.9
New York	9	249	48	107	44.9	29	36	80.6	28	33	18	0	125	13.9
St. Louis	9	257	46	119	38.7	26	29	89.7	32	34	25	1	118	13.1
Boston	9	232	48	117	41.0	19	27	70.4	26	19	38	1	115	12.8
Chicago	9	245	39	104	37.5	26	28	92.9	37	38	23	0	104	11.6
Cincinnati	9	253	43	113	38.1	18	22	81.8	30	30	30	1	104	11.6
Los Angeles	9	237	42	100	42.0	18	20	90.0	28	33	36	1	102	11.3
Detroit	9	254	40	96	41.7	14	19	73.7	28	31	16	0	94	10.4
TOTALS	81	2249	423	982	43.1	223	266	83.8	265	303	246	6	1069	13.2

NBA RECORD

	G.	Min.	FG	FGA	FG%	FT	FTA	FT%	R	A	PF	D	Pts.	Ave.
1964–65 Balt.	77	1250	154	411	37.5	99	136	72.8	140	200	196	1	407	5.3
1965–66 Phila.	80	2196	296	799	37.0	128	172	74.4	169	273	250	6	720	9.0
1966–67 Phila.	81	2249	423	982	43.1	223	266	83.8	265	303	246	6	1069	13.2
TOTALS	238	5695	873	2192	39.8	450	574	78.4	574	776	692	13	2196	9.2

PLAYOFF RECORD

	G.	Min.	FG	FGA	FG%	FT	FTA	FT%	R	A	PF	D	Pts.	Ave.
1964–65 Balt.	10	162	29	63	46.0	15	20	75.0	20	18	28	1	73	7.3
1965–66 Phila.	5	156	25	77	32.5	15	22	68.2	15	18	18	0	65	13.0
1966–67 Phila.	15	476	109	244	44.7	45	58	77.6	42	61	58	0	263	17.5
TOTALS	30	794	163	384	42.4	75	100	75.0	77	97	104	1	401	13.4

Larry Costello

Birth Date—July 2, 1931 Height—6-1
Weight—188 Residence—Minoa, New York

Playing his 12th season in NBA, being only active player left from 1954–55 campaign . . . Bothered by leg injuries again last season and played in only 49 games. . . . Started year as regular guard until hurt . . . Managed to score 380 points for a 7.8 average in his return to the game after a year's absence . . . Still one of best foul shooters and made 90.2 percent of his shots . . . One of few two-handed set shooters left in the game . . . Began NBA career with Philadelphia Warriors and then was traded to Syracuse Nats before club was transferred here . . . Considered one of the top defensive guards in the game and one of the best playmakers.

LARRY COSTELLO'S 1966-67 SCORING VS. EACH NBA RIVAL

	G.	Min.	FG	FGA	FG%	FT	FTA	FT%	R	A	PF	D	Pts.	Ave.
Detroit	5	115	17	41	41.5	16	18	88.9	6	16	16	0	50	10.0
Chicago	6	118	21	38	55.3	13	15	86.7	15	21	21	0	55	9.2
St. Louis	5	102	16	33	48.5	14	15	93.3	9	17	9	0	46	9.2
San Francisco	6	97	15	29	51.7	18	20	90.0	17	15	18	1	48	8.0
Baltimore	7	146	19	45	42.2	14	17	82.4	24	24	18	0	52	7.4
Los Angeles	4	69	8	15	53.3	11	11	100.0	2	10	14	1	27	6.9
Boston	4	94	9	29	31.0	9	11	81.8	5	11	14	0	27	6.8
New York	7	152	14	41	34.1	18	19	94.7	16	14	16	0	46	6.6
Cincinnati	5	83	11	22	50.0	7	7	100.0	9	12	15	0	29	5.8
TOTALS	49	976	130	293	44.4	120	133	90.2	103	140	141	2	380	7.8

NBA RECORD

	G.	Min.	FG	FGA	FG%	FT	FTA	FT%	R	A	PF	D	Pts.	Ave.
1954–55 Phila.	19	463	46	139	33.1	26	32	81.3	49	78	37	0	118	6.2
1956–57 Phila.	72	2111	186	497	37.4	175	222	78.8	323	236	182	2	547	7.6
1957–58 Syr.	72	2746	378	888	42.6	320	378	84.7	378	317	246	3	1076	14.9
1958–59 Syr.	70	2750	414	948	43.7	280	349	80.2	365	379	263	7	1108	15.8
1959–60 Syr.	71	2469	372	822	45.2	249	289	86.1	388	446	234	4	993	14.0
1960–61 Syr.	75	2167	407	844	48.2	270	338	79.9	292	413	286	9	1084	14.5
1961–62 Syr.	63	1854	310	726	42.7	247	295	83.7	245	358	220	5	867	13.7
1962–63 Syr.	78	2066	285	660	43.2	288	327	88.7*	337	334	259	4	858	11.0
1963–64 Phila.	45	1137	191	408	47.6	147	170	86.5	105	169	150	3	529	11.8
1964–65 Phila.	64	1967	309	695	44.5	243	277	82.7*	169	275	242	10	861	13.5
1966–67 Phila.	49	976	130	293	44.4	120	133	90.2	103	140	141	2	380	7.8
TOTALS	678	20706	3028	6920	43.8	2365	2810	84.2	2754	3145	2260	49	8421	12.4

*Led League

PLAYOFF RECORD

	G.	Min.	FG	FGA	FG%	FT	FTA	FT%	R	A	PF	D	Pts.	Ave.
1956–57 Phila.	2	16	3	8	37.5	0	1	0.0	5	2	3	0	6	3.0
1957–58 Syr.	3	134	10	34	29.4	14	14	100.0	25	12	6	0	34	11.3
1958–59 Syr.	9	361	54	121	44.6	51	61	83.6	53	54	40	2	159	17.7
1959–60 Syr.	3	122	20	47	42.5	10	12	83.3	14	20	15	1	50	16.7
1960–61 Syr.	8	269	42	103	40.8	47	55	85.4	35	52	39	3	131	16.4
1961–62 Syr.	5	167	22	51	43.1	29	33	87.9	16	28	21	0	73	14.6
1962–63 Syr.	5	134	16	37	43.2	19	23	82.6	4	23	27	2	51	10.2
1963–64 Phila.	5	36	3	14	21.4	10	10	100.0	3	4	14	1	16	3.2
1964–65 Phila.	10	207	22	53	41.5	11	16	68.8	12	20	43	2	55	5.5
1966–67 Phila.	2	25	6	8	75.0	5	5	100.0	4	3	2	0	17	8.5
TOTALS	52	1471	198	476	41.6	196	230	85.2	171	218	210	11	592	11.4

Matt Guokas

Birth Date—February 25, 1944 Height—6-6
Weight—170 Residence—Bryn Mawr, Pa.

Ready for his second year of NBA play . . . Gained stature as one of the circuit's top rookies at the end of last season . . . The former St. Joseph's College ace gathered momentum and by last third of the campaign was No. 1 sub in the guard spot . . . Came through with pressure-packed performances in playoffs . . . Continued his spectacular ball handling from college days . . . Originally picked as No. 1 draft choice of club in 1966 . . . Son of Matt, Sr., who played for the champion Philadelphia Warriors in 1946–47 . . . Showed coolness in crucial phases of games and picked up in scoring . . . Had 105 assists as tyro.

MATT GUOKAS' 1966-67 SCORING VS. EACH NBA RIVAL

	G.	Min.	FG	FGA	FG%	FT	FTA	FT%	R	A	PF	D	Pts.	Ave.
Los Angeles	8	111	11	24	45.8	6	10	60.0	10	17	8	0	28	3.5
San Francisco	7	69	9	22	40.9	6	9	33.3	8	12	7	0	24	3.4
Baltimore	9	95	10	23	43.5	10	16	62.5	8	13	10	0	30	3.3
Cincinnati	9	145	12	37	32.4	5	5	100.0	12	14	13	0	29	3.2
Boston	6	97	8	25	32.0	3	6	50.0	11	12	12	0	19	3.2
St. Louis	8	80	9	17	52.9	5	11	45.5	11	13	9	0	23	2.9
Chicago	9	87	8	24	33.3	9	13	69.2	7	14	5	0	25	2.8
Detroit	8	76	9	24	37.5	3	7	42.9	14	6	13	0	21	2.6
New York	5	48	3	7	42.9	2	4	50.0	2	4	5	0	8	1.6
TOTALS	69	808	79	203	38.9	49	81	60.5	83	105	82	0	207	3.0

PLAYOFF RECORD

	G.	Min.	FG	FGA	FG%	FT	FTA	FT%	R	A	PF	D	Pts.	Ave.
1966–67 Phila.	15	252	26	64	40.6	13	17	76.5	30	23	33	0	65	4.3

Billy Melchionni

Birth Date—October 19, 1944 Height—6–1
Weight—170 Residence—Bryn Mawr, Pa.

Entering second year in professional ranks . . . Demonstrated a sharp-shooting eye in his rookie year . . . Delighted fans with his flashy shooting and his ability to go on hot streaks . . . Used principally in shooting guard spot behind Hal Greer . . . Tallied 315 points in 75 games and was credited with 98 assists . . . Played collegiate ball at Vilianova where his 27.6 average ranked him ninth in nation . . . Also picked as most valuable player in Big Five and in the N.I.T. . . . Is one of the fastest players on team and is adept on the fast break . . . Called for six-month Army reserve duty during playoffs and rejoined team in time for training drills.

BILLY MELCHIONNI'S 1966–67 SCORING VS. EACH NBA RIVAL

	G.	Min.	FG	FGA	FG%	FT	FTA	FT%	R	A	PF	D	Pts.	Ave.
Detroit	9	108	23	59	39.0	13	17	76.5	18	15	9	0	59	6.6
Baltimore	9	101	22	57	38.6	2	4	50.0	29	16	10	0	46	5.1
Cincinnati	8	57	15	30	50.0	7	11	63.6	14	10	7	0	37	4.6
Boston	7	64	16	37	43.2	0	1	0.0	4	8	9	0	32	4.6
San Francisco	8	60	17	35	48.6	2	5	40.0	7	11	7	0	36	4.5
St. Louis	7	75	11	31	35.5	5	5	100.0	6	17	6	0	27	3.9
Los Angeles	7	82	13	41	31.7	1	3	33.3	8	7	10	0	27	3.9
Chicago	9	78	9	34	26.5	9	13	69.2	9	9	8	0	27	3.0
New York	9	67	12	29	41.4	0	1	0.0	3	5	7	0	24	2.7
TOTALS	73	692	138	353	39.1	39	60	65.0	98	98	73	0	315	4.3

PLAYOFF RECORD

	G.	Min.	FG	FGA	FG%	FT	FTA	FT%	R	A	PF	D	Pts.	Ave.
1966–67 Phila.	1	5	0	2	0.0	0	2	0.0	3	1	0	0	0	0.0

Irv Kosloff . . . President of the 76ers . . . Key figure in the return of professional basketball to the city after the departure of the Warriors . . . His wise draft choices and trades helped 76ers win Eastern title in three years and NBA crown in four . . . Restored the NBA to the local scene by teaming with the late Ike Richman to purchase the Syracuse Nats' franchise in May 1963 . . . A staunch booster and follower of major league basketball since the game was reinstituted here in 1946 . . . A graduate of Temple University after an athletic career at Southern High School . . . President of the Roosevelt Paper Company, one of America's largest firms in that field . . . Club's representative on the NBA's Board of Governors.

Dr. Jack Ramsay . . . Serving his second season as general manager of the club . . . Directed front office in his "rookie" year as team won NBA title . . . His duties include negotiating contracts with players, setting up exhibition and regular season schedule, and supervising promotional, ticket selling, and other business operations . . . Rated one of the nation's foremost basketball coaches during his eleven seasons at St. Joseph's College where he started as a coach and eventually rose to a combination athletic director and court mentor . . . His record was 234-72 for a .764 percentage and his teams vied in ten post season tourneys, won or shared seven Big Five titles and captured seven Middle Atlantic Conference University Division championships . . . Earlier coached high school basketball after playing at St. Joseph's and in Eastern League . . . Wrote book, "Pressure Basketball" . . . Earned Master's and Doctor's degrees in education at Penn.

Trainer Al Domenico is one of the outstanding trainers in the NBA. He has had 14 years of experience training athletes in various fields. He has a vast storehouse of knowledge concerning injuries athletes receive during the course of a contest. His rapid diagnosis and treatment quickly has restored many a 76er to action. Al began his career as a student trainer at North Catholic High School and later served in that capacity for the Camden Bullets in the Eastern League, for the Jersey Devils, the Roller Derby, and for wrestling. He began his tenure in the NBA as a visiting team trainer and in 1965 he was selected as the club's first full-time trainer. In addition to his training duties, Al also serves as traveling secretary of the club on road trips. He is a veteran of the Marine Medical Corps. He spent the summer conducting clinics.